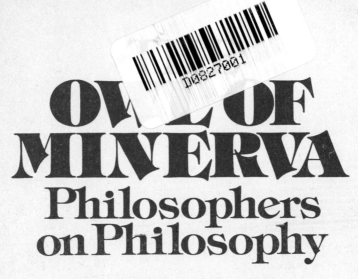

OWL OF MINERVA
Philosophers on Philosophy

Edited and with an Introduction by

Charles J. Bontempo

and

S. Jack Odell

Department of Philosophy
University of Maryland

McGraw-Hill Book Company

New York   St. Louis   San Francisco
Düsseldorf   Kuala Lumpur   London   Mexico
Montreal   New Delhi   Panama   Paris
São Paulo   Singapore   Sydney   Tokyo   Toronto

Library of Congress Cataloging in Publication Data

Bontempo, Charles J.
  The owl of Minerva.

  Bibliography: p.
  Includes index.
  1. Philosophy—Addresses, essays, lectures.
I. Odell, S. Jack, date   joint author. II. Title.
B53.B578   190   74-31440
ISBN 0-07-006480-6
ISBN 0-07-006481-4 (pbk.)
  234567890 BPBP 79876

The editors for this book were Nancy Tressel and Cheryl Love, the designer was Elaine Gongora, and the production supervisor was Milton Heiberg. It was set in Garamond by Cherry Hill Composition.

Printed and bound by the Book Press.

THE
OWL OF
MINERVA

To
Carol and Judith
Alexandra, Elizabeth, Erin, and Lynn

CONTENTS

CONTENTS

NOTES ON THE CONTRIBUTORS

SIR ALFRED J. AYER is the Wykeham Professor of Logic at Oxford University. He is the author of many articles and books in philosophy, including *Language, Truth and Logic,* 1936, *The Foundations of Empirical Knowledge,* 1940, and *The Problem of Knowledge,* 1956. He received his knighthood in 1970.

BRAND BLANSHARD is Emeritus Sterling Professor of Philosophy at Yale University. He served as President of the Eastern Division of the American Philosophical Association, 1942–1944, and President of the American Theological Society, 1955–1956. His many publications in philosophy include *The Nature of Thought,* 1939, *Reason and Goodness,* 1961, and *Reason and Analysis,* 1962. His work is soon to be the subject of a volume in the Library of Living Philosophers (*The Philosophy of Brand Blanshard,* ed. by Paul A. Schilpp).

REV. FREDERICK C. COPLESTON is Principal of Heythrop College at the University of London, Professor of the History of Philosophy at Heythrop, and Dean of the Faculty of Theology at the University of London. He is the author of several books and articles including *A History of Philosophy,* eight volumes, 1946–1966.

PAUL FEYERABEND is a Professor of Philosophy at the University of California at Berkeley. He is the author of numerous articles on philosophy, science, and the philosophy of science. He edited with Grover Maxwell *Mind, Matter and Method: Essays in Philosophy and Science in Honor of Herbert Feigl,* 1966.

MAX H. FISCH is Emeritus Professor of Philosophy at the University of Illinois at Urbana. He served as President of the Western Division of the American Philosophical Association, 1955–1956. He is the author of books and articles chiefly in the history of science, medicine, and philosophy, including *Philosophy in America* (with Paul Russell Anderson), 1939, and *Classic American Philosophers* (with A. W. Burks, Paul Henle, Otto Kraushaar, Philip B. Rice, Gail Kennedy, and Victor Lowe), 1951.

STUART N. HAMPSHIRE is Warden of Wadham College at Oxford University. He was Professor of Philosophy at Princeton University from 1963 to 1970. He served as President of the Eastern Division of the American Philosophical Association, 1969–1970. His many publications include *Spinoza,* 1951, *Thought and Action,* 1959, and *Freedom of the Individual,* 1965.

SIDNEY HOOK is Emeritus Professor of Philosophy at New York University. He served as President of the Eastern Division of the American Philosophical Association, 1959–1960. He is the author of numerous articles and books in philosophy and political and social theory, including *From Hegel to Marx,* 1933, *Social Myths and Democracy,* 1940, and *Political Power and Personal Freedom,* 1959.

PAUL LORENZEN is Professor of Philosophy at the University of Erlangen in West Germany. He is the author of numerous books and articles in philosophy, logic, and mathematics, including *Formale Logik,* 1958, *Normative Logic and Ethics,* 1969, and *Konstruktive Logik, Ethik und Wissenschaftstheorie* (with Oswald Schwemmer), 1973.

GABRIEL MARCEL, French existentialist philosopher and author, was a member of the Institut de France until his death in 1973. His many publications include *Metaphysical Journal,* 1927, and *Being the Mystery of Being* (Gifford Lectures), 1951.

HERBERT MARCUSE is Professor of Philosophy at the University of California at San Diego. He served as President of the Pacific Division of the American Philosophical Association, 1968–1969. His many publications include *Reason and Revolution: Hegel and the Rise of Social Theory,* 1941, *Soviet Marxism: A Critical Analysis,* 1958, and *One Dimensional Man: Studies in the Ideology of Advanced Industrial Society,* 1964.

SIR KARL POPPER is Emeritus Professor of Logic and Scientific Method at the University of London. His many publications include *The Logic of Scientific Discovery,* 1959, *The Open Society and Its Enemies,* 1945, and *Conjectures and Refutations,* 1972. His work is the subject of two volumes in the Library of Living Philosophers (*The Philosophy of Karl Popper,* ed. by Paul A. Schilpp, 1973). He received his knighthood in 1965.

WILLARD VAN ORMAN QUINE is Edgar Pierce Professor of Philosophy at Harvard University. He served as President of the Association for Symbolic Logic, 1953–1956, and the Eastern Division of the American Philosophical Association, 1957–1958. He is the author of numerous articles and books on philosophy, logic, and the philosophy of logic, including *Methods of Logic,* 1950, *From a Logical Point of View,* 1953, and *Word and Object,* 1960.

ADAM SCHAFF is Professor of Philosophy at the University of Warsaw in Poland. He has published numerous articles and books in philosophy, including *Introduction to Semantics,* 1962, *A Philosophy of Man,* 1963, and *Marxism and the Human Individual,* 1970.

J. J. C. SMART is currently Reader in Philosophy at La Trobe University, Victoria, and is Emeritus Hughes Professor of Philosophy at the University of Adelaide in Australia. He is the author of many articles and several books in philosophy and the philosophy of science, including *An Outline of a System of Utilitarian Ethics,* 1961, and *Philosophy and Scientific Realism,* 1963.

ALAN WATTS was until his death in 1973 President of the Society for Comparative Philosophy in Sausalito, California. He was a free-lance philosopher chiefly interested in the religio-philosophical dialogue between Asia and the West. His many publications include

The Way of Zen, 1957, *Nature, Man and Woman,* 1958, and *The Book: On the Taboo against Knowing Who You Are,* 1966.

ALAN WHITE is Ferens Professor of Philosophy in the University of Hull in England. He has published many articles and several books in philosophy, including *Attention,* 1964, *Philosophy of Mind,* 1967, and *Truth,* 1970.

JOHN WISDOM was Professor of Philosophy at Cambridge University from 1934 until 1968, and is currently Professor of Philosophy at the University of Oregon. He served as President of the Pacific Division of the American Philosophical Association, 1970–1971. His many publications in philosophy include *Problems of Mind and Matter,* 1934, *Other Minds,* 1952, and *Philosophy and Psychoanalysis,* 1952.

PAUL ZIFF is William Rand Kenan, Jr., Professor of Philosophy at the University of North Carolina. He is the author of numerous articles in the philosophy of mind, aesthetics, and the philosophy of language. His books include *Semantic Analysis,* 1960, *Philosophic Turnings,* 1966, and *Understanding Understanding,* 1972.

PREFACE

Our aim is to present the views of leading contemporary philosophers on the nature and relevance of philosophy. We have tried to present a balanced representation of thinkers on these topics—both philosophically and geographically. Our contributors include logicians, social and political thinkers, historians of philosophy, linguistic analysts, philosophers of science and of ethics, an existentialist, and a thinker who has had a strong interest in Far Eastern thought. They are from the United States, England, Australia, and the European continent.

Most of our contributions were written especially for this volume. The exceptions are (1) three American Philosophical Association presidential addresses—the contributions of Max Fisch, Herbert Marcuse, and John Wisdom; (2) Sidney Hook's contribution, which is an extension of a previously published paper; (3) Brand Blanshard's contribution, which is a revision of a Mahlon Powell Lecture; and (4) W. V. Quine's contribution, which is a letter he wrote in response to some questions that were asked him concerning himself and philosophy.

We take this opportunity to acknowledge helpful suggestions from Samuel Gorovitz, James Lesher, Alan Pasch, and Moreland Perkins, of the University of Maryland. We thank Margaret-Mary Ryan and Helen Wade for typing both the manuscript and the heavy volume of correspondence that is connected with a book of this sort. Jack Odell also thanks the University of Maryland for a sabbatical leave (spring 1973), a part of which was used to prepare the present volume.

C.J.B.

S.J.O.

The owl of Minerva spreads its wings
only with the falling of the dusk.
—Hegel

THE OWL OF MINERVA

SOME APPROACHES
TO PHILOSOPHY

Charles J. Bontempo and S. Jack Odell

I

Philosophy is one of our oldest disciplines. It was taught over two thousand years ago in the Greek academies by Plato and Aristotle. Yet it is a curious fact that despite its long history philosophy is neither widely nor well understood. And this is especially true outside the circle of professional academics who present the subject to today's students and who work at its development through their research. Of course philosophy is known as a subject which deals with deep and basic questions, but all too often this is *all* that is understood of the subject. Moreover, even among professional, academic philosophers there is no consensus on how their subject is *best* understood and on what relevance their work has to our lives and our institutions, to our personal choices and hopes, and to our public policies and goals. Briefly, it is not clear what bearing philosophy has on those questions concerning the human predicament which disturb all of us.

These questions concerning the nature of philosophy and its relevance constitute the topics of this volume. We want to increase our understanding of what philosophy *is* and of what philosophers *do*. We want at least to begin to see what it is that we can reasonably expect from our subject, from those who are engaged in its study, and from those who are contributing to its development.

We shall soon see that understanding the nature of philosophy is by no means an easy task. For philosophy differs from other subjects in ways that complicate our topics and make our inquiry intricate. However, this should not diminish our hope for increased understanding, since we have some of the best resources available to help us in our inquiry. These appear in this volume in the form of statements on our topics by leading contemporary philosophers. Surely we shall be in a better position to advance our inquiry if we consider carefully what these practicing philosophers have to say about their subject as *they* see it.

Our task can be as beneficial as it is difficult. An increase in our understanding of the nature of our subject can better equip us to approach the works of those who call themselves "philosophers." Increased insight into *how* a philosopher might view his subject can improve our ability to understand, to appraise, and to appreciate his philosophical efforts.

Our interest in achieving such understanding goes beyond "purely academic" bounds. For philosophy today, perhaps more than any other discipline, is severely criticized on the grounds that it is not *relevant* to human problems; that philosophers have fragmented their subject into a series of technical problems which are unrelated to the human crisis problems of the day and which are, apparently, even unrelated to each other.

It is argued that philosophers have become a cloistered group of elite professionals who deliberately ignore the responsibilities of anguished decision making and counseling on matters of public policy as well as the urgent work of planning and participating in actions toward human and social goals. It is also argued that in assuming this unattractive posture, today's philosophers have distorted the *true nature and aims of their subject*.

More generally, it is argued that, in fact, there are few results with which all philosophers agree and that philosophy's record of achievement is disappointing not only to laymen, but to some of its best-trained and most dedicated professors and students. For these reasons, the critics continue, we find some of its most gifted practitioners, students, and teachers periodically slipping into profound disillusionment with their subject and with their peers. The result of which is that these talents are often permanently lost to a subject which has always been regarded as worthy of our most dedicated and serious minds. The critics of philosophy also maintain that it is because philosophy lacks relevance that there is so little interest in philosophy and so little understanding of the activities and results of contemporary philosophers outside of academic quarters.

Of course similar criticisms of philosophy and philosophers have been made throughout its history, ever since the ancient Sophist Thrasymachus contemptuously likened Socrates to a "sniffling" child[1] and Aristophanes caricatured him as "an amusing eccentric, a combination of pedant, paradox-monger, freethinker, and necromancer."[2] Indeed, there have even been voices from within philosophy itself that have used these criticisms as points of departure for their own approaches to the subject, e.g., existentialism, Marxism, and personalism.

But today these allegations have a special force for two reasons. First, the current social scene is undergoing far-reaching changes in which the dynamics of participatory democracy play a crucial role. It is not surprising that in this environment the philosopher (who is for many the thinker *par excellence* of the community) is scrutinized and is challenged to account for himself. He is asked for his position on this or that issue; he is asked to defend his position; he is asked to indicate what he is prepared to do to advance his position; and he is asked to *deliver* whatever he claims to be willing to contribute as a proponent of his position in the form of plans and actions toward some specific social objective.

Perhaps what is most interesting about these challenges is that the philosopher is often expected to respond in each case *as a philosopher*. This expectation is based on the belief that he is especially interested in issues and especially qualified to participate in programs by virtue of his training and talents as a philosopher since he is often identified (either rightly or wrongly) with a long line of social thinkers, like Plato, Aristotle, Hobbes, Locke, and Marx— thinkers whose views have made a marked difference in the events

---

[1] *The Republic of Plato*, book I, 343, trans. F. M. Cornford, Oxford University Press, New York, 1945.
[2] A. E. Taylor, *Socrates*, Doubleday & Company, Inc., Garden City, N.Y., 1952, p. 89.

of the past. Undoubtedly, these highly demanding expectations have been encouraged by the substantive treatment given to basic sociopolitical questions in works like Plato's *Republic*, a work that can be viewed as one of the most sustained, comprehensive, and detailed plans for sociopolitical relationships in the history of Western thought.

Now we consider the second reason why the charges against philosophy have a special force, and why they are particularly disturbing today. Here we need to take into account the self-image of past philosophers as compared to the self-image of their contemporary counterparts. We are told that the ancient philosophers viewed themselves as lovers of wisdom. They believed that their subject began in wonder and that in its more developed stages it was the "queen of the sciences." The value of the philosopher's special talents and training received no greater emphasis than in Plato's *Republic*, where Plato maintained that the success of any state, and especially the state he described, depended upon the proper exercise of *the* leadership role by philosophers.

> Unless either philosophers become kings in their countries or those who are now called kings and rulers come to be sufficiently inspired with a genuine desire for wisdom; unless, that is to say, political power and philosophy meet together . . . there can be no rest from troubles . . . for states, nor yet, as I believe, for all mankind; nor can this commonwealth which we have imagined ever till then see the light of day and grow to its full stature.[3]

Thus, the ancient philosophers and many of their successors maintained high aspirations with regard to what they thought they could achieve with their subject.

Now let us look at what some contemporary philosophers in this volume have to say about philosophy's past achievements and future promise. One such philosopher, Karl Popper (1), believes that professional philosophy "is in urgent need of . . . a defense of its existence" and that since Plato's time "megalomania has been the

---

[3] *The Republic of Plato*, book V, 473, trans. F. M. Cornford, Oxford University Press, New York, 1945.

philosopher's most widespread professional disease."[4] Commenting
on current philosophy he notes:

> Scholasticism, in the worst sense of the term, abounds; all the
> great ideas are buried in a flood of words. At the same time, a
> certain arrogance and rudeness—once a rarity in philosophical lit-
> erature—seems to be accepted, by the editors of many of the jour-
> nals, as a proof of boldness of thought and originality.

Another contemporary thinker, J. J. C. Smart (2), bemoans the
nature and extent of disagreement among philosophers: "The trouble about philosophy is not that we get disagreement about fundamental issues. Such disagreement occurs healthily in science. It is
that we get something like *total* disagreement or even total incomprehension." He also questions the "respectability" of the subject
by commenting: "Surely if philosophy were a respectable subject,
there would be general agreement as to what is and is not bosh, at
least among those who are paid large sums of money to teach it at
prestigious universities." Sidney Hook (3) describes this lack of
agreement as the "skeleton rattling in the philosophical cupboard."
  What is very disconcerting about these opinions of philosophy is
that they are not expressed in these cases by philosophical "radicals"
or "extremists," but by *well-established* members of the professional philosophical community, thinkers who have made contributions of significance to philosophy.

II

What can be said about these criticisms and charges against our
subject and against its practitioners? Surely, we shall be in a better
position to assess them once we increase our understanding of the
nature of our subject. It is difficult, for example, to determine
whether or not the failure to develop a body of results with which
all philosophers agree *should* be counted against philosophy. Of

---

[4] References to the papers of contributors to this volume appear within paren-
theses. This number corresponds to the author's entry in our Table of Contents.
This device is used for *initial* references and is dropped in subsequent references
to contributors. Conventional notes are used to refer to works outside of this
volume.

course we shall be concerned over this failure if we view philosophy as similar in nature, say, to science. On the other hand, if we see a similarity in nature between philosophy and art, as opposed to science, we shall probably not be seriously concerned.

This suggests that our judgment of the success or failure of philosophy will depend very much on our view of its nature, that is, on our view of what philosophy *is* and of what it *seeks to achieve*. It is important, therefore, that we consider how philosophy is similar to or differs from other subjects. As a part of this task, we should ask whether or not 'philosophy' can be defined—or at least characterized—in a way that distinguishes it from other subjects. We turn now to some thoughts on these questions. Later we return to the question concerning the relevance of philosophy.

III

Now the question "What is philosophy?" is certainly a familiar one for those of us involved in philosophical activities as practitioners, teachers, or students. Often the question arises in those ordinary circumstances in which inquiries concerning our activities and occupations are a part of the normal conversational preliminaries. We are first asked, "What is it that you do?" We respond, "I'm a philosopher," "I'm a teacher of philosophy," or "I'm a student of philosophy." Inevitably, it seems, we are faced with the difficult follow-on question, "What is philosophy?" which asks us to explain, define, or somehow characterize our subject.

It is interesting that, for example, bakers, teachers of law, and students of physics usually need not go through the same sequence of questions. For *their* replies to the initial question—"I'm a baker," "I'm a law teacher," or "I'm a student of physics"—seem sufficient to satisfy the questioner's interest. Apparently, by simply indicating their occupations they go a long way toward identifying the sorts of activities in which they are engaged, and the conversation is free to turn to the weather, sports, or the current headlines. Those involved in philosophy rarely get off this easily.

These questions and responses are apt to occur during a cocktail party, a holiday visit with family and friends, or a chance meeting on a plane. But the professional philosopher is apt to encounter the

6

same problem in discussions with his academic counterparts in other disciplines. "I have never understood exactly what it is that you people are about. Could you explain it?" This is not an uncommon request, and it may come from one's colleagues in engineering, chemistry, mathematics, or classical languages. Even those who have had a course or two in philosophy may comment: "I had a course in your subject when I was an undergraduate, but I never really understood what it was all about. Can you tell me?"

Many thinkers have believed that a good way to acquire an understanding of "what philosophy is all about" is through a study of its history. Some have said that this kind of study is a prerequisite to such understanding. Others have argued that it is the best or even the *only* way to reach an understanding of the nature of philosophy. We examine these suggestions as a part of what we term the *historical approach* to our question.

The Historical Approach

There is much to be said for the suggestion that a good way to gain insight into the nature of philosophy is by examining the works of those thinkers who are *historically* credited with philosophical contributions. Traditionally, this suggestion has been adopted and implemented in our universities by requiring students in philosophy programs to receive instruction and to pass examinations in the history of philosophy. Some thinkers would say that there now appears to be considerable agreement among historians of philosophy on those figures selected for treatment in such courses. And they would note that in our better works on the history of philosophy, we find extensive overlap among those figures whose views are presented. For these reasons these thinkers claim that this approach provides a common focal point of interest.

There is evidence that this approach has achieved at least some measure of success. Despite our earlier observation that some former students of philosophy are puzzled concerning the nature of philosophy, it is *also* true that many students who study the historical philosophical figures come away with the conviction that through these thinkers they have been introduced to a manner and level of thought that, for the most part, is new to them. Often such students come to understand a range of problems which, very likely, would not have occurred to them without exposure to these thinkers. Experiences of this kind have unquestionably contributed to an improved understanding of the nature of philosophy, if only by providing an opportunity to acquire such understanding through a kind of "direct acquaintance" with the philosophical thought of the past.

In addition, we have the testimony of many contemporary professional philosophers who maintain that their philosophical activities are continuous with and connected to the works of their predecessors. They claim that there is a set of problems which has been and always will be characteristic of the philosophical enterprise. In this volume, Stuart Hampshire (4) maintains that this link with the past is so important that those who are unfamiliar with the works of the principal philosophers of the past (as well as those of the present) are "almost certainly disqualified" from contributing to the substantial issues of philosophy. Surely one would expect that most major philosophers today and throughout history have studied and been influenced by their predecessors. (As an obvious historical example we cite the chain of student-teacher relationships of Socrates, Plato, and Aristotle.)

Some thinkers have made much stronger claims for the historical approach. For example, as Martin Heidegger sees it, "we can ask the question, 'What is philosophy?' only if we enter into a discussion with the thinking of the Greek world...."[5] According to Heidegger, we cannot understand philosophy if we break with the past and especially if we break with the thought of the ancient Greeks, for philosophy is an adoption and transformation of what the Greeks have given us. Heidegger is maintaining, then, that the historical approach is the only satisfactory path toward an understanding of the nature of philosophy.

Although there is certainly much to be said for this approach, there have also been serious objections raised against it. Some of these objections have been based on the claim that philosophy has

_____

[5] Martin Heidegger, *What Is Philosophy?* trans. William Kluback and Jean T. Wilde, Twayne Publishers, Inc., New York, 1958, p. 35.

changed so drastically in the twentieth century that we can distinguish between an "old" and "new" philosophy, or a "prescientific" and a "scientific" philosophy. The former is supposedly characterized by excesses of speculation and an unreasonable demand for absolutely certain knowledge of the physical world. The "new" philosophy, of course, is described in terms of the opposite of each of these characteristics.[6] It has been argued that since there are such sharp differences between the "new" and the "old" philosophies, the historical approach is not only unprofitable, but runs a serious risk of being misleading and even harmful, especially when it is mismanaged. This mismanagement takes the form of a lack of objectivity which results in a "glorification of the philosophies of the past."[7] According to some, this can give rise to an *elitist* view of philosophy and philosophers, in which philosophy is viewed as a special subject—reserved only for those with extraordinary talents —whose method, problems, and aims are completely beyond the reach of the ordinary man. According to this elitist view, we can expect no aid from the thought of those who do not approach the subject with these esoteric talents and special historical training.[8]

This elitist view is at odds with a popular conception of philosophy in which every man, whether he be a cab driver, longshoreman, or fisherman, is thought capable of developing interesting views on the nature of man and on man's relationship to his universe. Such a person may never have heard of Plato or Aristotle; but if he were told about them, he might well recognize that what he had been doing in his own deliberations was in some way similar to the sort of thing they did. Indeed, there is a "cracker-barrel" view of the philosopher which characterizes him as just such a person—one whose age and life experiences make what he says instructive and valuable, although he has had none of the formal training of the professional or academic thinker. Now it is even

---

[6] For example, this characterization is given by Hans Reichenbach, *The Rise of Scientific Philosophy*, University of California Press, Berkeley, 1951.

[7] Ibid., p. 325.

[8] This elitist view has not always been associated with the historical approach. For Heidegger, mastery of Greek thought and culture would constitute the qualifications necessary for membership in this elite. However, others would suggest different conditions of membership.

possible that a person meeting this description could have something to say which would be considered noteworthy by professional and academic philosophers. (We tend to believe it much less likely that we could find such a contribution being made to a discipline like mathematics by one who is similarly untrained in that subject.)

Not every opponent of the elitist view would be content to let the case against this view turn on the existence or nonexistence of such exceptional persons. For example, Karl Popper claims that in fact *every* man and woman is a philosopher—not a professional or academic philosopher, of course, but nonetheless a philosopher.[9] He concedes that there have been only a few truly great philosophers and that what they produced is of great importance. Nevertheless, as he puts it, "philosophy does not depend on them in the sense in which painting depends on the great painters or music on the great composers."

As Popper sees it, all men and women take attitudes and have uncritical convictions or prejudices regarding such things as life and death. He regards these attitudes and prejudices as "theories which they unconsciously take for granted, or which they have absorbed from their intellectual environment or from tradition." The difference between professional philosophers and ordinary men who are also philosophers is that the former recognize that the attitudes and prejudices of the ordinary man are in fact *theories* which need to be critically examined. The need for people who critically examine such theories and the problems associated with them is, for Popper, the only justification for professional philosophy.

Another objection to the historical approach is based on the distinction between philosophy and intellectual history, or the history of ideas. It is argued that it is one thing to philosophize and another thing to describe the views of philosophers in their historical context. Generally, philosophers are interested in *arguments* relating to views on basic notions like *truth, the good*, and *certainty*. They are concerned with the truth or falsity of the suppositions

---

[9] Popper's comments here are in response to Friedrich Waismann, whose views are expressed in his paper "How I See Philosophy," in A. J. Ayer (ed.), *Logical Positivism*, The Free Press of Glencoe, Inc., New York, 1959, pp. 345–380.

that might enter into such arguments and with the correctness of inferences that are made on the basis of such suppositions. Roughly, they examine ideas and the purported connections among these ideas. On the other hand, the historian of ideas is concerned with relating a thinker's ideas to his historical context and with explaining divergent ideas among such thinkers in terms of differences in these contexts.

It is also argued that unless these activities are clearly distinguished they are apt to be confused. Such confusion has certainly occurred in the past. Some claim that this confusion has sometimes produced an insidious form of historicism according to which philosophical ideas are interpreted and appraised by reference to (1) the social conditions under which they developed, i.e., their "source," and (2) their influence on those conditions, i.e., their "historical significance." It is also claimed that some representatives of the historicist approach go on to identify or define "historical significance" in terms of their *own* social goals. They judge a view favorably if it seems to them to promote their social goals; otherwise they judge the view unfavorably. Thus, if a philosophical theory is construed as supporting the *status quo* and if they favor *sustaining* current conditions, they will judge the theory positively. (Others who favor a change in the same conditions might judge the same view negatively.)

The form of historicism described in (1) involves an obvious mistake in reasoning, the genetic fallacy, in which a view is philosophically appraised on the basis of its *origins* rather than its *soundness*. The form described in (2) confuses "historical significance" with soundness. Here a criterion of appraisal that *might be* appropriate in one area, history, is inappropriately adopted and applied in another area, philosophy.

Other critics are not impressed by the claim that there is considerable agreement among historians of philosophy concerning which thinkers are to be counted among the philosophers. They argue that the history of our subject presents a wide and variegated range of ideas and theories. Therefore, the view of philosophy one develops based on its historical study will depend on which thinkers are selected for study—and on where and how the emphasis is placed in such historical treatments. Moreover, they add, the criteria used in selection and emphasis are themselves problematic.

It is also noted by these critics that *contemporary* treatments of philosophical topics and problems are apt to be clearer and more precise than the historical treatments of the same topics. For this reason, students are less likely to be distracted by controversy over how a thinker is to be correctly interpreted.

In evaluating the arguments surrounding the historical approach we suggest (in addition to our earlier observations) that undoubtedly philosophy has changed significantly in our century as the result of the works of Frege, Russell, Whitehead, Moore, Carnap, and Wittgenstein.[10] Indeed, there is much to be said for the claim that the later work of Wittgenstein alone constitutes a conception of philosophical activity which is in many ways fundamentally different than what preceded it. Moreover, it has been noted that one can find few, if any, allusions to or reliance upon his predecessors in his work. Also there can be little doubt that recent philosophers have become more deliberate, methodical, and rigorous in the development and use of analytic skills and techniques. However, it is *not* clear that all of this amounts to a total break with the past—to a complete revolution in philosophy. Recent work in the history of philosophy shows that there is a long historical tradition going back to Plato and Aristotle which also makes use of analytic skills and techniques. Alan White (5) notes some examples in his essay. The striking originality of the conception introduced by Wittgenstein is readily acknowledged. Yet even among those who put this approach to use today, there are some who believe that the method associated with it is not suitable for the exercise of *all* the functions and tasks properly within the scope of philosophy. Thus, any suggestion that the "new" philosophy is *entirely* new, or even that it is so different from what preceded it as to make a study of philosophy's history useless for our purposes, must be seriously questioned.

We note also that while it is important to distinguish philosophy

---

[10] Many facets of these changes are well documented in A. J. Ayer et al., *The Revolution in Philosophy*, The Macmillan Company, New York, 1960.

from the history of ideas, it is also important to distinguish the history of *ideas* from the history of *philosophy*. Surely, there is ample evidence that we can understand and appraise the works of past philosophers for their soundness, i.e., from a philosophical standpoint. The works of past philosophers can be treated in terms of their cogency and general *philosophical* merit, apart from their "historical significance" and historical context. This is just the sort of approach that is taken by many historians of philosophy. And this is just what distinguishes the history of philosophy from the history of ideas.

But we should not overlook the fact that there have been valuable contributions made to philosophy by historians of ideas—those who have examined past philosophical works *in their historical contexts*. It is just this sort of approach which often enriches our interpretation and understanding of the works of the historical figures.

For many it is difficult to see how the works of the historical figures could be *completely* ignored in an attempt to understand philosophy's nature. Gabriel Marcel (6) suggests that such disregard for the history of our subject constitutes a serious form of ingratitude—based on a failure to acknowledge our debt to the past. Such ingratitude could be perilous and costly to us even though the historical approach may not be the only way to arrive at an understanding of our subject.

Finally, we observe that the proponents of the historical approach are not actually providing us with a *direct* answer to the question "What is philosophy?" Instead they are presenting what they believe is the preferred avenue for *developing an understanding of its nature*. Often, as Heidegger does, they will point to a historical figure or period as the specific, concrete exemplification of what this nature is. For Heidegger, its nature is "essentially Greek." Thus for him the nature of philosophy cannot be described without reference to this historical period, and an understanding of this nature cannot be achieved without direct acquaintance with the thought and culture of this period. There is, then, a pragmatic dimension to his response to our question: one comes to see the nature of philosophy only by accepting his invitation to become historically involved with the culture and thought of this period.

The Activity Approach

One direct approach to our subject is to identify philosophy as an activity and to explain how it differs from or resembles other activities. Here we will focus on (1) *what* philosophy seeks to achieve—the aims of the activity—and (2) *how* it seeks to achieve these aims—the methods or techniques used to achieve them. We will also have to consider the material or subject matter to which the methods or techniques are applied.

Obviously philosophy differs from other activities like field hockey, calisthenics, and acrobatics in a way that mathematics, journalism, and architecture differ from the same activities. Philosophy is, first of all, an intellectual rather than a physical activity. As such, it can be viewed simply as an attempt to provide answers to questions, an aim which it shares with other intellectual activities.

Now it is in characterizing the nature of its questions and answers that we are confronted with a fundamental difference in conviction among philosophers. Isaiah Berlin has suggested that this difference was noted by the Greek poet Archilochus in his remark, "The fox knows many things, but the hedgehog knows one big thing."[11] Presumably the difference the poet is marking is in the *kind* of questions with which a thinker deals.

The philosophical foxes see philosophy primarily as a critical activity with aims similar to those of other critical activities: providing the solutions to specific problems.[12] (It would be unusual to find a critical thinker who would maintain that his competency in philosophy makes him particularly qualified to provide answers to those "large" questions concerning one's place and purpose in the universe.)

---

[11] Isaiah Berlin, *The Hedgehog and the Fox: An Essay on Tolstoy's View of History*, Simon and Schuster, New York, 1966, p. 1. Professor Berlin construes the poet's remark as applying to thinkers in general and not specifically to philosophers.

[12] In our descriptions of the two philosophical types we have interpreted and extended Professor Berlin's characterizations considerably, and on some key points differ in our descriptions. A similar distinction is systematically applied to philosophers by C. D. Broad. See "Critical and Speculative Philosophy," in J. H. Muirhead (ed.), *Contemporary British Philosophy*, First Series, George Allen & Unwin, Ltd., London, 1924, pp. 75–100.

The techniques they apply to problems are generally characterized as analytic. The techniques of logical and linguistic analysis are usually indispensable tools. The philosophical fox, like any good analytic thinker, proceeds on a piecemeal basis toward a solution to a definite problem. Moreover, what he says about one problem need not have a bearing on his solutions to other problems. It is in this sense that he can be said "to know many things." He thinks of his work as at least moderately technical, requiring a recognizable degree of competency in the use of his tools.

What are some of his problems or questions? He is concerned with analyzing concepts like *existence, knowledge, belief, certainty, cause, action, perception, emotion.* He is interested in solutions to problems like the problems of induction, analyticity, personal identity.

What are some of his *specific* analytic techniques? His techniques range from the formal logical techniques of Bertrand Russell, who is grappling with the correct analysis of referring phrases, to the semantic and grammatical techniques of J. L. Austin, who is trying to explain the significance of the distinction between an interrogatory and a relative pronoun for the problem of other minds (i.e., Do any minds other than my own exist?). The critical philosopher might present an argument based on recognition of a formal fallacy or of a category mistake. He might argue by citing a paradigm case of "seeing a table," by citing a counterexample, or by appealing to a difference in the "surface and depth grammar" of an expression.

Finally there is the method which we term "critical constructivism" and which is represented in the works of Rudolf Carnap, G. Bergman, Nelson Goodman, and W. V. Quine. With this method the philosopher tries to develop a constructed language which will express accurately and completely all that needs to be stated, *and nothing more,* concerning a problem area.[13] A variation on this approach is represented in this volume by Paul Lorenzen (7).

One of the often-cited benefits of the critical view is that it puts philosophy on an equal footing with other technical disciplines

---

[13] Here we acknowledge that we have ignored some important differences in approach among these thinkers.

insofar as it gives philosophers a set of techniques whose use can be shared in a way that enables one technician to communicate with others in his field—and even to corroborate the results obtained by others through the use of these techniques. It has been the hope of those who see philosophy in this way that this shared competence would produce a body of results on which there would be wide agreement.

Nonetheless, the extent to which such results have been achieved is questioned by some of our contemporaries—even among those who might be sympathetic with the general view of philosophy as a critical activity. Sidney Hook suggests that although there have been unquestionable advances in the level of complexity of the techniques used by many critical thinkers, the use of such techniques has not produced any significant consensus on solutions to specific philosophical problems. Hook cites several problems which many philosophers once regarded as solved but which are no longer regarded as solved by many of the same thinkers. Hook concludes that philosophy "has become more scientific without the fruits of science." For some, Hook's observation will suggest a *general* problem for the critical philosopher. They will argue that it is necessary for the critical philosopher to formulate and agree upon criteria which can be used to determine that a proposed solution to a philosophical problem is adequate to the problem addressed.[14]

It is important for purposes of our inquiry to observe that although it is characteristic of the critical philosopher to use *some* analytic techniques, there are actually divergent opinions among such thinkers concerning the relative merits of various of these techniques. In short, they do not agree on the efficacy of each such technique. Furthermore they differ in their views on the proper objects or subject matter of philosophical analysis. To some extent, at least, these divergent views can be attributed to their different views on the *specific* aims of the critical activity (as opposed to their *general* agreement on the critical approach itself). For example, Alan White sees philosophy primarily as conceptual analysis

---

[14] Of course one might argue here that the nature of philosophical problems makes it impossible (and even undesirable) to formulate such criteria.

whose specific aim is the discovery of "the necessary characteristics" of things. He presents a clear account of the techniques of ordinary language analysis in which he shows how these techniques are actually applied, and he performs the very difficult task of explaining the significance, in terms of this aim, of the results so achieved. White disagrees with those we have categorized as constructivists. He maintains that insofar as the aim of constructivism is to develop a language which would correlate exactly logical and linguistic differences, it is both impossible and undesirable. J. J. C. Smart agrees with White that philosophy is conceptual analysis, but he argues that as such it cannot be completely autonomous; it must depend ultimately on a test of "scientific plausibility," the meaning of which Smart explains in his essay.

Concerning the subject matter of philosophical inquiry, some critical thinkers believe that what should be analyzed are the concepts of common sense as they are found in ordinary discourse. Others believe that what should be analyzed are concepts as they are found in the language of science. Still others believe that concepts from *both* areas constitute the proper objects of philosophical investigation. Max Fisch (8) views philosophy as a critical activity, but views language as only *one* of our many social institutions that should be the object of the philosopher's critical study.

We have come to see that there are important differences among critical philosophers on those major elements in terms of which the critical activity is characterized: aims, techniques, and subject matter.

The philosophical hedgehog, who "knows one big thing," has a very different view of his activity. His aim is to provide answers to "large" questions, e.g., "What is the nature of the universe?" and "What is man's place in the scheme of things?" In so doing he develops one grand system, a single world view (*Weltanschauung*) that is, as Professor Berlin puts it, "less or more coherent."[15] His system will represent what the philosopher has synthesized and interpreted from the findings of science, history, common sense, art, law, or some combination of these. He is by no means reluctant to

---

[15] Berlin, loc. cit.

draw upon his personal experience as a source of data to be interpreted and synthesized. His interpretation and synthesis are often based upon a single insight or "vision" in terms of which his data are interpreted and organized. This insight constitutes the "one big thing" referred to by Archilochus. Sometimes what he gains through such insight becomes the single, universal organizing principle for that synthesis of all the data which he seeks to achieve. Perhaps Plato, with his theory of forms, and certainly Hegel, with his dialectical, triadic movement of history, represent this view of philosophy. Notice that the philosophical hedgehog does not hesitate to speculate in arriving at organizing principles, in formulating generalizations to cover all of the data he wants to take into account, or in filling gaps in what he claims for his body of knowledge.

Notice also that the philosophical hedgehog does not regard it as *outside the scope of his activity* to provide answers to questions concerning the human predicament. He is fully prepared to tell us what, if anything, is the purpose of our lives and how we should conduct ourselves to realize this purpose. In fact, for many, one of the compelling features of this approach to philosophy is that it seeks to provide a set of comprehensive answers to a broad range of questions.

On the negative side, the problems with this view of philosophy are well known. It is argued that it has resulted in excesses of speculation that go far beyond what is warranted by its data. It allows for a degree of subjectivism in interpreting the data it purports to take into account that, for many, is reckless. At its worst, it makes claims to knowledge that run counter to our current body of scientific knowledge.

Critics of this view also claim that the speculative philosopher is presumptuous in expecting to be able to achieve his aim—that the familiarity with the broad range of data that is required for his task is beyond the power of a single thinker, or even a committee of such thinkers. They maintain too that those best equipped to speculate on observed phenomena are the scientists who have a working familiarity with the data involved in their specialized areas. Also, some point out that once we rely on creative insight or "vision" for the discovery *and validation* of our primary organizing principles, we open the floodgates of philosophy to prophets, poets, visionaries, and even soothsayers and that the evaluation of the system or world views so developed will depend primarily on that insight or vision with which each of us happens to be in tune.

Considerations of this sort motivated the attempts of the early positivists to rule such speculative activity out of philosophy. Although many philosophers concede that there are serious difficulties with positivism, they share the basic motivation of the positivists. They believe that the speculative philosopher's tendency toward excesses of the imagination—all in the name of "creative insight"—should be checked and harnessed.

As Berlin indicates, it would be a mistake to cling for too long to our two categories of fox and hedgehog.[16] Many of the contributions to this volume reflect the view that although philosophers should certainly avoid what J. J. C. Smart calls the "mad speculation" of many earlier hedgehogs, there is unquestionably a place in philosophy for at least a *disciplined* form of speculation, synthesis, and even creative insight.[17] Some thinkers, like Frederick Copleston (9), maintain that analysis and synthesis are both integral parts of the philosophical enterprise. While contending that philosophy can never be divorced from science, Karl Popper sees philosophy's main task as critical speculation about the universe and about "our place" in it including our "powers of knowing" and our "powers for good and evil."

Although he deplores the unharnessed speculation of many philosophers, Brand Blanshard (10) argues that in trying to achieve his aim of understanding and explaining the world, the philosopher supplements science through both criticism and synthesis. Philosophy, he maintains, is "the criticism and the completion of science." Stuart Hampshire contends that there is no *single* correct method in philosophy and even that insight unsupported by "rigorous argument" has been useful in philosophy in the past.

Those who take the view that both criticism and speculation are

---

16 Ibid., p. 2.
17 We do not suggest that all of these thinkers give the same weight to the value of speculative activity.

important dimensions of philosophical activity also try to explain how philosophy differs from other inquiries which exhibit both dimensions, e.g., physics, psychology, linguistics. For example, Blanshard maintains that philosophy's activities are logically "before" and "after" the activities of science. He states that philosophy questions the *starting points* or suppositions of the special sciences and synthesizes the *results* of science and common sense.

Adam Schaff (11) maintains that philosophy differs from other scientific activities insofar as it deals with statements of a higher level of generality than those statements which are characteristic of the sciences. Schaff states that philosophy arrives at its statements through a different process or procedure. The procedure by which they are established is neither inductive nor deductive; and their proof or refutation is not possible. Yet such statements, Schaff maintains, are essential elements in "a unified scientific image of the world."

In concluding the discussion of the *activity approach* to philosophy we observe that some thinkers might object to the emphasis we have placed on philosophy as an intellectual activity. For example, Alan Watts (12) expresses the view that academic philosophy today is pursuing the unattainable in its attempts to translate what there is to be known into verbal descriptions and explanations. The philosopher, he says, *must* replace verbalization with what Watts terms variously "contemplative mysticism," "interior empiricism," and "idealess contemplation." The aim of the philosopher, for Watts, is to remain silent, to experience through the senses what *is*, as opposed to what is represented in common language, and to do so without comment.

Paul Feyerabend (13) believes that the philosopher could benefit considerably by departing from the conventional approach to his subject and problems. Taking his cue from the use of literary devices by Plato, Feyerabend suggests the use of an entirely different medium of expression for the philosopher. He suggests that philosophers utilize the resources and techniques of film making to develop and present their ideas.

Readers may now be struck by the great variety of views on the nature of philosophy. This variety has been noted by some philosophers who urge us to recognize that when we actually look at philosophy as it has been and as it is practiced and taught, we find no *single* set of characteristics—no necessary and sufficient conditions that warrant the application of the term 'philosophy' to a single subject or a single activity. This is the basis for the next approach to our question.

The Pragmatic Approach

At first blush this approach is quite simple. It is sometimes adopted by teachers of introductory philosophy at the start of their courses. Instead of introducing their subject by trying to define it, they explain that their students will come to understand what philosophy is by engaging in those activities which comprise the course: reading and study of the texts, and discussion of the topics which arise in connection with the texts and lectures. Briefly, this pedagogical strategy is based on the conviction that students and others *best* learn what philosophy is by *doing* philosophy.

In support of this approach it is sometimes noted that it works well for other disciplines. For example, physicists usually do not open their lectures by *defining* physics. Instead they "get on directly with the business at hand." Unfortunately, this approach does not seem to succeed for philosophy as it does for physics. We have already noted that students of philosophy are often at just as much of a loss to say what philosophy is *after* courses in philosophy as they are *before* entering their coursework.

There are more serious objections. The instructor who adopts this approach may well be experiencing his own doubts and questions concerning the nature of his subject. He may find that he is not able to say exactly what his subject is even though he pursues it very satisfactorily on a professional basis. (It is interesting that musicians and novelists may similarly pursue their activities very successfully even though, at the same time, they may be unable to define or adequately explain the nature of "music" or "the novel.")

In addition, many philosophers observe that although they once thought they knew what philosophy is, they either are no longer sure or find that their view of it has changed significantly. A. J. Ayer (14) and J. J. C. Smart explain that their views of philosophy have undergone changes at different times in their philosophical careers.

Some thinkers contend that these difficulties reveal a basic mistake in the way we have approached our question. They argue that these problems arise because philosophy has no essential nature, that there are no necessary and sufficient conditions for the correct application of the term 'philosophy'. They would have us recognize that the only reason we are tempted to think that philosophy has an essential nature is because we have not looked carefully enough at all the things which are called 'philosophy'.

This way of approaching our topic can be called (borrowing from Wittgenstein) the family resemblance approach. Careful scrutiny of various members of the same family reveals that some of them share certain body types, others certain facial characteristics, and others, say, certain mannerisms. But such scrutiny also reveals that there is no *single* characteristic or set of characteristics which each of them possesses. Moreover, comparison of different members of a given family results in the recognition that there are significant differences between them. Certain individual members of the family may, in fact, have more in common with members of other families than they do with many members of their own family. The fact that we are able to recognize a resemblance among members of the same family is not because we recognize some characteristic or set of characteristics which they all have in common, but rather because we recognize a set of characteristics which overlap and criss-cross among the members of that family. Wittgenstein would have us see that general terms, for example, 'number' or 'game', are properly understood only if they are viewed as family resemblance terms. Which is to say, according to the way we read the analogy to families, that various games (like the members of a family) may resemble each other in spite of the fact that there is no single characteristic or set of characteristics which they have in common. We also have to recognize that there are significant differences among the activities which we refer to by the word 'games'. Football and chess are games, yet when we examine them we note, for example, that in some important respects football has more in common with calisthenics and big business than it has with chess; and chess has more in common with logic and mathematics than it does with football.

Extending this way of thinking to cover the word 'philosophy', we get the view that if we *look* carefully at the many activities, topics, and problems which come under the heading of 'philosophy', we will see that there is *no* characteristic or characteristics which they all share and which they alone share.

We see this view, which asks us to *look* at philosophy, as an extension of the pragmatic approach—an extension which is made in order to overcome the difficulties cited above. In this volume J. J. C. Smart states that philosophy is a family resemblance concept. We suggest that Paul Ziff's statement (15) can be interpreted along these lines.[18]

W. V. Quine (16) also takes what we regard as a pragmatic approach to our topic. Yet he sees philosophy somewhat differently than those who hold the family resemblance view. He claims that 'philosophy' is "one of a number of blanket terms used by deans and librarians" to group "the myriad topics and problems of science and scholarship under a manageable number of headings." He agrees with those who take the family resemblance approach that the boundaries for the use of this term are by no means well fixed. For Quine its use reflects no common core of competence as does the term 'medicine', since, he contends, philosophy is not a "unified profession" as is medicine. For Quine the way in which the term 'philosophy' is used does not aid us in understanding the nature of our subject. For him the term functions as a label, a kind of extension to a library catalog scheme. The boundaries for its correct application are fluid, like the boundaries for the correct application of geographic regional terms, for example, 'Northwest' and 'Southeast'.

The family resemblance approach will be persuasive for many readers, since it emphasizes the importance of an actual examination of philosophical activity. In so doing, it directs us in a way that resembles any sound empirical inquiry, and it appears to give what-

---

[18] But then perhaps Ziff's statement is best appreciated if one does not attempt to categorize it.

ever results we achieve a firm empirical basis. Yet it has difficulties related to the notion of family resemblance itself, which are still under discussion in the philosophical literature today. It is beyond our scope here to go deeply into this discussion.

In connection with Quine's view we note that it derives much of its force from the difficulties we encounter in fixing the *outer* boundaries for the correct application of the term 'philosophy'. Let us look again at the example relating to the term 'game'. Undoubtedly, there are some activities which we consider borderline cases of games. Nonetheless there are many other activities which we count as games with complete confidence. And there are activities which we count as philosophical with a similar degree of confidence. For example, we would confidently agree that certain works written by Plato are unquestionably philosophical and are philosophical in the same sense as, say, certain works of Aristotle. This judgment is based on the conviction that their approach and subject matter exhibit some common feature or features. We may have difficulties in identifying and explaining these features. But we have no difficulty in deciding that those who produce these works are correctly termed 'philosophers'.

We can extend this reasoning even further. Librarians or deans may disagree about the correct classification of the works of a Paul Tillich. Is he theologian or philosopher? Similar problems occur with Einstein. Is he philosopher or scientist? However, they have no difficulty in classifying the works of a Kant, Hume, or Moore. The boundaries of our subject may indeed be fluid rather than permanently fixed. They may well be, as Quine suggests, akin to regional boundaries connoted by terms like 'Northeast' and 'Middle Atlantic'. But we should not forget that these fluid geographic boundaries are still sufficiently clear to keep us from including New York within those boundaries which we understand as encompassing, say, the Northwest or Southeastern regions. The boundaries may be fluid at the outer edges. But they are not, nor *can* they be, *totally* capricious in their movements.

Of course those who subscribe to the family resemblance approach to philosophy would contend that the reason we have no difficulty in recognizing that there are activities which we count as philosophy with complete confidence is that there is a set of characteristics which overlap and criss-cross throughout the works of thinkers like Plato and Aristotle. In short, we recognize a family resemblance. And such recognition would explain why the boundaries of the term 'philosophy' are not, nor can they be, totally capricious in their movements.

The Paradigm Case Approach

Thus far we have concentrated exclusively on philosophy itself in an attempt to specify what it is, and we have pretty much ignored those persons who profess and study our subject, the philosophers. It might be argued that this is a mistake. Perhaps we can more readily achieve progress in our effort to increase our understanding of philosophy if we concentrate on the philosophers themselves, if we ask what it is that sets the philosopher apart. Some contend that in so doing we can distinguish the "real" philosopher from others, and then by characterizing *his* activities and *his* interests, we will capture the "essence" of our subject.

Our problems here are obvious. On what basis do we select the *real* philosophers? Admittedly, professional philosophers often single out colleagues as "real philosophers," but it is not altogether clear how they are using this term in so doing. They may be using it to suggest that the person to whom it is applied is highly productive, that he produces more than most of his colleagues. But, obviously, we need to ask how production is measured. One way, of course, is to count his publications in philosophy.

But then what would count as a "publication in philosophy"? Would we count only those papers which appear in such journals as *Mind, The Philosophical Review,* or *The Journal of Philosophy*? Or would a publication of a work on contemporary linguistic theory in a journal of linguistics be counted as a publication in philosophy? All of this aside, the term is sometimes applied to someone who has published little or nothing in philosophy. For example, we recognize Socrates as a "real philosopher," and as far as we know, he published nothing.

Finally, we note a general difficulty with this approach. Trying to understand exactly what it is to be a real philosopher by examination of a paradigm case is like trying to understand exactly what a game is by restricting one's attention to football. Unquestionably football is a paradigm case of a game. Nevertheless, if one restricts his attention to football, he will almost certainly fail to understand what it is to be a game. Similarly, if one restricts his attention to Socrates as paradigmatic of what it is to be a real philosopher, one's picture of the real philosopher is apt to be that the real philosopher is concerned with determining what is the proper business of a human being. One usually sees Socrates engaged in dialogues with slaves, freemen, aristocrats, prostitutes, ladies, politicians. This is done with a purpose, and this purpose seems to be to enlighten the other person. To use a contemporary term, Socrates seems to be trying to "expand the consciousness" of those about him. He is very much a teacher; the teacher's function is an inseparable part of our concept of him as a philosopher. He does not offer a final solution to human problems. Socrates is satisfied to see that you have self-doubts, that you surrender your dogmas, that you begin to question those about you, and that you question yourself. His gift is not contentment, complacency, or well-being, but sagacity, curiosity, and honesty.

But if one selects Kant as his paradigm of the philosopher, a much different picture emerges. He is a man happy to live what is apparently an orderly, middle-class life. He worked at philosophy in a way that resembles the contemporary professional in other fields. (Note Alan Watts's disappointment with what he regards as the middle-class, nine-to-five, briefcase-in-hand life styles of many contemporary philosophers.)

Again, if we think of Epicurus as a paradigm case of a philosopher, we are presented with a view which differs from that of Socrates and from that of Kant. Epicurus gives us a picture of the philosopher as a wise and contented man who has benefited considerably from his long years. He gives counsel on how to live—a prescription for "the full rich life." His picture contrasts with that of Socrates, who assiduously avoided giving such counsel. Socrates sought to enlighten his listeners, but he encouraged critical doubt about the way in which they conducted their lives, and he proclaimed his inability to give pat answers to such questions.

Perhaps the key to understanding the *genuine*, or "real," philosopher is to be found in the *attitude* with which he performs his work. The real philosopher, it might be said, exhibits a full, intense commitment to his work, as Socrates did. He is the sort of person who devotes very little effort to accumulating wealth, cultivating friends, advancing his status in the community, or amusing himself with the theatre, concerts, fashions of the day, or other conventional sources of diversion. The idea of a hobby is foreign and abhorrent to him. The "real" philosopher, it might be argued, spends most of his time doing philosophy.

This is an attractive portrayal of the "real" philosopher, but it does not withstand critical appraisal. First, intense commitment of this kind is exhibited by many persons *outside* of philosophy. Artists, politicians, mathematicians, poets, and sports *aficionados* sometimes exhibit such commitment to their areas of interest. For this reason, passionate commitment alone cannot be a sufficient condition for use of the term 'real philosopher'. Moreover, it is not clear that this sort of single-minded dedication is even necessary. Recall the accounts we have of Hume's life. Here is one of our outstanding modern thinkers who lived a well-balanced life, who enjoyed the pleasures of the salons of his day and doubtless fully appreciated the subtleties and skill of a game of billiards as well as the delights of the dining table.

Thus far our aim has been to present some of the problems which arise in the attempt to characterize philosophy. It would be a mistake to conclude from our presentation that *none* of the approaches we have described is viable, or that none of them is to be preferred over any of the others, for there may well be satisfactory and persuasive answers to the questions we have raised regarding each approach. For this reason the reader is encouraged to examine carefully the statements of the philosophers in this volume where he may find what he takes to be satisfactory answers to these questions.

As we have already suggested, our evaluation of the charge that contemporary philosophy is not relevant might depend very much on *how* we see philosophy. Needless to say, it is not our aim in this introduction to provide a conclusive answer to the question "What

is philosophy?" Let us now proceed to consider the charge that
philosophy is irrelevant.

IV

In considering the charge pertaining to the *relevance* of philosophy, we employ a technique that is familiar to students and practitioners of our subject. First we identify and explain various senses
of this crucial term in order to clarify the charge. We shall see that
this charge can be interpreted in several ways, and that the issues
it raises differ depending upon the interpretation given to it. For
each sense of the crucial term that is distinguished and for each
corresponding interpretation of the charge, we then give some of
the main replies that might be made to it. We also begin to show
how the effects of the charge vary depending upon the approach to
philosophy one espouses. In this way we hope to illuminate key
issues the charge raises, as well as the logic of the arguments which
surround these issues.

The success of this technique does not require us to restrict ourselves to what the critics have said concerning the interpretation of
their charge. Often the critics do not explain how their charge is to
be construed; they do not state which of the various senses of the
term 'relevant' they intend when they make the charge. It is one of
the advantages of the technique we are using that we can proceed
despite their failure to identify *the* sense or senses in which they
claim that philosophy is not relevant. With this technique we try
to make clear the alternative, plausible interpretations of this term
so that we will better understand what the critics intend by the
charge. (A complete analysis of this sort would take into account
all of the pertinent interpretations in this manner. We do not pretend that our analysis is exhaustive. We note especially that we will
not discuss *all* of the issues raised by the various interpretations we
provide of the charge that philosophy is irrelevant.)

We sometimes say that the data produced in an empirical, scientific inquiry is 'relevant' to a hypothesis. Similarly we say that the
testimony of a witness is 'relevant' to the defendant's guilt (or
innocence). In an empirical inquiry we use the term in this way to

note that the data constitute evidence which tends to confirm or disconfirm the hypothesis in question. In applying the term to the testimony of a witness, we are noting that the data so *presented* constitutes evidence bearing upon the legal question at hand. *We call this the evidential sense of the term 'relevant'.*

There is another use of the term readily recognized by students of logic, in which we say that one statement is relevant to another in the sense that the former supports the latter, as a *premise* supports a *conclusion* in formal inferences. Examples are easily cited from introductory logic texts. The generalization "All union leaders oppose wage controls" is relevant in this sense to "George Meany opposes wage controls." Once we include the additional premise "George Meany is a union leader," we have met the requirements for a sound argument. *Thus our generalization represents one class of statements which can be what we term strictly relevant to the truth or falsity of some claim.*

It is clear that those we have classified as *speculative* philosophers believe that it is well within the scope of their philosophical activities to select, interpret, and present "data" that are *evidentially relevant* to sociopolitical problems and to problems relating to the human predicament. For example, many would interpret the detailed treatment of the master-servant relationship given by Hegel as data which are *evidentially relevant* to problems in human relations—problems which always confront teacher and student, employer and employee, and, perhaps, husband and wife.

These philosophers argue that many of these "data" do not receive adequate treatment by the sciences. It has been claimed that in part this is what has prompted outstanding existentialists to use the novel and the theatre as vehicles to present "data" which they believe have significance for the human predicament.

It is also clear that the speculative philosophers regard it as within their proper scope to formulate generalizations that enter into our thinking in ways which they believe *can* be strictly relevant to conclusions concerning each man's purposes, problems, and roles in the general scheme of things.

Let us suppose, for example, that a speculative philosopher formulates several generalizations such as these: (1) Historical events take place according to a definite pattern, say a pattern modeled on the movements of a pendulum in which there is movement from very tradition-bound conservatism, on one hand, to a progressive, change-oriented liberalism, on the other. (2) The position of the pendulum, i.e., the sociopolitical climate, can be determined and even anticipated through various clues, such as the dominant literary, dramatic, musical, and other artistic motifs, styles, or movements of the period. For example, this speculative philosopher maintains that in music the well-structured, even cadences and harmonies of a Haydn or Brahms are indicators of a conservative period, while the "loosely" structured, uneven cadences and dissonant chords of a Stravinsky or Bartök are indicators of a liberal period. (3) The highest form of morality consists of actions which are "in tune" with the temper or spirit of the times. That is, during a conservative period, *what is right* is what sustains tradition; and during a liberal period, *what is right* is what promotes change.

Now it is easy to see how these generalizations can be construed as starting points or premises on the basis of which one might derive conclusions which easily serve to direct one's sociopolitical and ethical conduct. They can be viewed as providing a basis for action—a framework within which one's sociopolitical and ethical decisions are made and as a basis for position statements on sociopolitical questions. If I know that my historical period is characterized by an extreme liberalism and that my actions and choices (as a moral person) should be in keeping with the mood or spirit of my period, I have a well-delineated framework within which I can exercise my options.

Of course this is at best only a caricature of our leading speculative philosophers. Nevertheless this caricature of speculative philosophy is not unheard of within philosophy for the very reason that generalizations of this *sort* have, in fact, been *presented and used* by some philosophers—at least roughly as we have presented and used them here. These statements might be generalizations concerning economic phenomena (Marx), historical events (Hegel), or human existence (Sartre). For such speculative philosophers, *formulating* and *using* generalizations in this way is an important facet of the *synthesis* so necessary to the formation of a world view, a total outlook or perspective.[19]

Now the critical philosopher, on the other hand, is often taken to task by critics for *not* producing results which can be either *evidentially relevant* or *strictly relevant* to current sociopolitical issues or to questions concerning the human predicament.

Many of these critical thinkers would enter a demurrer to this complaint. They would concede that their work is not relevant in either of these ways. They would also argue that the development and presentation of such data and such generalizations are definitely *outside* of their scope. They view these as tasks proper to history or to social sciences like political science, economics, psychology, and sociology; and they insist that they are by no means qualified by their philosophical training for such tasks.

Some critical philosophers would also contend that the outcome of this speculative activity is presumably either (1) a body of factual data or (2) a class of general statements which are descriptive, i.e., which *describe* events, things, etc. As such, they would argue these factual data and general statements cannot in themselves do the job which the speculative philosopher wants them to do. They claim that the speculative philosopher is looking for support for conclusions which, at bottom, tell us what we *ought* to do. Such statements are prescriptive—they *prescribe* conduct and actions. And statements of this sort appear to be required to satisfy the critic's demand for direction and counsel in the choices we must all make in our daily lives.

These critical thinkers agree with Hume that we cannot derive prescriptive (or normative) conclusions from such *descriptive* statements; we cannot derive a statement of what *ought* to be from one or more statements about what *is*.[20] (We shall see that this distinction between descriptive and prescriptive statements is important in connection with another interpretation of the charge of irrelevance.)

---

[19] We acknowledge the difficulties some philosophers will find in calling our sample expressions "generalizations."

[20] There are, of course, other issues involved here. Discussion of them is omitted because of the constraints on the scope of our treatment.

It is important to note that many critical thinkers believe that they *do* have a critical function to perform with respect to such statements. They believe that they can apply their critical skills to the *interpretation* of such evidentially relevant data and to the methodology used in formulating descriptive generalizations. Beyond this, some thinkers, like Sidney Hook, observe that a thorough familiarity with the findings of the social scientist is required for those philosophers who are interested in engaging in social philosophy.

V

Finalliy, we identify a use of the term 'relevance' that has gained considerable currency today. It is often found in discussions of sociopolitical issues when one party characterizes an activity, position, program, plan, or action as *irrelevant* to some avowed sociopolitical objectives. Often the speaker means that the former do not serve to advance or further such objectives. Sometimes the same complaint is voiced with respect to philosophy by saying that philosophy is not *useful*, that it does not contribute to the realization of the avowed objectives.[21] This is the *same* sense of 'relevant' in which it is argued that a classical education is irrelevant to the social objective of equipping minority group members for a place in our competitive, technological job market. *We call this the objectives-oriented use of the term.*

It is this use of the term that Herbert Marcuse (17) seems to have in mind when he argues for a basic redirection of our philosophical efforts. Marcuse contends that "reality . . . has invalidated the historical relevance of philosophy." He sees "pure" philosophy today as "*reduced* to the order of an intellectual exercise. . . ." Marcuse expresses what he regards as this *irrelevance* of philosophy to avowed objectives as follows:

---

[21] 'Useful' and 'relevant' overlap here. There are other ways in which these two terms overlap. But they should be distinguished because a critic *might* acknowledge that the works of some philosophers appear to be *relevant* but still maintain that philosophy is not *useful* since there is no agreement among philosophers that these works are *sound*.

What is the point in subtle epistemological investigations when science and technology, not unduly worried about the foundations of their knowledge, increase daily their mastery of nature and man? What is the point of a linguistic analysis which steers clear of the transformation of language (ordinary language!) into an instrument of political control? What is the point in philosophical reflections on the meaning of good and evil when Auschwitz, the Indonesian massacres, and the war in Vietnam provide a definition which suffocates all discussion on ethics? And what is the point in further philosophical occupation with Reason and Freedom when the resources and the features of a rational society, and the need for liberation are all too clear, and the problem is, not their concept but the political practice of their realization?

Apparently Marcuse is arguing that the work of contemporary philosophers does not *advance* such objectives as the "mastery of nature and man," "political control," and "liberation," and hence is not relevant in this *objectives-oriented* sense.

For many critics, this call for objectives-oriented, relevant activity is a demand that the philosopher commit himself to the realization of such objectives *and* that he redirect his efforts *as a philosopher* to activities which count in those arenas where sociopolitical processes are played out.

Some critical philosophers will be quick to point out that participation in these activities presupposes a prescriptive or normative judgment with respect to the values associated with such objectives. They will cite the difficulty involved in attempting to derive prescriptive conclusions from descriptive premises which has already been noted. But there are additional problems here.

Let us consider that to a large degree the thrust of Marcuse's charges is directed against those philosophers who see philosophy primarily as linguistic or logical analysis. These philosophers are the "purists" whom many critics forcefully reprimand for reasons similar to those given by Marcuse.

We suggest that this is due to a feature of their philosophical approach which is more basic to their approach and which applies more generally to restrict the scope of their activities than does the distinction between prescriptive and descriptive statements. This feature of their approach rules out of their direct philosophical concern a class of statements of which prescriptive statements are only one subclass.[22] We shall see that this feature very likely accounts for their reluctance to do *relevant* philosophy in the previous senses identified, as well as in the *objectives-oriented* sense of the term 'relevant' which we are now discussing. This feature involves a distinction which is discussed by several of our contributors, including Alan White, J. J. C. Smart, and Frederick Copleston.

We recall our earlier observation that the *primary* aim of many critical philosophers is in the correct analysis of concepts like *truth, knowledge, certainty, good,* or *cause.* These thinkers distinguish between first- and second-order inquiries and regard such analysis as part of a *second-order* inquiry. Very briefly, such analysis consists in determining *what it means to say,* for example, that one event is the cause of another event. This is to be distinguished from the *first-order* inquiry, in which one tries to determine what events, *in fact,* are the causes of other events. According to these thinkers the philosopher concerns himself with the correct analysis of *cause,* but not with identifying specific causes of other events. As Alan White puts it, the *philosopher* conducts a second-order inquiry into those characteristics a thing must have if it is to fall into the class of causes. The specification of such characteristics is the *aim* of philosophical analysis. On the other hand, it is the *scientist* who determines that some specific event is the cause of some other specific event.

These critical philosophers go on to explain that as philosophers their scope is *restricted* to such second-order inquiries. As White puts it, "philosophy has no interest in *what* things, if any, *are,* e.g., just or known [first order], but only in what it is *to be* just or known [second order]."[23]

There are several observations relating to this distinction that deserve notice. Some of these introduce various ironic turns which

---

[22] We should be careful here. We are not suggesting that these philosophers do not share Marcuse's interest in advancing any of the objectives he cites. The point here is that where they do share such concern, they do so as conscientious citizens and not as philosophers.

[23] Our italics. We note that not all critical philosophers are convinced that this distinction between first- and second-order levels of inquiry can be sustained. For example, J. J. C. Smart observes that if Quine's view on the analytic-synthetic distinction is correct, then it may *not* be possible to sustain this distinction.

the discussion among philosophers concerning this distinction has taken. An examination of these will be instructive for our purposes.

One of the most obvious of these ironic turns arises simply from the circumstances surrounding one notable instance in which this distinction came into play; it occurred in a discussion of the ethical views of Bertrand Russell, and is discussed by Copleston in his contribution to this volume.[24] First, consider that Russell's life was indisputably rich with relevant activities—in any interesting sense of that term—not the least of which were activities in which he espoused and advanced many of the causes of an enlightened liberalism on the basis of his preference for the ethical values associated with such a sociopolitical approach. At the same time, Russell had argued *philosophically* for an emotive analysis of certain basic ethical terms. According to this *philosophical* position, to say that a thing is, say, *good* is only to express one's feelings or attitudes toward that thing. On this view, what one expresses here is not capable of validation or verification of any sort simply because one is not expressing anything other than his emotions or attitudes. This led some philosophers to charge that Russell's *philosophical emotivism* was at odds with his *espousal of humanitarian and liberal values and causes*. Critics of Russell asked how one who maintained that to say that something is good is only to express one's favorable attitude toward that thing could *also* espouse various causes with which a definite set of values or "goods" are associated. They felt that Russell's emotivism barred him from trying to persuade or convince others as to what things are good.

Russell, in turn, maintained that there was no inconsistency involved in this position.[25] In *our* terms, Russell argued that there was no inconsistency between his particular first- and second-order views.

Now many philosophers have extended his contention to cover, more generally, the relationship between any first- and second-order analysis in ethics and in other areas of philosophy. They maintain that there is no logical connection between one's second-order views in ethics (how we analyze basic ethical concepts like *good* and

---

[24] See, for example, Justus Buchler, "Russell and the Principles of Ethics," in Paul Arthur Schilpp (ed.), *The Philosophy of Bertrand Russell*, 3d ed., Tudor Publishing Company, New York, 1951, pp. 511–535.

[25] Bertrand Russell, "Reply to Criticisms," in ibid., p. 724.

right), and one's first-order views in that field (*what* we identify as *good, right*). Of course it is also ironic that *this* position results in the apparent gap between philosophy and self-commitment that is noted by Copleston.

Now we are in a position to complete the picture. Those critical philosophers who fall under Marcuse's criticisms would reply that the objectives Marcuse wishes to advance imply commitment to a set of values. As philosophers they cannot argue for such values, since such arguments take them into the area of *first*-order inquiry. As philosophers they are limited to inquiries concerning what it means to say that something is ethically valuable or good. But they do not see it as their task to identify *what* is ethically valuable or good.

When this basic distinction between the two levels of analysis is coupled with a view of philosophy as consisting *exclusively* in *second*-order analysis, we can easily see how critics would regard the work of those so-called purists as *irrelevant* to current socio-political and ethical issues.

This is a mistake. And to show that this is a mistake we need only point to Alan White's notion of a "conceptual derivation" in which second-order statements can serve as premises in deductive inferences whose conclusions, we suggest, could constitute position statements on such issues. In such a derivation a conclusion is derived from at least one premise whose acceptability is based on the second-order analysis of a particular concept which functions as a key element in the derivation. White's example is as follows:

> . . . if it is true that young people are interested only in what affects themselves, then, if an analysis of *interest* in terms of an *inclination to pay attention* is correct, it would be true that young people are inclined to pay attention only to what affects themselves.

Specifically, White's example suggests to us that the apparent gap between philosophy and commitment might be closed by combining the results of second-order inquiries (in his example, the "analysis of *interest* in terms of *inclination to pay attention*") with the results of first-order inquiries ("young people are interested only in what affects themselves").

Thus even if there is a logical gap between first- and second-order inquiries, it is still possible to combine results from these two levels of inquiry in ways that can make second-order statements relevant to the crisis problems of the day—relevant in both the strict and the objectives-oriented senses. If we consider the use of similar second-order results for the concepts of *right, duty, justice,* and *equality,* their relevance to today's crisis problems becomes an important challenge. We suggest that the application of second-order results in this way is a task for the social philosopher and more generally, perhaps, for applied—as opposed to "pure"—philosophy.

In addition we refer the reader to Hook's essay, where he will find what we believe is another interesting application of second-order analysis in dealing with current problems and programs relating to equal opportunity.

The reader might still ask what can be said of the philosopher who takes the purist approach to his subject and restricts his work as a philosopher to second-order inquiries.[26] We suggest that if the philosopher takes this distinction seriously, then *perhaps* we demand too much of him by asking that he commit himself *as a philosopher* to the advancement of objectives we espouse. Of course this does not imply that we cannot appeal to him, in behalf of our objectives, as a citizen—or as one who shares our concern for a particular set of values. Nor does it prevent him from responding with enthusiasm to our appeal. Beyond this, however, when we demand that he respond as a philosopher, what we require of him may result in a violation of the integrity of his philosophical thinking. And in so doing we may resemble those who ran short of patience and understanding in the court of Athens over two thousand years ago and finally issued that terrible judgment condemning Socrates to death after hearing him deliver what Karl Popper calls an "impressive apology of philosophy."

The study of philosophy is to be recommended for many reasons which are unrelated to the stand one takes regarding the philoso-

---

[26] What follows here can also be said of the philosopher who confines himself generally to the pursuit of those theoretical interests to which Quine refers in his comments.

pher's responsibility to deal with social and political issues. We shall mention a few of them.

It can assist us in developing alternative views which might not otherwise occur to us. For example, no one who has read Sartre, as well as other existential writers, can help but recognize that if Sartre is correct in holding that God does not exist and hence cannot dictate what is to be regarded as right or wrong, good or bad, then it is extremely difficult to justify one's own beliefs concerning these basic ethical questions. Such an awareness frequently leads one to consider in great detail various nontheistic ethical theories in the hope that some objective grounds regarding right and wrong will be found.

In addition, anyone who seriously reads such philosophers as Leibniz, Spinoza, Hegel, and MacTaggart is very apt to profit from the way these men viewed the universe. Whether or not one adopts their ways of looking at or understanding the universe, one is still made aware of the capacity that the human mind has for creating alternative ways of viewing the world. And this awareness can lead to a more creative approach to matters close to one's own immediate concerns. Such philosophers, like poets, painters, sculptors, and musicians, are capable generally of enriching our lives, by showing us a wide range of unfamiliar alternatives and possibilities.

The study of philosophy can also assist us by sharpening our abilities to detect the ambiguities which occur in ordinary speech and which affect our thinking. One who has read philosophers like Russell, Moore, Austin, or Wittgenstein, to name only a few, cannot help but recognize ambiguities in the thinking of others as well as in his own thinking. For example, the distinction between 'possible for' and 'possible that' develops a certain critical awareness as regards any claims to the effect that *something is possible.* The lawyer who compassionately responds to his client's demands to know whether or not the governor is going to commute his sentence by claiming, "It's possible," will find himself hard pressed if his client is aware of the distinction between 'possible for' and 'possible that'. For the lawyer is apt to be informed by his client that if the lawyer means that it's possible *for* the governor to do so, the client is unimpressed. Any governor has it in his power to commute a sentence, and in fact it is possible *for* this governor to do so even if he has already made it clear to the lawyer that he does not plan to do so. The client wants to know whether it is possible *that* the governor will do so. In other words, is there any evidence or reason for thinking that the governor will commute his sentence?

The contributions of philosophy are to a large degree those of rational and theoretical inquiry. Indeed, some thinkers maintain that it is primarily because philosophy has been so much a theoretical inquiry that there are no results in philosophy on which all philosophers agree. Thus J. O. Urmson explains that "whenever within any field of philosophy (or what has hitherto been counted as philosophy) we find a sure method or procedure and an agreed way of testing hypotheses we cease to call that field philosophy any longer. Philosophy is thus the fissiparous mother of all the sciences."[27]

Some critics would be willing to concede much of what has been said in defense of the study of philosophy in general. Yet they would claim that there are specific areas within philosophy, and usually they cite epistemology, which are so abstract as to be of little or no value in practice. John Wisdom (18) attempts to answer this kind of objection. He argues that the study of epistemology can lead to enlightenment which is of value to us in practice.

VI

Of course there is a great deal more to be said about our topics. And again we direct the reader to the statements by our contributors, where many of their views which we have described only briefly are more adequately presented and more fully developed.

We believe that the current critics of philosophy and philosophers, like their historical predecessors, do our subject a service by stimulating the sort of critical self-examination among philosophers which is provided by our contributors. We believe that the variety of thought presented in our contributors' statements shows that, in Sidney Hook's words, "the great philosophers are not men of one

---

[27] J. O. Urmson, "Introduction," in J. O. Urmson (ed.), *The Concise Encyclopaedia of Western Philosophy and Philosophers*, Hutchinson and Co. (Publishers), Ltd., London, 1960, p. 11.

note, or of one season, or of one mood." Finally, we believe that philosophy's critics can ignore what the philosophers have said here only out of a disinterest and impatience which would make the critics mean judges of those whom they charge—and which would betray a lack of that sense of history which is, after all, the basis of the wisdom we all seek.

ONE

HOW I SEE PHILOSOPHY

Karl R. Popper

I

There is a famous and spirited paper by my late friend Friedrich Waismann under this title.[1] I admire much in his paper, and there are even a number of points in it with which I can agree, even though my approach is totally different from his.

Fritz Waismann and many of his colleagues take it for granted that philosophers are a special kind of people, and that philosophy can be looked upon as their peculiar activity. And what he tries to do, in his paper, is to show, with the help of examples, what constitutes the distinctive character of a philosopher, and the distinctive character of philosophy, if compared with other academic subjects such as mathematics or physics. Thus he tries, especially, to give a description of the interests and activities of contemporary academic philosophers, and of the sense in which they can be said to carry on what philosophers did in the past.

Not only is all this very interesting, but Waismann's paper exhibits a considerable degree of personal engagement in these academic activities, and even of excitement. Clearly, he himself is a philosopher, body and soul, in the sense of this special group of philosophers, and clearly, he wishes to convey to us something of the excitement which is shared by the members of this somewhat exclusive community.

---

[1] F. Waismann, in H. D. Lewis (ed.), *Contemporary British Philosophy*, Third Series, 2d ed., George Allen & Unwin, Ltd., London, 1961, pp. 447–490.

II

The way I see philosophy is totally different. I think that all men and all women are philosophers, though some are more so than others. I agree that there is such a thing as a distinctive and exclusive group of people, the academic philosophers, but I am far from sharing Waismann's enthusiasm about their activities and their approach. On the contrary, I feel that there is much to be said for those (they are, in my view, philosophers of a kind) who are suspicious of academic philosophy. At any rate, I am deeply opposed to an idea (a philosophical idea) whose influence, unexamined and never mentioned, pervades Waismann's brilliant essay: I mean the idea of an intellectual and philosophical *élite*.[2]

I admit, of course, that there have been a few truly great philosophers, and also a small number of philosophers who, though admirable in many ways, just missed being great. But although what they have produced ought to be of major importance for any academic philosopher, philosophy does not depend on them in the sense in which painting depends upon the great painters or music upon the great composers. Besides, great philosophy—for example, that of the pre-Socratics—antedates all academies and all professions.

III

In my own view, professional philosophy has not done too well. It is in urgent need of an *apologia pro vita sua*—a defense of its existence.

I even feel that the fact that I am a professional philosopher myself establishes a serious case against me: I feel it as an accusation. I must plead guilty, and offer, like Socrates, my apology.

I refer to Plato's *The Apology of Socrates* because of all works on philosophy ever written I like it best. I conjecture that it is historically true—that it tells us, by and large, what Socrates said before the Athenian court. I like it because here speaks a man,

---

[2] This idea comes to the fore in such remarks of Waismann's as "Indeed, a philosopher is a man who senses as it were hidden crevices in the build of our concepts where others only see the smooth path of commonplaceness before them." Ibid., p. 448.

modest and fearless. And his apology is very simple: he insists that he is aware of his limitations, not wise, except possibly in his awareness of the fact that he is not wise; and that he is a critic, especially of all high-sounding jargon, yet a friend of his fellow men and a good citizen.

This is not only the apology of Socrates, but it is in my view an impressive apology for philosophy.

IV

But let us look at the case for the prosecution against philosophy. Many philosophers, and among them some of the greatest, have not done too well. Even Plato, the greatest, deepest, and most gifted of all philosophers, had an outlook on human life which I find repulsive and indeed horrifying. Yet he was not only a great philosopher and the founder of the greatest professional school of philosophy, but a great and inspired poet; and he wrote, among other beautiful works, *The Apology of Socrates*.

What ailed him, and so many professional philosophers after him, was that, in stark contrast to Socrates, he believed in the *élite*: in the Kingdom of Philosophy. While Socrates demanded that the statesman should be wise, that is, aware of how little he knows, Plato demanded that the wise, the learned philosophers, should be absolute rulers. Ever since Plato, megalomania has been the philosophers' most widespread occupational disease.

David Hume, who was not a professional philosopher, and who was, next to Socrates, perhaps the most candid and well-balanced of all philosophers and a thoroughly modest, rational, and reasonably dispassionate man, was led, by an unfortunate and mistaken theory of knowledge which taught him to distrust his own very remarkable powers of reason, to the terrible doctrine, "Reason is, and ought only to be, the slave of the passions, and can never pretend to any other office than to serve and obey them."[3] I am ready to admit that nothing great has ever been achieved without passion, but I believe in the very opposite of Hume's statement. The taming of our pas-

---

[3] David Hume, *A Treatise of Human Nature*, ed. Selby-Bigge, Clarendon Press, Oxford, 1888 (and many later editions), book II, part III, sec. III, p. 415.

sions by that limited reasonableness of which we may be capable is, in my view, the only hope for mankind.

Spinoza, the saint among the great philosophers and like Socrates and like Hume not a philosopher by profession, taught almost exactly the opposite to Hume, but in a way which I, for one, hold to be not only mistaken but also ethically unacceptable. He was a determinist (as was Hume), and human freedom consisted for him solely in having a clear, distinct, and adequate understanding of the true causes of our actions: "An affect, which is a passion, ceases to be a passion as soon as we form a clear and distinct idea of it."[4] As long as it is a passion, we are in its clutches and unfree; once we have a clear and distinct idea of it, we are still determined by it, but we have transformed it into part of our reason. And this alone is freedom.

I regard this teaching as an untenable and dangerous form of rationalism, even though I am a rationalist of sorts myself. First of all, I do not believe in determinism, and I do not think that Spinoza or anybody else has produced strong arguments in its support, or in support of a reconciliation of determinism with human freedom (and thus with common sense). It seems to me that Spinoza's determinism is a typical philosopher's mistake, even though it is of course true that much of what we are doing (but not all) is determined and even predictable. Secondly, though it may be true in some sense that an excess of what Spinoza means by 'passion' makes us unfree, his formula would make us not responsible for our actions whenever we cannot form a clear, distinct, and adequate rational idea of the motives of our actions. But, I assert, we never can; and although to be reasonable in our actions and in our dealings with our fellow creatures is, I think, a most important aim (and Spinoza certainly thought so too), I do not think it an aim which we can ever say that we have reached.

Kant, one of the few admirable and highly original thinkers among professional philosophers, tried to solve Hume's problem of the rejection of reason, and Spinoza's problem of determinism; yet he failed in both attempts.

---

[4] Benedictus de Spinoza, *Ethics*, book V, proposition III.

These are some of the greatest philosophers, philosophers whom I truly admire. You will understand why I feel that philosophy has not done too well, and why I feel so apologetic about it.

V

I was never, like my friends Fritz Waismann, Herbert Feigl, Victor Kraft, Hans Hahn, Karl Menger, Philipp Frank, Rudolf Carnap, and Franz Urbach, a member of the Vienna Circle of logical positivists; in fact, Otto Neurath called me "the official opposition." I was never invited to any of the meetings of the Circle, I suppose owing to my well-known opposition to positivism. (I would have been delighted to accept an invitation, for not only were some of the members of the Circle personal friends of mine, but I also had the greatest admiration for some of the other members.) Under the influence of Ludwig Wittgenstein's *Tractatus Logico-Philosophicus*, the Circle had become not only antimetaphysical, but antiphilosophical. Schlick, the leader of the Circle,[5] formulated this by way of the prophecy that philosophy, "which never talks sense but only meaningless nonsense," will soon disappear, because philosophers will find that their audience, tired of empty tirades, has gone away.

Waismann agreed with Wittgenstein and Schlick for many years. I think I can detect in his enthusiasm for philosophy the enthusiasm of the convert.

I always defended philosophy and even metaphysics against the Circle, even though I had to admit that philosophers had not been doing too well. For I believed that many people, and I among them, had genuine philosophical problems of various degrees of seriousness and difficulty, and that these problems were not all insoluble.

Indeed the existence of urgent and serious philosophical problems and the need to discuss them critically is, in my view, the only apology for what may be called professional or academic philosophy.

Wittgenstein and the Vienna Circle denied the existence of serious philosophical problems.

According to the end of the *Tractatus*, the apparent problems of

---

[5] The Vienna Circle was, in fact, Schlick's private seminar, and members were personally invited by Schlick.

philosophy (including those of the *Tractatus* itself) are pseudo-problems which arise from speaking without having given meaning to all one's words. This theory may be regarded as inspired by Russell's solution of the logical paradoxes as pseudo-propositions which are neither true nor false but meaningless. This led to the modern philosophical technique of branding all sorts of inconvenient propositions or problems as 'meaningless'. The later Wittgenstein used to speak of "puzzles," caused by the philosophical misuse of language. I can only say that if I had no serious philosophical problems and no hope of solving them, I should have no excuse for being a philosopher: to my mind, there would be no apology for philosophy.

VI

In this section I will list certain views of philosophy and certain activities that are often taken to be characteristic of philosophy which I, for one, find unsatisfactory. The section could be entitled "How I Do Not See Philosophy."

1. I do not see philosophy as the solving of linguistic puzzles.

2. I do not see philosophy as a series of works of art, as striking and original pictures of the world, or as clever and unusual ways of describing the world. I think that if we look upon philosophy in this way, we do a great injustice to the great philosophers. The great philosophers were not engaged in an aesthetic endeavor. They did not try to be architects of clever systems; but they were, first of all, like the great scientists, seekers after truth—after true solutions of genuine problems. No, I see the history of philosophy essentially as one of the search for truth, and I reject the *purely* aesthetic view of it, even though beauty is important in philosophy as well as in science.

I am all for intellectual boldness. We cannot be intellectual cowards and seekers for truth at the same time. A seeker for truth has to dare to be wise—he has to dare to be a revolutionary in the field of thought.

3. I do not see the long history of philosophical systems as one of intellectual edifices in which all possible ideas are tried out,

and in which truth may perhaps come to light as a by-product. I believe that we are doing an injustice to the truly great philosophers of the past if we doubt for a moment that every one of them would have discarded his system (as he should have done) had he become convinced that, although perhaps brilliant, it was not a step on the way to truth. (This, incidentally, is the reason why I do not regard Fichte or Hegel as real philosophers: I mistrust their devotion to truth.)

4. I do not see philosophy as an attempt either to clarify or to analyze or to "explicate" concepts, or words, or languages.

Concepts or words are mere tools for formulating propositions, conjectures, and theories. Concepts or words cannot be true in themselves; they merely serve human descriptive and argumentative language. Our aim should not be to analyze *meanings*, but to seek for interesting and important *truths*; that is, for true *theories*.

5. I do not see philosophy as a way of being clever.

6. I do not see philosophy as a kind of intellectual therapy (Wittgenstein), an activity of helping people out of philosophical perplexities. To my mind, Wittgenstein (in his later work) did not show the fly the way out of the bottle. Rather, I see in the fly, unable to escape from the bottle, a striking self-portrait of Wittgenstein.

7. I do not see philosophy as a study of how to express things more precisely or exactly. Precision and exactness are not intellectual values in themselves, and we should never try to be more precise or exact than is demanded by the problem in hand.

8. Accordingly, I do not see philosophy as an attempt to provide the foundations or the conceptual framework for solving problems which may turn up in the nearer or the more distant future. John Locke did so; he wanted to write an essay on ethics, and considered it necessary first to provide the conceptual preliminaries.

His *Essay* consists of these preliminaries, and British philosophy has ever since (with very few exceptions such as some of the political essays of Hume) remained bogged down in preliminaries.

9. Nor do I see philosophy as an expression of the spirit of the time. This is a Hegelian idea which does not stand up to criticism. Fashions there are in philosophy, as there are in science. But

a genuine searcher for truth will not follow fashion; he will distrust fashions and even fight them.

VII

All men and all women are philosophers; or, let us say, if they are not conscious of having philosophical problems, they have, at any rate, philosophical prejudices. Most of these are theories which they unconsciously take for granted, or which they have absorbed from their intellectual environment or from tradition.

Since few of these theories are consciously held, they are prejudices in the sense that they are held without critical examination, even though they may be of great importance for the practical actions of people, and for their whole life.

It is an apology for the existence of professional philosophy that men are needed who *examine critically* these widespread and influential theories.

This is the insecure starting point of all science and of all philosophy. All philosophy must start from the dubious and often pernicious views of uncritical common sense. Its aim is enlightened, critical, common sense: a view nearer to the truth, and with a less pernicious influence on human life.

VIII

Let me present some examples of widespread philosophical prejudices.

There is a very influential philosophical view of life to the effect that whenever something happens in this world that is really bad (or that we dislike), then there must be somebody intentionally responsible for it; somebody who has done it. This view is very old. In Homer the envy and the anger of the gods were responsible for most of the terrible things that happened in the field before Troy, and to Troy itself; and it was Poseidon who was responsible for the misadventures of Odysseus. In later Christian thought it is the Devil who is responsible for evil; in vulgar Marxism it is the conspiracy of the greedy capitalists that prevents the coming of socialism and the establishment of heaven on earth.

The theory which sees war, poverty, and unemployment as the

result of some evil intention, of some sinister design, is part of common sense, but it is uncritical. I have called this uncritical commonsense theory the *conspiracy theory of society*. One might even call it the conspiracy theory of the world. It is widely held and, in the form of a search for scapegoats, it has inspired much political strife and has created much avoidable suffering.

One aspect of the conspiracy theory of society is that it encourages real conspiracies. But a critical investigation shows that conspiracies hardly ever attain their aims. Lenin, who held the conspiracy theory, was a conspirator, and so were Mussolini and Hitler. But Lenin's aims were not realized in Russia, nor were Mussolini's or Hitler's aims realized in Italy or Germany. All these conspirators became conspirators because they believed in an uncritical conspiracy theory of society.

It may perhaps be a modest but not quite insignificant contribution to philosophy to draw attention to the mistakes of the conspiracy theory of society. Moreover this contribution leads to further contributions such as to the discovery of the significance for society of the *unintended consequences* of human actions, and to the suggestion that we regard it as the aim of the theoretical social sciences to discover those social relations which produce the unintended consequences of our actions.

Take the problem of war. Even a critical philosopher of the status of Bertrand Russell believes that we have to explain wars by psychological motives—by human aggressiveness. I do not deny the existence of aggressiveness, but I am surprised that Russell did not see that most wars in modern times have been inspired by fear of aggression rather than by personal aggressiveness. They have been either ideological wars inspired by the fear of the power of some conspiracy, or wars which nobody wanted but which came about as the result of fear inspired by some objective situation. One example is the mutual fear of aggression which leads to an armaments race and thence to war; perhaps to a preventive war such as even Russell, who was an enemy of war and of aggression, recommended for a time, fearing (rightly) that Russia would soon have the hydrogen bomb. (Nobody wanted the bomb; it was the fear that Hitler would monopolize it which led to its construction.)

Or take a different example of a philosophical prejudice. There is the prejudice that a man's opinions are always determined by his self-interest. This doctrine (which may be described as a degenerate form of Hume's doctrine that reason is, and ought to be, the slave of the passions) is not as a rule applied to oneself (this was done by Hume, who taught modesty and skepticism with respect to our powers of reason, his own included), but it is as a rule only applied to the other fellow—whose opinion differs from our own. It prevents us from listening patiently, and from taking seriously opinions which are opposed to our own, because we explain them by the other fellow's interests. But this makes rational discussion impossible. It leads to a deterioration of our natural curiosity, our interest in finding out the truth about things. In place of the important question "What is the truth about this matter?" it puts the less important question "What is your self-interest, what are your motives?" It prevents us from learning from people whose opinions differ from our own, and it leads to a dissolution of the unity of mankind, a unity that is based on our common rationality.

A similar philosophical prejudice is the thesis, at present immensely influential, that rational discussion is possible only between people who agree on fundamentals. This pernicious doctrine implies that rational or critical discussion about fundamentals is impossible, and it leads to consequences as undesirable as those of the doctrine discussed before.

These doctrines are held by many people, but they belong to a field of philosophy which has been one of the main concerns of many professional philosophers: *the theory of knowledge.*

IX

As I see it, the problems of the theory of knowledge form the very heart of philosophy, both of uncritical or popular commonsense philosophy and of academic philosophy. They are even decisive for the theory of ethics (as Jacques Monod has recently reminded us[6]).

Put in a simple way, the main problem here as in other regions of philosophy is the conflict between "epistemological" optimism and

[6] Jacques Monod, *Chance and Necessity*, Alfred A. Knopf, Inc., New York, 1971.

"epistemological" pessimism. Can we know? How much can we know? While the epistemological optimist believes in the possibility of human knowledge, the pessimist believes that genuine knowledge is beyond human powers.

I am an admirer of common sense, though not of all of it; I hold that common sense is our only possible starting point. But we should not attempt to erect an edifice of secure knowledge upon it, but rather criticize it and improve upon it. Thus I am a common-sense realist; I believe in the reality of matter (which I think is the very paradigm of what the word 'real' is meant to denote); and for this reason I should call myself a 'materialist', were it not for the fact that this term also denotes a creed that (a) takes matter as essentially irreducible, and (b) denies the reality of immaterial fields of forces and, of course, also of mind, or consciousness; and of anything else but matter.

I follow common sense in holding that there is both matter ('world 1') and mind ('world 2'), and other things to boot, such as the products of the human mind, which include our scientific conjectures, theories, and problems ('world 3'); in other words, I am a commonsense pluralist. I am very ready to have this position criticized and replaced by a sounder one, *but all the critical arguments against it which are known to me are, in my opinion, invalid.* (Incidentally, I regard the pluralism here described as needed for ethics.)

All the arguments that have been advanced against a pluralistic realism are based, in the last instance, upon an *uncritical acceptance of the commonsense theory of knowledge* which I regard as the weakest part of common sense.

The commonsense theory of knowledge is highly optimistic insofar as it equates *knowledge* with *certain knowledge*; everything conjectural is, so it holds, not really 'knowledge'. I dismiss this argument as merely verbal; I would readily admit that the term 'knowledge' carries in all languages known to me the connotation of certainty; but the commonsense program of starting from what appears the most certain or basic knowledge available (observational knowledge) in order to erect on these foundations an edifice of knowledge does not stand up to criticism.

It leads, incidentally, to two non-commonsensical views of reality, which stand in direct contradiction to each other.

1. Immaterialism (Berkeley, Hume, Mach)
2. Behaviorist materialism (Watson, Skinner)

The first of these denies the reality of matter, because the only certain and secure basis of our knowledge consists of our own *perceptual experiences*; and these remain, forever, immaterial.

The second denies the existence of mind (and, incidentally, of human freedom), because all we can really *observe* is human behavior which is in every way like animal behavior (except that it incorporates a wide and important field, 'linguistic behavior').

Both these theories are based upon the invalid commonsense theory of knowledge which leads to the traditional but invalid criticism of the commonsense theory of reality. Both these theories are not ethically neutral, but pernicious: if I wish to comfort a weeping child, I do not wish to stop some irritating perceptions (of mine or of yours); nor do I wish to change the child's behavior; or to stop drops of water from running down its cheeks. No, my motives are different—undemonstrable, underivable, but *human.*

Immaterialism (which owes its origin to the insistence of Descartes—who was of course no immaterialist—that we must start from an indubitable basis such as the knowledge of our own existence) reached its culmination at the turn of the century with Ernst Mach, but has now lost most of its influence. It is no longer fashionable.

Behaviorism—the denial of the existence of mind—is very fashionable at present. Although extolling observation, it not only flies in the face of all human experience, but it tries to derive from its theories an ethically horrible theory—the theory of conditioning[7]—although no ethical theory is, in fact, derivable from human nature

---

[7] The conditioner's dream of omnipotence may be found in Watson's *Behaviorism* and also in the work of Skinner (for example, *Beyond Freedom and Dignity,* Knopf, New York, 1971). I may quote from Watson: "Give me a dozen healthy infants . . . and I'll guarantee to take any one at random and train him to become any type of specialist I might select—doctor, lawyer, artist . . . [or] thief" (J. B. Watson, *Behaviorism,* 2d ed., Routledge, London, 1931, p. 104). Thus everything will depend on the morals of the omnipotent conditioner. (Yet according to the conditioners, these morals are nothing but the product of conditioning.)

(as Jacques Monod has rightly emphasized;[8] see also my *Open Society and Its Enemies*[9]). It is to be hoped that this fashion, based upon an uncritical acceptance of the commonsense theory of knowledge whose untenability I have tried to establish,[10] will one day lose its influence.

X

As I see philosophy, it ought never to be, and indeed it never can be, divorced from science. Historically, all Western science is an offspring of Greek philosophical speculation about the cosmos, the world order; the common ancestors of all scientists and all philosophers are Homer, Hesiod, and the pre-Socratics. Central for them is the inquiry about the structure of our world, and our place in this world including the problem of our knowledge of this world (a problem which, as I see it, remains decisive for all philosophy). And it is the critical inquiry into the sciences, their findings, and their methods which remains a characteristic of philosophical inquiry, even after the sciences have broken away from it. Newton's *Mathematical Principles of Natural Philosophy* marks, in my opinion, the greatest event, the greatest intellectual revolution, in the history of mankind. It marks the fulfillment of a dream that was two thousand years old; it marks the maturation of science, and its break away from philosophy. But Newton himself, like all great scientists, remained a philosopher; and in spite of the perfectionism which pervades his work, he remained a critical thinker, a searcher, and skeptical of his own theories. Thus he wrote in his letter to Bentley (February 25, 1693) of his own theory which involves action at a distance (italics mine):

> That gravity should be innate, inherent, and essential to matter, *so that one body may act upon another at a distance* ... is to me so great an absurdity that I believe no man who has in philosophical matters a competent faculty of thinking can ever fall into it.

---

[8] See note 6.
[9] K. R. Popper, *The Open Society and Its Enemies,* Routledge & Kegan Paul, Ltd., London, 1945, 5th ed., 1969; Princeton University Press, Princeton, N.J., 5th ed., 1966, and Princeton paperback, 1971.
[10] See for example K. R. Popper, *Objective Knowledge: An Evolutionary Approach*, Clarendon Press, Oxford, and Oxford University Press, New York, 1972 (especially chap. 2).

It is his own theory of action at a distance which led him necessarily to both skepticism and mysticism. He reasoned that if all the vastly distant regions of space can interact instantaneously with each other, then this must be due to the omnipresence at the same time of one and the same being in all regions—to the omnipresence of God. It was thus the attempt to solve this problem of action at a distance which led Newton to his mystical theory according to which space is the sensorium of God; a theory in which he transcended science and which combined into one, critical and speculative philosophy and speculative religion. We know that Einstein was similarly motivated.

XI

I admit that there are some very subtle problems in philosophy which have their natural and indeed their only place in academic philosophy, for example, the problems of mathematical logic and, more generally, the philosophy of mathematics; and I am greatly impressed by the astounding progress made in these fields in our century.

But as far as academic philosophy in general is concerned, I am worried by the influence of what Berkeley used to call the "minute philosophers." Admittedly, criticism is the lifeblood of philosophy; yet a minute criticism of minute points without an understanding of the great problems of cosmology, of human knowledge, of ethics, and of political philosophy, and without a serious and devoted attempt to solve them, appears to me fatal. It almost looks as if every printed passage which might with some effort be misunderstood or misinterpreted is good enough to justify the writing of another critical philosophical paper. Scholasticism, in the worst sense of the term, abounds; all the great ideas are buried in a flood of words. At the same time, a certain arrogance and rudeness— once a rarity in philosophical literature—seems to be accepted, by the editors of many of the journals, as a proof of boldness of thought and originality.

I believe it is the duty of every intellectual to be aware of the privileged position he is in. He has a duty to write as simply and clearly as he can, and in as civilized a manner as he can; and never to forget either the great problems which beset mankind and which demand new and bold but patient thought, or the Socratic modesty of the man who knows how little he knows. As against the minute philosophers with their minute problems, I think that the main task of philosophy is to speculate critically about the universe and about our place in the universe, including our powers of knowing and our powers for good and evil.

XII

I might perhaps end with a bit of decidedly nonacademic philosophy.

One of the astronauts involved in the first visit to the moon is credited with a simple, wise, and beautiful remark which he made on his return. It ran as follows (I am quoting from memory): "I have seen some planets in my day, but give me the earth every time." I think this is not only wisdom, but philosophical wisdom. We do not know how it is that we are alive on this wonderful little planet—or why there should be something like life, to make our planet so beautiful. But here we are, and we have every reason to wonder at it, and to feel grateful for it. It comes close to being a miracle. For all that science can tell us, the universe is almost empty of matter; and where there is matter, it is almost everywhere in a chaotic state, and uninhabitable. There may be many other planets with life on them. Yet if we pick out at random a place in the universe, then the probability (calculated on the basis of our somewhat dubious current cosmology) of finding a life-carrying body at that place will be zero, or almost zero. So life has at any rate the value of something rare; it is precious. We are inclined to forget this, and treat life cheaply, perhaps out of thoughtlessness; or perhaps because this beautiful earth of ours is, no doubt, a bit overcrowded.

All men are philosophers, because in one way or other all take up an attitude toward life and death. There are those who think that life is valueless because it has an end. They do not think that the opposite argument might also be proposed: that if there were no end to life, it would have no value; that it is, in part, the ever-present danger of losing it which helps to bring home to us the value of life.

TWO

MY SEMANTIC ASCENTS AND DESCENTS

J. J. C. Smart

It seems clear that the concept of philosophy is a family resemblance one, so that no general definition of it can be given. However, one important characteristic of the family is that of being in some sense a *conceptual* inquiry, and so a science can be thought of as bordering on philosophy to the extent to which it raises within itself problems of a conceptual nature. Consider a typical meeting of a university philosophy club. It will be unusual to find an organic chemist in the audience. Organic chemists do not talk much with philosophers because although their problems may be difficult and in certain ways sophisticated ones, the conceptual guidelines of their science are pretty well agreed upon. Contrast mathematical physicists, who come up against such questions as the following one.

With one experimental arrangement you can determine the position of an electron. With another experimental arrangement you can determine the momentum of an electron. There is no experimental arrangement by which you can determine both the position and momentum of an electron. This is no mere practical impossibility. The mathematics of the theory shows that a contradiction would arise if we supposed that the electron had at one and the same time both a determinate momentum and a determinate position (even though we could not in fact measure both of them). Hence there naturally arises the so-called Copenhagen interpretation of quantum mechanics, whereby the states of a particle are relations to experimental arrangements. Thus the position of the electron is a relation to an experimental arrangement of one sort, and the momentum of the electron is a relation to an experimental arrangement of another sort. However, we get into an infinite regress if we suppose that the properties of the experimental arrangement (or the particles making it up) are themselves relations between the experimental arrangement and yet other experimental arrangements. That is, the positions and momenta of the components of the experimental arrangement have to be positions and momenta as in classical physics. This reliance upon classical physics for the theory of the experimental arrangement is embraced by adherents of the Copenhagen interpretation, but by others it may be seen as a serious weakness in quantum mechanics. Surely a physical theory ought to be a theory of everything in the universe, including the measuring instruments which are needed to test the theory. Or again, like P. K. Feyerabend[1] in an important recent paper, a person may feel this uneasiness while yet conceding that the Copenhagen interpretation of quantum mechanics is the only viable one which has been produced, and that, indeed, to get an interpretation which did not produce this sort of uneasiness in us, a radically new theory of microphysics would have to be discovered.

This brief excursus into the interpretation of quantum mechanics shows the way in which theoretical physicists are brought up against conceptual questions, questions about the general structure of their theories. They get into debates about what sorts of theories are intellectually satisfactory. Where the organic chemist debates about whether a particular theory is a good one or not, the theoretical physicist is drawn into a debate about what it is for a theory to be a good one. Is inability to provide within itself a theory of measuring instruments to be regarded as a defect in existing quantum mechanics? To ask this question is to get involved in issues, such as that between realism and instrumentalism, which are typically philosophical, i.e., part of the stock in trade of people who are normally called 'philosophers'.

---

[1] Paul K. Feyerabend, "On a Recent Critique of Complementarity," *Philosophy of Science,* 35 (1968), 309–331, and 36 (1969), 82–105.

It should be noted, however, that the conceptual investigations undertaken by physicists are not done merely for their own sakes. When the physicist discusses and compares various sorts of physical theory he does so because he wishes to know which sort of theory it would be best to adopt, or which sort of theory should be viewed with suspicion (even despite undoubted success in predicting empirical facts). So in the last resort his conceptual investigation is done in the interests of finding out what the universe is like. Conceptual issues need not be factually neutral. W. V. Quine has drawn attention to the phenomenon of semantic ascent,[2] in which we go from debate about things to debate about our talk about things. This is especially valuable when it is not agreed as to whether the ostensible objects of our discourse exist. (Whether or not we believe in phlogiston, we can discuss the role of the word 'phlogiston' in a chemical theory.) Semantic ascent implies also the possibility of semantic descent: the settling of conceptual questions can influence our beliefs about what the world in fact is like.

I have argued that activities which most of us would regard as "philosophical" occur in mathematical physics. Since mathematical physics is generally regarded as a highly respectable subject, this suggests that philosophy is a respectable subject. However, when we look at the profession of philosophy itself, we may begin to doubt this supposed respectability. This is because there do not seem to be any agreed standards in philosophy. Consider the writings of a certain sort of phenomenologist or existentialist. To many philosophers, including myself, they seem to be not only incomprehensible but to be utter bosh. Whether such writings really are bosh or not, it does seem to be an empirical fact that there are groups within the philosophy profession between whom dialogue does not seem to be possible. It almost seems, sometimes, that though phenomenologists, existentialists, and a certain sort of Thomist are interested in concepts, their interest is often not so much to clarify concepts as to muddy them up. Perhaps muddy reflection on concepts produces certain emotions, such as *angst*,

---

[2] W. V. Quine, *Word and Object*, The M.I.T. Press, Cambridge, Mass., 1969, pp. 270–276.

which are prized by some of these philosophers. (It is odd that *angst* should be prized. Contrast David Hume's short autobiography, in which he expresses his calm and cheerful reflections on his own imminent death. He was singularly free of *angst*, which I should have thought was good both for him and for his friends and for those of us who read his words.) No doubt the reason why the purveyors of *angst* are thought of as falling under the family resemblance concept *philosopher* is that they are, in their own strange way, engaged with concepts and interested in the nature of the universe.

I cannot, however, disguise the fact that this division and lack of communication between parts of the philosophy profession does worry me. Surely if philosophy were a respectable subject, there would be general agreement as to what is and is not bosh, at least among those who are paid large sums of money to teach it at prestigious universities. Compare the situation in mathematical physics. There may be disagreement over the goodness or badness of the Copenhagen interpretation of quantum mechanics. Nevertheless there is a very definite way in which those who so disagree do speak the same language. They have a great body of techniques in common. They can handle matrices and differential equations, they play around with Hilbert space, they write down bras and kets, they understand how sophisticated experiments are done, and so on. There is a body of expertise which gives them *discipline*. This common discipline prevents their seeming to one another as mad or beyond the reach of reason, however much they may differ on fundamental issues. The trouble about philosophy is not that we get disagreement about fundamental issues. Such disagreement occurs healthily in science. It is that we get something like *total* disagreement or even total incomprehension.

A similar background of discipline is building up among professional philosophers. In order for a student to understand a great deal of current philosophy, it is necessary for him to familiarize himself with quantification theory, Gödel's and Church's theorems, Tarski's definition of truth, and so on. Consider, as a somewhat random example, the sort of background needed for reading such an article as W. V. Quine's "Implicit Definition Sustained."[3] This background of shared discipline can do much to prevent the sort of philosophy which we teach our students from degenerating into either verbalistic triviality or mad speculation. A generation or two ago a background of discipline in the form of Greek scholarship performed a similar function for Oxford philosophy. However, in this case the discipline was more adventitious. Except insofar as Plato and Aristotle could be regarded as mines for arguments which could be applied in contemporary contexts—and surely before long the mines would be worked out—Greek scholarship was not a tool for philosophers in the way in which contemporary logic, recursive function theory, and semantics are. Another background of shared discipline which has also prevented a large group of philosophers from disintegrating too much into different factions has been familiarity with a certain corpus of philosophical writing, e.g., Locke, Hume, Moore, Russell, Wittgenstein, Carnap (to mention only philosophers who are no longer alive). However, since the purveyors of *angst* can point to their own more literary and dark corpus of philosophers (Hegel, Kierkegaard, Nietzsche, Husserl, Heidegger, et al.), it is dangerous to rely on any purely philosophical corpus as the disciplinary backbone. It is better to stress logic, semantics, and the like—disciplines which are mathematical or scientific rather than philosophical, but which provide tools for philosophical disputation or results which are of philosophical interest. I have moments of despair about philosophy when I think of how so much phenomenological and existentialist philosophy seems such sheer bosh that I cannot even begin to read it, and I wonder whether philosophy is a proper subject. In such moments I tend to cheer myself up by reflecting that if the student reads Quine's philosophy he at least learns some logic, and if he reads Adolf Grünbaum's he at least learns some physics! However, this is rather a last line of defense.

I wish now to pass on to a more domestic sort of disagreement about philosophical method: a disagreement with philosophers with whom I can still do business and who are not separated from me

---

[3] Reprinted in W. V. Quine, *The Ways of Paradox*, Random House, Inc., New York, 1966.

by a vast gulf as are the purveyors of *angst*. Since this more domestic disagreement can be illustrated by comparing different temporal segments of myself, I can perhaps best illustrate it by engaging in some mild autobiography.

When I was a boy I read such books as Eddington's *Nature of the Physical World*,[4] which I now recognize to be partly philosophical, though when I tried to read G. E. Moore's *Ethics*,[5] I was quite baffled. Indeed Moore was a friend of my parents in Cambridge, and all that I then knew about philosophy was that it was whatever it was that Moore did for a living! We moved to Glasgow when my father was appointed Regius Professor of Astronomy there, and I entered Glasgow University to do mathematics and physics (or 'natural philosophy' as it was called there). It was necessary to do two other subjects for one year, and I picked on what was then called 'logic' because it seemed to be the most mathematical nonmathematical subject. 'Logic' in Glasgow really meant 'philosophy' (though moral philosophy had a separate department), and the professor was C. A. Campbell. I got enthusiastic about philosophy and went on with it, so that mathematics took second place. I was able to see how Campbell out-Bradleyed F. H. Bradley. When war service took me to India, this adventitious circumstance got me reading the *Upanishads* and *Bhagavad Gītā* in translation, as well as accounts of the Advaita Vedānta, and I recognized in the Advaitin's Brahman or Atman the suprarational absolute of C. A. Campbell. I was interested to try to find self-referential inconsistencies in this sort of position. Whether or not I succeeded is another matter. In reacting against this sort of idealist philosophy I was much influenced by D. R. Cousin, who was the one empiricist in the department at Glasgow. I found it harder to get puzzled about problems of ethics; when I read *Principia Ethica*[6] it seemed to give all the answers, and I thought it a fine thing to devote myself to increasing the amount of the nonnatural quality, goodness, in the world. This now seems rather an odd thought, though with the metaphysics

---

[4] A. S. Eddington, *The Nature of the Physical World*, Cambridge University Press, London, 1928.
[5] G. E. Moore, *Ethics*, Williams and Norgate, London, 1912.
[6] G. E. Moore, *Principia Ethica*, Cambridge University Press, London, 1903.

taken out of it I still think that this sort of utilitarianism provides an attractive basis for ethics.

It can be seen therefore that when I went to Oxford to do postgraduate work in philosophy I was groping my way in a metaphysical fog, and the sort of account of philosophy which was being purveyed by Gilbert Ryle came as a liberation. According to this account philosophy was a second-order activity, "talk about talk" as Ryle put it, or as he put it in an early paper, "the detection of the sources in linguistic idioms of recurrent misconstructions and absurd theories."[7] There seemed to be two good things about this. In the first place, it seemed to make philosophy secure as a profession. Philosophy seemed to have acquired a respectable place in the republic of letters as a second-order activity, so that it would not all hive off into special sciences in the way in which psychology had recently done. And this secure place could be seen not to depend on the existence of intuitive, transcendental, or otherwise mysteriously nonscientific modes of knowing. In the second place, the Rylean philosophy pleasingly exorcised a lot of mysterious and ghostly entities. When I was an inexperienced student at Glasgow I saw a review of Brand Blanshard's *Nature of Thought*[8] and thought to myself: "What a clever chap Blanshard must be. What a queer stuff thought must be! Is it some sort of fluid? How does one find out about it? I know how to do experiments with electricity, but how does one do them with thought?" Of course when I looked at the book it turned out unexcitingly to be just another (however excellent) book of idealist philosophy. How good it was to get to Oxford and to find the mind vanishing into behavior dispositions! All seemed clear for a physicalist world view, with cybernetics one day explaining the dispositions. Of course in the intellectual climate of Oxford at that time one would not ever admit explicitly that there were "world views," but to me the appeal of Ryle's talk about talk was nevertheless that it cleared a lot of lum-

---

[7] G. Ryle, "Systematically Misleading Expressions," reprinted in A. G. N. Flew (ed.), *Logic and Language*, First Series, Basil Blackwell & Mott, Ltd., Oxford, 1951.
[8] Brand Blanshard, *The Nature of Thought*, George Allen & Unwin, Ltd., London, 1939.

ber away and did in fact give rise to a certain implicit way of looking at the world.

Besides being influenced by Ryle, I was also much impressed by F. Waismann and G. A. Paul, and by the sort of second-hand Wittgensteinianism which was in the air generally. This second-hand Wittgensteinianism was partly characterized by talk of "this is the language game" and by a certain unacknowledged verificationism. Unacknowledged and even consciously denied presuppositions are of course the most insidious ones. This sort of Wittgensteinianism helped me to avoid facing certain important issues for some time, and in particular the question of whether I could honestly continue the practice of religion, to which I was emotionally very drawn despite the fact that another side of my nature craved an austerer metaphysics. What finally made me break with religion was getting interested in biology, largely because of the excellent biological discussion group which centered on the zoology department of the University of Adelaide. When one comes to see man as a zoological species, a lot of the Christian story seems most unplausibly anthropocentric. Moreover, how can one think biologically of immortality and of prayer? Could there be an information-flow model of prayer? Such questions could no longer be blocked by evasive Wittgensteinian talk about language games.

This made it clear to me how much more potent than neo-Wittgensteinian philosophical analysis were considerations of scientific plausibility. At first I had felt that these considerations were merely part of philosophical heuristics; that is, if philosophical analysis in the Rylean or neo-Wittgensteinian manner suggested a conclusion which was scientifically unplausible, then we should consider that there was probably an undetected fallacy in the philosophical arguments.[9] For example, Oxford philosophers were rejecting Rylean behaviorism, and they thought of materialism as even beyond the pale of serious discussion. If their arguments were correct, then these philosophers were surely committed to irreducible psychical entities which did not seem to fit in happily with physics and biology. This suggested to me that we should look again at the argu-

---

[9] See my note "Plausible Reasoning in Philosophy," *Mind*, 66 (1957), 75–78.

ments against behaviorism and materialism. At this stage, however, I still thought of philosophy as an autonomous *a priori* discipline, so that these considerations of scientific plausibility could be heuristic only. I drew the analogy with G. Polya's well-known heuristics for mathematics.[10] He made use of inductive and plausible arguments which could not belong to the corpus of mathematics itself, which is a system of rigorous proof in accordance with the rules of deductive logic.

However, I later came to think that the plausible reasoning in philosophy which I had advocated could not be merely heuristic. Despite all the brave words of the neo-Wittgensteinians, conceptual problems were not being resolved to the satisfaction of all concerned; there was nothing analogous to the agreement which mathematicians reached by means of their proofs. The neo-Wittgensteinians had of course themselves stressed certain differences between philosophical arguments and mathematical proofs, but nevertheless they did think that their methods would lead to assured results in an *a priori* manner. The empirical fact unfortunately was that philosophers continued to disagree as they had always done in the past, and the fly often remained obdurately within the fly bottle.[11] It therefore began to look as though there was something wrong with the neo-Wittgensteinian conception of philosophy. I began to think that considerations of scientific plausibility had their own rightful place in settling philosophical disputes, and that they were not mere heuristics paving the way for future proofs. Indeed they appeared more convincing than merely *a priori* or analytic philosophical argument could be on its own.[12]

This can be illustrated by a controversy in which once more I engaged in friendly debate with my old mentor C. A. Campbell. When not concerned with his suprarational absolute (which, of

---

[10] G. Polya, *Mathematics and Plausible Reasoning*, Princeton University Press, Princeton, N.J., 1954.
[11] Cf. L. Wittgenstein, *Philosophical Investigations*, Basil Blackwell & Mott. Ltd., Oxford, 1953, Section 309.
[12] See my paper "Philosophy and Scientific Plausibility," in P. K. Feyerabend and G. Maxwell (eds.), *Mind, Matter and Method: Essays in Honor of Herbert Feigl*, The University of Minnesota Press, Minneapolis, 1966.

necessity, was most of the time), Campbell argued for many philosophical theses about the phenomenal (as opposed to noumenal) world. In particular he defended a libertarian theory of free will. I thought that I had a knockdown argument against such a theory. I gave a Laplacean definition of determinism and defined pure chance as the negation of determinism. These definitions seemed to be natural ones, and they implied that an action had to be either determined or a matter of pure chance, so that no third possibility (acting from Campbellian free will) was left open.[13] However, in discussion with various philosophers it soon became apparent that libertarians (including Campbell himself)[14] were not willing to accept my definition of 'pure chance', but within the field demarcated by me as 'pure chance' they distinguished two possibilities, (1) pure chance and (2) free action. Of course such philosophers then have the problem of explaining what they mean by 'free will' and 'pure chance', since neither can now be defined as the negation of determinism. This pushes the libertarian into problems about meaning, and so I still think that the original argument does good, in bringing to light difficulties in the libertarian's position. However, it is manifestly not an apodeictic refutation. In the end the strategy is to force the libertarian into adopting more and more unplausible assumptions. Of course what is thought plausible depends on the person in question; for example, one man may judge theology in the light of scientific plausibility, while another may judge science in the light of theological plausibility. However, those libertarians who prize scientific plausibility may be brought to feel doubts about their theory when they are asked to reflect on how a libertarian free will can be explained in terms of mechanistic biology. How could mutations in DNA molecules lead to the existence of such a transcendent entity?

This all too sketchy account of a philosophical controversy has been intended to illustrate the thesis that you cannot refute another

---

[13] See my article "Free-Will, Praise and Blame," *Mind*, 70 (1960), 291–306.
[14] See C. A. Campbell, "Professor Smart on Free-Will, Praise and Blame," *Mind*, 72 (1963), 400–405.

philosopher merely by *a priori* argument, but you may use argument in order to push him into having to rely on premises which he (or others) may feel to be unplausible in the light of total science. This account of philosophy as dependent on considerations of scientific plausibility explains why philosophers need to engage in conceptual investigations, but it implies that these conceptual investigations do not have the sort of autonomy and independence of scientific theories which the neo-Wittgensteinians have held that they have. The view of philosophy to which I have come is not very different from Quine's, since Quine has been concerned to work out a canonical notation in which to express total science.[15] This is no accident. Quine's criticisms of the analytic-synthetic distinction[16] broke down the distinction between the conceptual and the factual, and hence shed doubt on the autonomy of philosophy as a second-order activity. Also Quine's writings stimulate reflection on different formulations of set theory. This reminds us that what is ruled out as ungrammatical or nonsensical according to one form of theory may turn out as simply unprovable (or even provably false) in another formulation. This helps to break down the Rylean notion of a *category mistake* as something different in kind from ordinary factual error.[17] Unfortunately this breaking down of the sense-nonsense versus true-false dichotomy implies that I cannot give a *clear* account of what I have meant when earlier in this essay I have said that some subjects are more concerned with "conceptual matters" than are others. The best I have been able to do is to illustrate the notion of *being more concerned with conceptual matters* by giving examples.

When one adopts the criterion of scientific plausibility one tends to get a certain way of looking at the universe, which is to see it *sub specie aeternitatis*. The phrase of course comes from Spinoza,

---

15 See Quine, *Word and Object*.
16 W. V. Quine, *From a Logical Point of View*, 2d ed., Harper & Row, Publishers, Incorporated, New York, 1961, chap. 2.
17 See my paper "Nonsense," in W. H. Capitan and D. D. Merrill (eds.), *Metaphysics and Explanation*, The University of Pittsburgh Press, Pittsburgh, 1966.

and in Spinoza's philosophy to see something *sub specie aeternitatis* implies seeing it as occurring by something like logical necessity. Of course I do not wish to include this as part of the connotation of the phrase as I use it. To see the world *sub specie aeternitatis* is to see it apart from any particular or human perspective. Theoretical language of science facilitates this vision of the world because it contains no indexical words like 'I', 'you', 'here', 'now', 'past', 'present', and 'future', and its laws can be expressed in tenseless language. Moreover, it contains no words for secondary qualities, such as colors, which though in a sense perfectly objective are of interest only because of the specific structures of the perceptual mechanisms of *Homo sapiens*. Other attitudes are of course possible. Some may prefer to see the world in perspective, so that, as F. P. Ramsey put it, "The foreground is occupied by human beings and the stars are all as small as threepenny bits."[18] So far this is a matter of taste, but in the case of Ramsey there was surely also intellectual error (in the shape of phenomenalism), since he went on to say, "I don't really believe in astronomy, except as a complicated description of part of the course of human and possibly animal sensation." Apart from the usual neo-Wittgensteinian arguments which have been brought against it we may surely reject phenomenalism as quite unplausible. It is too much to believe that the world should consist of sequences of sensations which are just *as if* they were caused by enduring physical objects. The implausibility of phenomenalism is quite closely related to its anthropocentricity (or at any rate sentience centeredness).

My interest in seeing the world *sub specie aeternitatis* is not shared by some influential contemporary philosophers who are primarily interested in man's ordinary commonsense picture of the world.[19] A few years ago there were some discussions by philosophers of the question of whether there could be disparate spaces

---

18 F. P. Ramsey, *The Foundations of Mathematics*, Kegan Paul, London, 1931, p. 291.
19 For an advocacy of anthropocentricity in philosophy see the remarks by P. F. Strawson on p. 141 of Bryan Magee (ed.), *Modern British Philosophy*, Martin Secker & Warburg, Ltd., London, 1971.

and times.[20] The details do not matter here, but what worried me about these discussions was that much of the argument was carried on by considering what certain tribes would say if certain strange things happened in their experience, or what we should say if certain strange things happened in our experience. The turn the discussion took perhaps depended on a neo-Kantian shift (rather characteristic of some recent Oxford philosophy) from talking about X to talking about *our experience* of X. That is, the discussion was often almost anthropological, whereas in reply I suggested that it was more relevant to argue mathematically, for example, to point out that two disparate 4-spaces (space-times) can be embedded in a 5-dimensional space.[21] Of course denizens of one 4-space might know nothing of the other 4-spaces, and so they might not need to use the concept of disparate 4-spaces. However, I slightly adapted a speculation by the physicist F. R. Stannard[22] to show how a hypothesis about disparate space-times might even come to have some tenuous relationship with observation. This, then, illustrates a divergence in philosophical method between myself and some of my contemporaries. It is, however, not a really wide one, as is the divergence between both myself and these contemporaries on the one hand and the purveyors of *angst* on the other hand!

So far I have not said much about ethics. Ethics is part of philosophy not only for obvious historical reasons (because Plato, Aristotle, et al., wrote about it) but also because it gives rise to many conceptual problems. Suffice to say that I have been interested to defend act utilitarianism, which has the sort of universality and generality which can appeal to one who is concerned with the world *sub specie aeternitatis*. Its supreme principle would be as applicable if we had to deal with beings from Alpha Centauri as it is in dealing with members of *Homo sapiens*, as well as horses, dogs,

---

[20] See Anthony Quinton, "Spaces and Times," *Philosophy*, 37 (1962), 130–147; R. G. Swinburne, "Times," *Analysis*, 25 (1964–65), 47–50; A. Skillen, "The Myth of Temporal Division," *Analysis*, 25, 44–47; Martin Hollis, "Box and Cox," *Philosophy*, 42 (1967), 75–78.

[21] See my article "The Unity of Space-Time: Mathematics versus Myth-Making," *Australasian Journal of Philosophy*, 45 (1967), 214–217.

[22] See F. R. Stannard, "Symmetry of the Time-Axis," *Nature*, 211 (1966), 693–695.

etc. Act utilitarianism appeals as a possible "cosmic ethics." (It is, of course, not necessarily the only system of ethics that does so.)

Another branch of study which has traditionally been regarded as part of philosophy is political philosophy. Once more this may be for the historical reason that many great metaphysicians and epistemologists have also written about politics. Of course they have often written about mathematics and physics too, but the fact that these require special mathematical and experimental techniques and expertise may partly explain why they are not taught within philosophy departments. Another reason, no doubt, is the high proportion of conceptual questions which arise in the writings of traditional philosophers who have discussed political theory. However, my own opinion (for what it is worth) is that on the whole there is not much new conceptual work to be done in this area, and what there is can be done with quite an elementary knowledge of general philosophy. Political philosophy is concerned with the best ways of organizing human society and requires empirical more than conceptual ability, and I tend to think that it is probably best done within politics departments of universities. However, this preference is a practical and undogmatic one: there certainly are political philosophers who are fun to have around, and I do not wish to lose their company if they happen to be in my own department! Another reason why I do not want to be too dogmatic about whether political philosophy should be regarded as philosophy proper is that the extension of the term "philosopher" is one of the things which philosophers do not agree about. I have no more academic right to object to a philosophical colleague lecturing about politics than he has to object to me if I encroach on physics. My proposal is pragmatic only and in accordance with a general view that tight departmental boundaries are unjustifiable.

At present we live in a very politically conscious age, and my feeling that political philosophy is best not done in philosophy departments will not meet with approval from those who wish philosophy to be "socially relevant." In reply I should like to make two points.

First of all, it is a shame that philosophers should be persecuted so much with demands for social relevance. No doubt some of the radical young may feel this way even about subjects like topology, botany, and mechanical engineering, but they do tend to scream at philosophers more than at most other people. One of the worst features of the demand for social relevance is that it is frequently coupled with a contempt for intellectual curiosity as such. Let me put the denigrator of intellectual curiosity on the horns of a dilemma. Consider the arms race. This is a positive feedback process which we all deplore but which is very hard to stop. Now either it can be stopped or it cannot be stopped. If it cannot be stopped, we are all doomed, and to satisfy intellectual curiosity can do no harm and will give us some pleasure during the period before the final catastrophe. Alternatively it can be stopped. But if it can be stopped, it will require much high-powered thought to discover *how* to stop it. Probably many highly abstract intellectual tools, such as the theory of games, will be needed. These intellectual tools tend to be acquired only by those students who have enough intellectual curiosity to enjoy the hard and difficult work of acquiring them. So once more intellectual curiosity is a good thing. The antiscientific young often blame science for our present troubles (overpopulation, pollution, destructive weapons). They perhaps have too rosy a picture of earlier ages when babies died young, few people had meat to eat, teeth had to be removed without anaesthetics, and all sorts of horrible diseases flourished. However, let us concede that science may have made the world a worse place in which to live. It is still fallacious to go on to say that we should give up thinking in a scientific way. If science has got us into this fix, it will be nothing less than science which will get us out of it again. (This is not to deny that other conditions may be needed too, such as a change of heart.) And if science will not get us out of our fix and we really are doomed, is this a reason for forgoing the higher intellectual activities in the time which remains to us? If a ship is sinking, the passengers need not revert to barbarism.

The second point which I wish to make about the social relevance of philosophy follows on naturally from the first point. If intellectual sophistication really is needed to get us out of our present troubles, then a really tough sophisticated philosophical education is a good thing. Those philosophers who prefer to lecture on topical themes of immediately obvious social concern do so at the cost of not lecturing on abstract, sophisticated tough philosophical questions. In their courses they may deal with certain rather elementary conceptual confusions, but there is so much empirical content in their courses that the student does not get scope for really advanced conceptual work, as he does when discussing, say, Quine on the indeterminacy of translation. So the students do not get the really sophisticated conceptual training which they can apply later in other fields, perhaps socially relevant ones. In other words, philosophy can be most socially relevant by being true to itself and not setting out directly to be socially relevant.

THREE

PHILOSOPHY AND PUBLIC POLICY

Sidney Hook

To anyone who believes that there is a body of philosophical knowledge comparable to the bodies of knowledge acquired in other disciplines the very topics of this collection of essays must seem anomalous. A series of essays entitled *The Nature of Chemistry* or *The Nature of Mathematics* would strike the reader as rather bizarre if they expressed different conceptions of what the subject matter of chemistry or mathematics was. To be sure there could legitimately be different analyses of the subject matter, different metascientific and metamathematical interpretations, but in every case this would presuppose the existence of, and agreement upon, certain truths whose cumulative development constituted the subject matter being discoursed about. Scientists do not disagree about the validity of specific laws that have been established, nor do mathematicians disagree about the validity of specific theorems. But there is not a single piece of philosophical knowledge, not a single philosophical proposition, on which philosophers are all agreed.

It was Arthur O. Lovejoy who many years ago called attention to this skeleton rattling in the philosophical cupboard. And although he proposed that philosophy become empirical in order to reach conclusions that could be universally agreed upon by all qualified

NOTE: Professor Hook's contribution is an extension of a paper with the same title that appeared in *The Journal of Philosophy*, vol. LXVII, no. 14 (July 23, 1970), pp. 461–470.

investigators, he never showed how it could be done. Since his time the scandal of philosophical disagreement, if anything, has become more pronounced. When he wrote, there seemed to be rather general agreement among philosophers that what G. E. Moore called "the naturalistic fallacy" was a fallacy and that J. S. Mill had committed it, that there was a sharp distinction between analytic and synthetic judgments, that there were no *a priori* synthetic judgments (including that assertion), and that the truths of logic and mathematics were valid no matter what. Today every one of these positions has been controverted by highly qualified professional philosophers. Every traditional philosophical position is just as much in dispute, when it emerges into the focus of attention, as in the past.

Does this mean that there has been no progress in philosophy? If progress is measured in the same way as it is in fields like medicine or physics, by increase in systematized knowledge and control, then we must answer in the negative. But if the index of progress is depth, complexity, and subtlety of analysis or the level and rigor of argument, then undoubtedly there has been progress. Nonetheless such progress, instead of diminishing disagreement, preserves it and sometimes intensifies it. It has not led to any body of philosophic truths that would warrant reference to philosophic knowledge. Only the style of thinking has changed. It has become more scientific without the fruits of science.

It is at this point that philosophers are tempted to abandon the claim to be in the possession of any knowledge, and to surrender the quest for knowledge to ordinary commonsense experience and the sciences which have developed from it. Philosophy is then defined as an activity, an activity of conceptual or categorial analysis which results not in knowledge but in clarification. There are some difficulties with this view, too. This kind of analysis is not restricted to philosophers. At some point every scientist raises questions about his fundamental organizing terms. But more important, there is no more agreement about the upshot of this analysis than about substantive conclusions. The conceptual or categorial analyses of scientists seem to be controlled by the state of scientific knowledge or by the bearing they have on integrating what is known and furthering more fruitful inquiries. Thus Einstein's analysis of the concept of simultaneity and contention that the simultaneity of events was relative, not absolute, recommended itself in terms of the consequences of its use. But there does not seem to be any comparable way of determining the relative validity of different philosophic analyses of the concepts of "matter," "self," "consciousness," "individual."

At the present juncture of philosophical thought it seems appropriate, therefore, to present one's conception of philosophy as a *proposal* in the light of the state of affairs described above. To the extent that the proposal is accepted, cooperative inquiry may result in common findings and agreement comparable to some extent to the universally agreed-upon conclusions of scientific inquiry. But even if the scandal of philosophical disagreement persists, this would not be fatal either to professional activity or popular interest in what goes by the name of philosophy, but only to pretentious claims to be in possession of genuine knowledge. It may be that philosophy can continue as an autonomous intellectual activity regardless of whether there is anything like philosophic knowledge or truth, just as artistic and religious activities are enjoyed regardless of whether or not there are any such things as universally agreed-upon "artistic truths" or "religious truths"—about which I myself am very skeptical.

I

Together with a few other American philosophers who have studied with or been influenced by John Dewey, I have always believed that philosophy is legitimately concerned with large problems of human affairs, that philosophers should have something to say to their fellow citizens and not only to their professional colleagues. To those of us who have held this point of view, there is something ironical about the mounting surge of impassioned interest in public policy that has suddenly developed among those hitherto indifferent to its themes. When this is accompanied by zealous and sometimes self-righteous demands that philosophers *do* something about the state of the world, that they offer programs and solutions to the perplexing problems from which the community suffers, the situation becomes not so much ironical as one of dramatic parody.

I say "dramatic parody" because it sometimes sounds as if philosophers were being urged to become merely social reformers, to play the role that we were falsely taxed with advocating by influential critics among an earlier generation of philosophers. We were condemned for conceiving of philosophy in a way that betrayed its true vocation, for reducing it from a position of proud autonomy to that of handmaiden to the progressive politics of the age.

The charge was false. It is true that John Dewey as a *citizen* was a great social reformer. And it is true that he believed that the central and continuing concern of philosophy involved problems of moral choice and policy on which all reflective human beings must act. But this does not entail the view that *philosophy* is social-reformist or revolutionary or counterrevolutionary. And still less does it justify any demand that philosophers, organized as a *professional* association to further the interests of philosophic study and the teaching of philosophy, take stands on specific political issues or programs except those that bear on their freedom to pursue their professional activity.

I propose to consider afresh the relation between philosophy and public affairs and draw some conclusions on how philosophers should conceive their role with respect to its problems. The easiest and least rewarding approach to the issues is the question-begging procedure of defining philosophy in terms of one's own partisan philosophical standpoint, and then reading off what is included or excluded from the circle of its implications. Surely a more fruitful and less partisan approach is the denotative, historical one. Let us ask, What are the criteria by which until now thinkers have been included in a history of philosophy as distinct from a history of physics or mathematics or psychology? Why do we include Descartes, Leibniz, Hobbes, and Spinoza in a history of philosophy, and not merely as figures in chapters of the histories of physics, mathematics, or psychology? I believe the reason is that all of them are concerned at some point with the nature of value, with the nature of the good in man or society or history. The most comprehensive as well as the most adequate conception of philosophy that emerges from the history of philosophy is that it is *the normative consideration of human values.* Another way of putting this is that philosophy is a study of existence and possibility from the standpoint of value and its bearing on human conduct. This, it seems to me, is the central thread of continuity in the history of philosophy from Socrates to John Dewey. It envelops even those who, on skeptical or metaethical grounds, have concluded that philosophy has nothing cognitively meaningful to say about human values.

If this is what philosophy has been, or even if it is taken only as a proposal of what it should be, it is altogether natural for the community to turn to the philosopher in expectation of finding some wise guidance or some integrated outlook on life. For whatever else wisdom is, it is insight into the nature, interrelation, and career of values in human experience. If philosophers can provide no wisdom, the community turns to others for guidance and enlightenment—traditionally to its priests and prophets, to its poets and dramatists, and in periods of crisis to faith healers, confidence men, and other creatures of the intellectual underworld.

Obviously the philosopher is not unique in his concern with values and with the rational grounds for value-decisions. All men are concerned with problems of human conduct, but what others do episodically the professional philosopher does systematically.

The great difficulty with this conception of philosophy is that it seems unrelated to so many other philosophical concerns—epistemological, ontological, and logical—which for many, if not most, philosophers constitute the very heart of their discipline. How are these technical philosophical problems and questions, like the theory of universals or the knowledge of other people's minds or the analysis of analyticity, encompassed in this view of philosophy?

Two possible answers to this question have a bearing on our theme. One answer is that the perennial problems of philosophy are directly or indirectly bound up with problems of human value, with the quest for wisdom or a satisfactory way of life. The proper ordering of human conduct depends upon knowledge of self and mind, and this in turn upon knowledge of society and history, of the world and its environing cosmos; and both kinds of knowledge, insofar as they differ from opinion, guesswork, or hearsay, are assured by the tested methods of critical inquiry.

This is no new conception of man in the universe. Nor is it an expression of scientism. From time immemorial the pursuit of wisdom or the definition and achievement of the good life has been related to other things. This holds true not only for Western culture, but for all cultures known to man. A simple and amusing illustration of this is provided in a text from Confucius in the sixth century before our era:

> The ancients who desired to cast light on illustrious virtues throughout the kingdom, first ordered well their own states. Wishing to order well their states, they first regulated their families. Wishing to regulate their families, they first cultivated their persons. Wishing to cultivate their persons, they first rectified their hearts. Wishing to rectify their hearts, they first sought to be sincere in their thoughts. Wishing to be sincere in their thoughts, they first extended to the utmost their knowledge; such extension of knowledge lay in the investigation of things.
>
> Things being investigated, knowledge became complete. Their knowledge being complete, their thoughts were sincere. Their thoughts being sincere, their hearts were then rectified. Their hearts being rectified, their persons were cultivated. Their persons being cultivated, their families were regulated. Their families being regulated, their states were rightly governed. Their states being rightly governed, the whole kingdom was made tranquil and happy.
>
> *Introduction to the Great Learning*

A more complex illustration is provided by John Dewey, who contends that the connection between philosophy and civilization is intrinsic. Whenever a civilization develops beyond the level of the merely customary and seeks to develop a reflective morality, it asks three questions. First, "What are the place and role of knowledge and reason in the conduct of life?" Second, "What are the constitution and structure of knowledge and reason in virtue of which they can perform the assigned function?" And growing out of this question, third, "What is the constitution of nature, of the universe, which renders possible and guarantees the conceptions of knowledge and of good that are reached?" On this view the quest for wisdom and for understanding the nature of reflective conduct provides the principle of relevance to philosophical inquiry as distinct from purely scientific inquiry. The discussion of public policy and of the value-decisions involved is an appropriate concern for philosophers, and one not unrelated to the ontological and epistemological questions, no matter how recondite and technical, with which professional philosophers deal.

There is an obvious objection to this first answer. It can be argued that the relationship between the quest for wisdom or the ideals of rational conduct, on the one hand, and the many problems in the different fields in which professional philosophers are engaged, on the other, is historical and accidental, not logical or necessary. Chesterton's landlady, who is rightfully, from the point of view of a landlady, more interested in the philosophy of her boarder than in the contents of his trunk, doesn't care a tinker's damn about her boarder's views on universals, the mind-body problems, induction, or the status of theoretical constructs and intervening variables. Whether he will pay his rent or skip may be more reliably inferred from his views on whether promises are *prima facie* binding or the justice of piecemeal appropriation of those who live on unearned income and allied ethical considerations than from his views on ontology or epistemology. A professional philosopher could support her indifference to these latter questions by defending with complex arguments the complete autonomy of moral judgment. The relationships among the various philosophical disciplines is a metaphilosophical problem, and still open.

Further, to the extent that this first answer presupposes that all knowledge either originally or ultimately arises from some practical interest or that thinking exists for the sake of action or application, one can challenge this with the contention that man has a natural curiosity to know for its own sake, and that this desire or drive, and not the practical necessities of living, feeds his metaphysical hunger. It also accounts for his absorption with the minutiae of the technical philosophical disciplines.

We are dealing with a highly tangled question posed by this first answer. It would require a volume to unravel it. But in a tentative way I believe it is justified to bring in a Scotch verdict: "Not proven." Although I believe that Peirce and Dewey are right in their claim that some activity or experiment ultimately enters into all scientific knowledge of fact, I do not believe that all scientific knowledge is acquired for some practical end or purpose. Aristotle's insights in the first paragraph of his *Metaphysics* seem to me to be valid. Even Dewey admits that the division between what is considered philosophical and scientific in the history of natural science is "often arbitrary." The speculative and broadly hypothetical phases of scientific thought can be considered philosophical independently of their bearing on the pursuit of wisdom or human values. But we must be clear that philosophy so conceived is ancillary to or anticipatory of specific scientific views especially in cosmogony and cosmology. Aristotle's view about the role of the heart, Kant's conception of the origin of the world—his acceptance of the nebular hypothesis—and Peirce's notions about the spontaneous generation of life are hardly of any concern to their philosophical successors.

Spin off, then, this kind of scientifically oriented philosophy from the traditional conceptions. Is what is now left essentially related to questions of normative analysis of values that ultimately affect, even when they are not directly affiliated with, issues of social and public policy?

I do not think so. Nor did Dewey, despite some occasional words to the contrary. There is something that Dewey himself recognizes as "a kind of music of ideas that appeals, apart from any question of empirical verification, to the minds of thinkers, who derive an emotional satisfaction from an imaginative play synthesis of ideas obtainable by them in no other way."[1] This is the aesthetic dimension of philosophy, philosophy for the fun of it, irrelevant to any social use and application.

We turn away, then, from the first answer to the question as to how the philosopher's concern with public policy can be justified, as untenable.

---

[1] John Dewey, "Philosophy," in *Encyclopaedia of the Social Sciences,* ed. Edwin R. A. Seligmann, The Macmillan Company, New York, 1933, vol. XII, p. 118.

II

This first answer was unnecessarily strong. For there is a second and less controversial answer that justifies concern with issues of public policy not as *the* philosopher's task, but as *one* of them. It makes problems of social and public policy a legitimate field of interest among others. This is a relatively humble view. It does not impose a duty or obligation on all philosophers to busy themselves with questions of this sort, but defends their right to do so against certain methodological purists, and against those whose conception of the subject matter of philosophical inquiry would exclude questions of public policy as improper themes of professional exploration and inquiry. Such purism is simply a form of intolerance, which would outlaw from the scope and sphere of philosophy important contributions to the discussion of human affairs by thinkers as disparate as Plato, Hegel, and John Stuart Mill. Such taboos are captious and arbitrary. But just as captious and arbitrary are those who would impose on all philosophers the necessity of taking a position as *philosophers* on those questions which as citizens they cannot escape. Questions of public policy should be the primary concern of those philosophers only who have a strong bent and special capacity for them.

The really important question for our purpose is, How should the philosopher *as* a philosopher proceed in his discussion of public affairs in contradistinction to others? Or, put differently, what can we expect from the contributions of the philosopher that would differentiate them from the contributions of the hosts of unphilosophical laymen already at work in the field?

First of all, we must expect of him a thorough familiarity with the subject matter—the facts in the case—with respect to which policy decisions are to be taken. This means that as a rule the philosopher is initially out of his field when he discusses questions of public policy. His training does not uniquely qualify him to master them. This mastery is a *sine qua non*, and not all the moral principles or sensitivities of conscience can compensate for its lack. Although no policy can be logically derived from any aggregation of facts, there are some facts that are sufficient in some problematic situations to invalidate policy proposals.

Not all philosophers who have suddenly turned to public affairs have shown that degree of familiarity with what they are talking about that we have a right to expect. For example, some philosophers have seriously asserted that United States economic involvement in various parts of the world is motivated primarily by the desire merely to exploit the peoples of those countries and that its only effect is to frustrate their economic plans, apparently unaware that the cessation of that involvement would spell death by starvation to tens of thousands in India, and great hardships to the peoples of Israel, Taiwan, and South Korea, to mention only a few countries. Problems of economic aid and kinds of aid are of tremendous complexity, and cannot be solved by outbursts of moral indignation.

Some philosophers have recently declared that repression in the United States is almost as bad today as it was in Hitler's Germany, thus convicting themselves not only of gross ignorance of what life was like under Hitler and of the unparalleled freedom of dissent in the United States today, but disarming themselves and others by this newly minted version of the theory of social fascism in the struggle against the dangers of a social backlash in the future.

The second thing we must expect from philosophers is a kind of methodological sophistication that either sharpens the issues at point in public controversy or discloses the absence of real or genuine issues, thus clarifying the options open for decision. For example, the confusion that attends the discussion of the self-incrimination clause of the Fifth Amendment is an intellectual scandal and contributes to the mischievous consequences of its abuse in every jurisdiction of the land. Philosophers could render a needed service in dissecting the tortured and tortuous reasoning of the courts. The problem of action, or what to do about the Fifth Amendment, is something else again. This involves a strategy for legislators beyond the competence of philosophical analysts.

The third kind of contribution a philosopher can make to the study and analysis of public policy is philosophical perspective. By this I mean, wherever it is relevant, the disentangling of ideological issues from factual ones. This is particularly important in discussions of birth control, abortion, suicide, and, in general, questions of church and state.

Perhaps the most important contribution the philosopher can make to the discussion of public affairs is to make explicit the ethical issues behind conflicting public policies and to relate them to the kind of society in which we want to live and to the kind of men and women we wish to see nurtured in such a society. It is here that the philosopher's professional interest in systematic moral evaluation, or his vocation as a moralist, should sensitize him to the presence of moral issues in what is sometimes regarded as a purely factual inquiry. The furious controversy over the implications of inquiries concerning genetic group differences is a case in point. Nothing significant in the way of civil rights and equal opportunities follows from any of the reported findings of differences in native capacities of different groups. Suppose in an individual family the IQs of the children range between upper and lower limits of 15 or 20 or even 30 points. Would anyone in his moral senses conclude that therefore this difference justified discrimination against any of the children with respect to their food, clothing, shelter, recreation, health care, and dignified treatment as human beings? There is a distinction between not having the relevant knowledge that would make a difference to our treatment of individuals and not knowing what difference any specific piece of relevant knowledge would make. The crucial questions in the treatment of religious, ethnic, and racial minorities are moral, and those who have thrown obscurantist blocks in the path of inquiry into questions of differential genetic capacities out of fear of the social consequences are fundamentally confused.

This confusion is not the monopoly of any one group whether "conservative" or "liberal"—terms that have become epithets of praise or abuse, not of reliable description. It is illustrated in some of the ways in which "the program of affirmative action" has been implemented. Designed to prevent discrimination in employment on the basis of irrelevant criteria of race, religion, sex, or national origin, in case after case it has resulted in forms of *reverse* discrimination in consequence of both logical and ethical error. The program recognizes that whenever there is unjust discrimination, sharp disproportions in the number of women and members of minorities result. It then infers from the existence of sharp disproportions in the sex and minority membership of the number of persons employed, evidence of invidious and unjust discrimination, thus overlooking the presence of other factors at work, like social stereotypes, that account for the disproportions. Condemning "quota" systems and efforts to achieve them, it imposes on universities "numerical goals" to be achieved within certain time schedules, overlooking the fact that "quotas" are "numerical goals," and that there is no difference in cognitive meaning between the commitment to "good faith" efforts to achieve quotas and the commitment to "good faith" efforts to achieve numerical goals. Finally, when partisans of the affirmative action program realize they are espousing a quota system, they justify reverse discrimination on the ground that it is a form of compensatory justice, as if the fact of injustices against the innocent victims of the past can absolve us from the odium of injustices against innocent victims in the present.

Finally, the philosopher must bring to his analysis of public affairs, no matter how passionate his moral concern, a kind of intellectual disengagement as a safeguard against one-sidedness, bias, and *parti pris*. We have plenty of fanatics and partisans at hand. There is no need for the philosopher to reinforce their shrill voices. In a world of widespread commitment to fixed causes and antecedently held conclusions, the philosopher must never surrender his objectivity. He must be prepared to recognize the truth when it is uttered even by those who are hated or condemned. This is extremely difficult, especially in the field of foreign policy, where a great deal of guesswork is involved. More important, it is a field in which errors are difficult to retrieve because even when they are acknowledged, the consequences of the original mistakes may alter the position to a point where what would have originally been the best alternative to begin with is no longer possible. To say that the foreign policy of the United States is not wise or sensible is not to say, as some philosophers have said, that it is all morally outrageous. And to deny that its policy is all morally outrageous is not to say that all of it is wise or sensible.

Listening to some philosophers indict the foreign policy of the United States since the Second World War, we hear merely a litany of horrors. There are horrible enough errors in the record to give all of us pause; but anyone who can mention that record without mentioning the fact that the United States withdrew its major forces from Europe while the Red Army was astride Europe, that it not only offered the Marshall Plan for the reconstruction of Europe but extended the offer to countries in the Communist orbit, that when the United States had the monopoly of atomic weapons and could have imposed its will on any nation of the world it offered to surrender that monopoly to an international authority— a concrete proposal for international socialism!—that it encouraged an agricultural and political revolution in Japan that restored it to greater heights of prosperity and with greater freedom than it ever enjoyed, that it has not ideologically interfered with its economic aid to Yugoslavia and other socialist and semisocialist regimes in Asia and Africa—anyone who fails to weigh these things and many others like them together with the errors in the balance of judgment is simply a propagandist.

The plain truth of the matter is that philosophers who have concerned themselves with public affairs in the past have not distinguished themselves by the cogency of their analysis or the accuracy of their predictions. For example, every one of the philosophers who ventured a judgment on the Munich settlement of 1938— Whitehead, Russell, Dewey, Santayana according to report—hailed it and urged its approval as the best insurance of peace. It turned out to be the worst.

Indeed, when one looks at the historical record of philosophical involvement in public affairs from Plato to the present, it can only inspire intellectual humility among those of us who are concerned with current issues. To speak only of our own century, we need only refer to Santayana's apologias for Mussolini and Stalin, Heidegger's support of Hitler, Sartre's and Merleau-Ponty's refusal to condemn the concentration-camp economy of the Soviet Union. Of course this is not the whole story. Although the record of Anglo-American philosophy is much better, Dewey's endorsement of the First World War and Russell's proposal for preventive nuclear war against the Soviet Union are evidence that philosophers can go as far astray as their unphilosophical colleagues and fellow citizens.

Seen in perspective, the faults of most philosophic treatments of public affairs flow not so much from defects of analysis as from mistakes of advocacy. This is brought out very well by John Stuart Mill in his analysis of the ethics of nonintervention, which still makes illuminating reading for our time. Although a position may be morally principled like "intervention to enforce non-intervention" when a people is struggling to defend its freedom and independence against despotism, it may not be prudent because of the likely consequences of the action. Mill makes one understand when we read his analysis how men of good will and intelligence can differ with each other. This makes his own conclusions far more weighty and persuasive than those by writers who arrogantly imply that none but fools or knaves can disagree with them. Much of politics is a choice of lesser evils in which the actual upshot of affairs depends upon contingent events. It is well to bear in mind that successful political action often depends upon timing and a discounting or reckoning in advance of what the other side will do.

There are some matters on which practical experience may be a better guide than pure theory. The very virtues of the thinker and man of vision—prolonged reflection, skepticism of one's own first principles, the long view, the attempt to see the situation from the standpoint of the other—may prove to be drawbacks in critical situations, when the fate of a people or a nation or a culture hangs in the balance. They may be sources of weakness when time is of the essence and action must be taken without the benefit of confirmed evidence. That is why as a rule philosophers *as* philosophers are not likely to make good public officials—the careers of John Stuart Mill and de Tocqueville as legislators were quite undistinguished—although in their capacity as citizens or even as party members they may be as good as their neighbors. Philosophers are better as critics than as intellectual laureates of the *status quo*. And this for several reasons. They have a keen sense of alternatives. They are likely to be more aware than others of the disparities between the ideal and the actual. And above all they cannot without stultification give their primary intellectual loyalty to any nation, cause, party, or organization, but only to the truth as they see it. That very commitment to truth should prevent them from using lies and certain selected truths that function as lies to further what they are convinced is a higher good or a holy cause.

As great and as important as the philosopher's insights may be for the illumination of public affairs of his own time, let us not deny that the outstanding philosophers of the past speak to us for other reasons. Their meaning for us today is found in some moral insight or vision that transcends the events of their own times. Public affairs and public policy do not exhaust the field of normative values. We read Hobbes and Hume, Spinoza and Kant, not because of their commentary upon and analysis of the public affairs of their day, but because of their visions of human excellence, their grasp of recurrent if not perennial problems of social life, and their insights into the condition of man. The great philosophers are not men of one note, or of one season, or of one mood. When they are in their time, they are not merely of their time. That is why Socrates, Plato, and Aristotle do not date in their central concerns, and still possess a freshness for sensitive and inquiring minds that have discounted their parochial setting.

The philosopher is uniquely a moral seer, a moralist, if you will, but not a moralizer or a priest or prophet. He is a lover and pursuer of wisdom wherever he finds himself, in any clime and in any culture. In the words of one whose soaring thought was much more impressive than his petty and uneventful life (Santayana):

> It is not easy for him [the philosopher] to shout or address a crowd; he must be silent for long periods, for he is watching stars that move slowly and in courses that it is possible though difficult to see; and he is crushing all things in his heart as in a winepress until his life and their secret flow out together.

FOUR

A STATEMENT
ABOUT PHILOSOPHY

Stuart Hampshire

There are six words which, taken together, mark the principal interests of philosophers, as philosophy is understood in the Greek and Western tradition. They are 'know', 'true', 'exist', 'same', 'cause', 'good'. No constructive philosopher has failed to have something to say about all, or most, of these notions. They are the most general organizing notions common to every type of discourse; so they are not the concern of specific positive sciences, but, being to the highest degree general, of philosophy. And a theory of any one of these notions—a theory of knowledge, of truth, and so on—tends to imply or contain a theory of all or most of the others. That philosophy tends to be systematic is therefore not a whim or an indulgence. If one tries to give an account of the nature of knowledge, one finds oneself also giving some account of truth and of existence.

So much is the general theory of philosophy to which I subscribe, abstracting from my own peculiar and limiting interests. These interests have been the same, in outline, since I first became determined to study philosophy, when I was a schoolboy. The center of this interest has always been the alleged uniqueness of human beings as having free will, or freedom of choice. Insofar as this claim is for some an attributable power that is nonnatural or supernatural, it has always seemed to me quite unacceptable. On the other hand I have thought that there is some traceable and intelligible peculiarity about the knowledge that men have of their own minds and of their own actions which accounts for a sense of freedom of choice.

The problem of freedom has therefore been for me a problem in the theory of knowledge, even though it is also evidently a problem in moral philosophy.

The theory of knowledge in which I was educated—namely, classical British empiricism—has seemed to me deficient in ignoring the contrasts, and the relation, between different kinds of empirical knowledge. More specifically, the classical empiricist theory of knowledge, as formulated in Hume, Mill, and Russell, ignored that relation between the activities of scanning and listening and their outcome in seeing and hearing which is essential to perception. Ignoring this relation, this theory neglected also the contrast between the knowledge that a man has of his own willed and attempted movements and the knowledge that he has of the changes in the environment, including some, but not all, of the changes in his own body. Empiricists take observation to be the foundation of all empirical knowledge; but their concept of observation has seemed to me defective because it implies that a human observer is a recording instrument which registers impressions received from the environment. But he is at least a recording instrument who uses himself to record impressions from the environment and to evaluate these impressions. His observation consists in doing something, even if it is only moving his eyes, and then noticing the effects that are of interest to him. Secondly, he takes account of his own position and his own actions in assessing any changes that he notices. He distinguishes between things as they appear to him and things as they really are by making allowances for his position, his actions, and the state of his perceptual apparatus. Thirdly, he uses a great bank of stored background knowledge in interpreting, and even correcting, the impressions that he receives; and the impressions are filtered by his expectations and intentions. He knows that they are.

The consequences of these deficiencies in the empiricist theory of knowledge first became clear to me in prewar discussions of the theory of perception, and specifically of the thesis of phenomenalism: the thesis that categorical statements about physical objects are in principle reducible to sets of hypothetical statements about sense-data. It was clear that the protases of the supposed hypothetical statements would need to refer to bodily movements and situations if the protases were to state the conditions under which sense-data of a determinate character would be obtained; the reference to the observer's body was ineliminable if a statement equivalent to the original perceptual claim about the external world was to be formulated. The discovery of this ineliminability suggested to me, in the years immediately before and after the war, that British empiricism was implicitly thinking of the observer as a transcendent observer to whom the physical world is presented and around whom it is arranged. As in Descartes, the observer was not represented in empiricist theories of knowledge as one body among others, perceiving the world from a determinate position and from a certain perspective within the world, and with consequent limitations of which he can be aware. Nor was any attention paid to the activity of the observer, experimenting with and using his senses and recording the effects of his experiments and exploration; rather, the observer seemed to be conceived as passively registering the impressions. This presupposition seemed in conflict with evidence from the psychology of perception.

For me the philosophical interest of the analysis of perceptual knowledge is precisely the interdependence between the two kinds of knowledge involved in perception: the knowledge that a man has of his own intentional movements and of his own aims and interests, and the knowledge that a man has of external objects observed. The relation between these distinct kinds of knowledge, clearly discernible in a coherent analysis of perception, seemed to me a pervasive relation which has to be studied in the philosophy of mind.

The analysis of statements about emotions requires that the distinction between kinds of knowledge be recognized; so does the analysis of the concept of thought. More generally, the paradoxes associated with the free-will controversy become intelligible when the points of intersection between the two kinds of knowledge are explained. The thesis of determinism often seems paradoxical principally because it is taken to imply that the only kind of knowledge that a man may have of his own interests, intentions, and beliefs is the same kind of knowledge that he may have of the interests, intentions, and beliefs of another person, as if there was no route to self-knowledge which was not also a route to knowledge of persons' states of mind and mental processes generally. We know this to be false. And this knowledge may be confused with another and quite independent proposition: that no causal explanation of standard form can be given of the mental states, or the dispositions, in question.

The two kinds of knowledge are distinguished from each other by the kind of support that must be forthcoming if a particular claim to knowledge is to be sustained under challenge—in this sense, by a difference of the source of knowledge. The knowledge that a man may claim to have of the world external to his own desires, thoughts, intentions, and feelings has to be arrived at in a respectable way if it is really knowledge and not just opinion. He has to be able to answer the question "How do you know?" satisfactorily. There is one exception to this general requirement: he may report his subjective impressions of the external world at a particular moment without committing himself to any statement about the real state of things; he is so far in the position of a man reporting his own sensations. In such cases a challenge to his claim to know does not take the form of "How do you know?"—of an inquiry into source—but only the form "Are you sure?"—with the implication that perhaps he has been careless or inaccurate in his description. In the relevant sense of 'external world', he is being noncommittal about the external world, and he is speaking only of himself; so he evidently has authority and is in the best position to judge.

Similarly a man has authority, and is in the best position to judge, when he speaks of his own thoughts, intentions, desires, and beliefs. His claims to knowledge in this sphere cannot be intelligibly challenged by the question "How do you know?" but only by the question "Are you sure?" Self-knowledge in these spheres is exposed to errors of various kinds: to self-deception, rationalization, and not being aware of, or not taking account of, less conscious desires, hopes, and expectations. These are the obvious, famous kinds of error. There are also often difficulties, and consequently often errors, in matching words to complex states of mind and to confused states of mind. Incorrigibility is not the mark of statements about mental states and processes, as some empiricist philosophers have claimed. On the contrary, most men are at many times oppressed by the difficulty of knowing what they want and what they believe, and remember important occasions when they have mistaken their own desires and sentiments. They are ready to believe, and reasonably to believe, that a friend is sometimes a better judge of what a man wants than is the subject himself. The subject is in the better position to judge; but it does not follow that he does not, in spite of this, fall into error, not because he has inadequate access to that which he is describing, but for other reasons.

The theory of knowledge that admits the contrast between self-knowledge and knowledge of the external world also insists that all statements are liable to error; different types of statement are distinctively liable to different types of error. Consequently an inductive argument from the evidence of parallel cases is never out of place, even if the argument concerns a man's revelations of his most intimate thoughts and feelings. One may still point to the evidence of parallel cases and persuade even the subject himself that he is probably mistaken in the account that he is giving. Perhaps he is exaggerating, or perhaps he is oversimplifying. Even in descriptions of sensations the subject may make an error in matching words to the phenomena, and a doctor, who has seen many similar cases, may be reasonably sure that he has made a mistake. I am not persuaded by philosophers who have made incorrigibility a distinguishing mark of statements about sensations and then extended the claim to avowals of mental states and processes generally. On the contrary, I have wished to argue that a man's desires, beliefs, and sentiments, so far from being transparent to him, are often half concealed and sometimes even wholly concealed from him; and that careful reflection upon the manifestations in behavior, and upon the causes of his states of mind, may change his beliefs about them.

I had distinguished two kinds of knowledge of mental states, the kind that is available to the subject, though he may make mistakes, and the kind that is available to an observer, who can judge only on the basis of the disclosures in speech, the behavior, and the expression of the subject, and on the general probabilities of the case. But I had not claimed that the distinction by source was also a distinction between the certain, or incorrigible, and the problematical and corrigible; nor had I claimed that the two kinds of knowledge are insulated from each other, in the sense that a conclusion arrived at by one route can never be overturned by the other. In an essay, "The Analogy of Feeling," I had argued that, at least where feelings and sentiments are in question, there is a circle of dependence of self-knowledge upon knowledge of others, and a dependence of knowledge of others upon knowledge of self: self-deception and deception provide potential cures for each other. We conjugate a common vocabulary of feelings and sentiments, and in the use of it I quite unavoidably try to see myself as others see me and try to project myself into the place of others, feeling what they feel. This reciprocity is the first condition of the intelligibility of the vocabulary of mental states. We each move constantly from the standpoint of agent and subject to the standpoint of observer, and this transition creates the circle of correction. I cannot know that I am intensely unhappy and am genuinely mourning the death of my friend unless I know what is generally counted as intense unhappiness; and I cannot know what is generally counted as intense unhappiness unless I have had some experience of intense feeling of some kind and of something like unhappiness. Thinking about one's own states of mind without thinking about others would be a barren and stultifying process; and trying to understand the desires and sentiments of others while eschewing self-knowledge would also be largely futile.

So much had been a line of thought about mental concepts and the conditions of their application, about the problem of other minds, and about the nature of the emotions and sentiments and of our knowledge of them. But along this path a further point about knowledge of mental states obtrudes itself and becomes unavoidable. However they may be characterized, intentional states, and the peculiar logic of reports of them, have been of interest to modern philosophers since Brentano. When I report my thoughts, whether they be beliefs, attitudes, sentiments, or meditations, I report on intentional states; and when I report what I am angry or frightened about or with, or otherwise specify the objects of my sentiments and attitudes, I report my thoughts, in the relevant sense of 'thought', and I report an intentional state. It is a well-known characteristic of statements about intentional states that they supply contexts in which the normal rules for existential commitment do not apply, in which normal entailments do not hold, and in which the normal substitution of identical terms is suspended. There is a further feature of statements that report intentional states: that the truth of the statement is not entirely independent of the subject's beliefs about its truth. This is the feature of the intentional states of persons, and of statements about them, which has seemed to me the most significant one, as far as traditional mind-body problems are concerned. It is significant also for many of the problems associated with free will.

A man is the authority on his own intentional states, although a fallible authority, because he is in part the author of them. His thought of the object of his fears, angers, hopes, and disappointments determines usually and in part, but not invariably and wholly, what he in fact fears, is angry with, hopes for, or is disappointed with. Usually the notional object (what he believes that he fears) is, in the normal case, the actual object of his sentiment, since he normally knows what he fears. But he might be untrivially confused in his identification of the object; or his behavior may show that his professed fear conceals another fear of which he is not aware, or which he has not admitted to himself. His thought in part determines the nature of the fear or hope, but not wholly; his behavior may show that the notional object of his fear masks the real object, which perhaps is clearly indicated by his actions. The subject himself may come to acknowledge that the real object cannot be that which he first indicated; he has to think again.

Generally, a man's attitude to his own sentiments and beliefs is not that of an interested inquirer into the facts, which usually is one's attitude toward the sentiments and beliefs of another. Rather one's own sentiments and beliefs are critically assessed and probed with some standard of defensibility or desirability in mind; this is the continuing, natural process of reflection, more explicit and verbalized in some people, but natural in all language users.

It is natural that men should often wish that they did not have the wishes and the sentiments that they do have and that they recognize as theirs. Possessing concepts, they will have second-order desires and attitudes. There are limits set to the sentiments and emotions that a man may experience by the limitation of his own thought; and his thought is in turn limited by his vocabulary. To expand the conceptual resources with which a man envisages the objects of his emotions is a way to expand (for good or for ill) the range of his emotions. Our emotional and sentimental interest in things is an interest in them under certain descriptions. We want things or we want to avoid them because in our thought they fall under certain descriptions and in our thought these descriptions have certain implications and associations. The descriptions drawn from the vocabulary of the culture in which we are educated enter into our sentiments, emotions, and tastes. If these were radically changed by learning new habits of thought and new classifications of persons and things, our emotional experience would be to some degree changed also.

So it has seemed to me that the peculiarities of our knowledge of mental states and processes, and also of psychology as a science, have become more intelligible to me. At no point is there anything mystical about the distinctions involved, nor is there an appeal to transcendental entities. Yet the distinctions serve to explain, to some degree at least, the reservations that one obscurely feels about the application, without qualification, of methods of explanation—which have dominated the physical sciences—to the mind. The wound and scar on a man's body are not changed by the subject's changing beliefs about them; they are independent objects. A man's sensations also do not change merely in virtue of changes in the subject's beliefs about them; at the most there might be an experimentally discoverable causal connection between a bodily sensation and a thought. But the relation between the subject's belief about the nature of his fear and the nature of the fear itself is more intimate than that. The connection can be specified in the following two ways (among others): (a) if the subject is sure, after reflecting on the question, that X is not the thing that he fears, but rather Y, then it cannot be the whole truth about his statement that X is the thing that he fears; if there are good grounds for judging that X, rather than Y, is what he fears, then his state of mind must at least be complex and confused; (*b*) if a man changes his opinion about his own fear (e.g., believes that it has gone), then his state must have, as a consequence, to some degree changed. His intentional states are never independent objects—independent, that is, of the subject's contemporary thought about them.

A man's beliefs and desires explain his actions, and his actions incorporate his intentions and aims. Statements about any one member of the triad belief, desire, and action are corrigible by reference to the other two; and one may infer statements about any one member of the triad from knowledge of the other two. Wanting something is an intentional state, and so also is a belief, and any other mode of thought. The intention and aim in or behind an action are the central cases of an intentional state. The statements that refer to desires and to thoughts of any kind, whether they are beliefs, intentions, hopes, ambitions, or sentiments, exhibit the peculiarities of oblique contexts; and to be sure of their truth one needs to be sure that one knows and understands the idiolect of the subject. This is the point at which the twin problems of mind-body relations and of causality and freedom come into view. The epistemological issues, which I have just mentioned, have always been for me of interest primarily because they are preliminaries to these two problems.

One further preliminary is needed: some inquiry into the methods of classification applied to mental states. Spinoza's account of the passions for me marked the next essential step: the sentiments and emotions are distinguished from each other in the *Ethics* by reference to the thoughts of the subject about the causes of the enjoyment or suffering which he is experiencing. There is therefore a theoretical component, a belief about causes, built into any ascription, to oneself or to another, of a sentiment or emotion or attitude of mind. "He is angry with X about Y" and "He is embarrassed about Z" are statements that attribute to the subject not only certain dispositions but also certain thoughts, including a thought about the cause of his own unpleasant feelings. If the subject changed his belief about the cause of his unpleasant feelings, he would have changed his belief about the correct diagnosis of his state of mind;

for embarrassment and depression are distinguished from cognate states in part by the types of incident that can cause them. Not just anything is a possible cause of embarrassment or depression, just as only certain kinds of behavior can be manifestations of embarrassment and depression.

If all the steps that I have outlined are correct and could be supported in detail, it follows that a man's states of mind, including among his states of mind his beliefs, can be changed by changing his beliefs about their causes. Such a change can occur, and does occur, in either of two ways: One becomes more systematic and critical in particular cases when one reflects on the factors that contribute, as one believes, to particular pleasant or unpleasant feelings, while still accepting the ordinary vocabulary of the emotions and the distinctions recognized in it. Or one might undergo a radical conversion, changing the general theory of the causes of pleasure and suffering which one applies to one's state of mind and to the states of mind of others. This last possibility is the one imagined by Spinoza when he imagined how men might be liberated from the passions that ordinarily lead to conflict and misery. They might learn that the ordinary diagnoses of states of mind are unscientific and unsystematic and presuppose a mind-body dualism which is incoherent and unacceptable, and that the causes of pleasure and suffering which are imputed are virtually never the true causes. Spinoza imagines living with a scientific grasp of the complexity of the causes that explain feelings of pleasure and suffering, and the dispositions associated with them. He imagines a consistent determinist, who also believes that every mental state and process is also a bodily state and process. Such a philosophical person will have rather different emotions, in virtue of classifying his own states differently; he will not crudely attribute to immediate and local causes those effects which he knows have in fact much more complex, and often more subjective, causes. He will impose a severely deterministic interpretation on his own passions, as on the passions of others. Not only that: he will live with the certainty that his thoughts have their physical embodiments which follow the laws of physics, as the thoughts themselves follow the laws of thought. He will always be aware of his general dependence on a long history of influences which stretches indefinitely into the past; he will be aware also of his power occasionally to be free of all external influences in his thinking and to be self-determining.

I have found my early intuitions about the extraordinary value of Spinoza's metaphysics gradually strengthened—above all the intuition that he had a theory of personality and of mind which now needs to be revived and reinterpreted. He seems to have prefigured, by a visionary guess, the direction in which the physical sciences would require psychology to move. In particular he understood the necessity of combining a consistent materialism with an account of self-knowledge and of reflection. He asked the necessary question, "What would be the situation of the moralist and philosopher who understood the identity of his own mental and physical states?" In the essay "A Kind of Materialism" (1970) I expounded Spinoza in this light. But I am well aware that this exposition falls short of being altogether convincing; the nature of the supposed relation between the thought in the mind and the bodily state that incorporates it is still obscure. Equally obscure is the scope of reflective thinking in modifying the states of mind which are incorporated in states of body, presumably in brain states and states of the nervous system. To interpreters of Spinoza this obscurity is known as the problem of the parallelism of the attributes.

It will be clear that my conception of philosophy does not exclude systematic metaphysics. On the contrary, I have found as many useful ideas in the rationalist philosophers as in the modern descriptive philosophers of the analytical school—useful, that is, to anyone interested in the mind-body relationship and the problem of human freedom. But there is one tenet of the great rationalist philosophers which seems to me quite incredible: the belief, or assumption, that it is possible to construct a philosophical system which has a claim to being accepted as true and adequate, in the sense that an experimentally confirmed scientific theory can be accepted as true and adequate. What one can do in philosophy, at the best, is to propose both clarifications and revisions of the conceptual scheme temporarily in use. It may happen, as with Spinoza's rejection of Cartesian dualism, that a philosophy comes too early to be immediately useful and suggestive. Spinoza had to be neglected for at least a century. Now the theory of mind-body identity can be put to a use, because inquiry into the structure of the brain and of the nervous system and into chemical control of mental illness has generated a set of conceptual problems to which Spinoza's grand solutions are relevant, or at least his claims are suggestive.

The rationalists certainly did not think of human knowledge as always and necessarily an inadequate and unsafe raft in an immense sea of ignorance. They did not think of our sciences as, first of all, human enterprises which have their history as part of social development, and which will reflect, in categories of explanation, both permanent and historically conditioned interests. These are the points at which I diverge from the rationalists. But at least Spinoza thought of human beings as greatly limited in their powers to grasp and to survey the natural order which must outrun their powers of perception and of understanding. His philosophy is by implication a polemic against anthropocentrism as much as it is a polemic against Christianity and Judaism. He does represent human intelligence as a not unnatural and not utterly discontinuous elaboration of structures found elsewhere in nature; and he always insists that our perceptual apparatus and our intelligence cannot exhaust the infinite variety and extent of nature. These are conclusions for which I am prepared to argue, although they are of course not conclusions that are to be in any sense proved.

I have brought the account almost up to the present. I believe that it is possible to show that there is an important difference between the explanation of mental phenomena and the explanation of physical phenomena, namely, that in the case of the former, knowledge of the cause will modify the effect when the knowing subject is also the object under study. Therefore the sciences concerned with states of mind—conspicuously sociology and psychology—have different prospects, and an extra complexity, when compared with the physical sciences. But this is not to deny that the physical sciences are likely to explain much of human behavior in their own terms as the functioning of the brain and the central nervous system are progressively explored.

The philosophy of mind is one area of philosophy in which speculation has been useful and in which I believe speculation can still be useful now. I do not believe that the philosophy of mind, or philosophical ethics founded upon it, can be made an exact inquiry, as some analytical philosophers have hoped. I do not believe that conclusive arguments leading to precise conclusions can be extracted from a study of mental concepts in use. I see no evidence, either from the past or from recent work, that the philosophy of mind can be made in any sense scientific, or even methodical. But there is good evidence that a close study of the actual uses of mental concepts is a very useful and suggestive preliminary to speculation about future forms of knowledge and of self-knowledge. To take one example, it is a long-standing question whether all thought must be, to some degree, conscious thought; and there is sometimes the suggestion that the concept of thought in ordinary use yields an affirmative answer, and that theoreticians who write of unconscious thoughts are extending the concept paradoxically. I think it can be shown that this is wrong, that ordinary speech presupposes that there are thoughts which are not conscious thoughts. Theories of the unconscious mind may be objectionable on other grounds, but not on this ground.

Philosophy has many parts, and different parts require different methods. In many parts of the philosophy of mathematics and of the philosophy of language, precise results and definite conclusions are obtainable. There is no such single thing as the right method in philosophy. In the philosophy of mind and in ethics, occasional insights unsupported by rigorous argument have in fact been as useful as strict argument. They may still be.

Of one conjunctive proposition I am certain: the issues here so cursorily mentioned are all significant and substantial issues which can be rationally discussed and clarified and which need to be clarified; and anyone who has not read the principal philosophers of the past and of the present carefully is certainly handicapped in contributing to them.

FIVE

CONCEPTUAL ANALYSIS

Alan R. White

One can distinguish between an attempt to discover any or all of the properties of something and an attempt to discover only those properties without which it would not be the kind of thing it is. This is related to the distinction which Plato made between studying the instances of something and studying the thing itself, e.g., between examining just acts and examining justice itself; which Aristotle made between, e.g., the study of *being* and the study of *being qua being*; and later philosophers, including Locke, made between an inquiry into the accidental and the essential properties of anything.

What philosophers throughout their history have sought are those characteristics of what they were examining, whether it be *knowledge, truth, necessity, mind, recklessness, value,* or *time,* in virtue of which it is what it is; those characteristics which are necessary to it and give its essence. Plato correctly, but unrevealingly, tells us that what makes something, e.g., an instance of justice, is the presence in it of justice itself. But he does not tell us what justice is except that we will see it in the afterlife. Even G. E. Moore was sometimes content to assure us that we would discover its nature by gazing at it when we called it before our mind. What most philosophers have been searching for is the nature of whatever makes something what it is.

It is because what philosophers seek are necessary characteristics, those without which things would not be what they are, that philosophical propositions, such as 'What is known to be so is so', 'Nothing moves', 'No empirical statement is known for certain', 'To be is to be perceived', 'We perceive only sense-data', etc., are either necessarily true or necessarily false. And hence, like the propositions of pure mathematics and unlike those of the natural sciences, they cannot be established by empirical methods.

Though things in nature have or lack the features in respect of which we can distinguish or classify them, they do not come to us distinguished or classified in various ways. This is a task we— whether we be animals, humans, or machines—have to perform. We have to consider them as either colored or plain, native or foreign, physical or nonphysical, old or new, square or oblong, relative to this or to that, etc. Which group a candidate falls into is not under our control, but which group it is considered a candidate for is. There are discriminations and classifications which no one has ever made; many which some people have never made; no doubt, many which no one could ever make; and perhaps, as Kant thought, many which we cannot help making. But those which do exist are discriminations and classifications which have been made. What makes anything an X is, therefore, its falling into the X class. The characteristics without which it would not be an X are the characteristics it has as a member of the class. And since classes are man-made, class-membership characteristics are man-made. These characteristics are not dependent on the characteristics of what is classified, or even on whether anything is thus classified. This is why philosophy has no interest in what things, if any, are, e.g., just or known, but only in what it is to be just or to be known.

We can, therefore, distinguish inquiries about the items which can fall into classes from inquiries about the classes into which they can fall, and for the sake of clarity call the former 'first-order' inquiries and the latter 'second-order' inquiries. The first-order inquiries are typical of the natural sciences, e.g., is this, or this kind of, chemical substance both soluble and magnetic? Are the effects of inflation also the causes of unemployment? Certain second-order inquiries, e.g., those about the biological, psychological, or sociological origin and growth of our classifications, are of a similar kind. There is, however, a type of second-order inquiry whose interest in the classifications is neither in that which falls into the classes nor in the origin of the classes, but in the interrelation of the classes.

For example, does being believed to be so involve being so? Is what is caused to be compelled to be? Can negligence only be inadvertent?

Because we have such an interest, we may also inquire, as did Kant and Strawson, whether there are certain classifications into which anything *must* fall. The failure to distinguish questions about distinctions from questions about what is thus distinguished is a major reason why for so many centuries philosophical problems were not clearly separated from scientific problems. The apparent insubstantiality of what is distinguished by psychological distinctions— e.g., *mind, intention, thought, will*—explains why psychology was the last science to be freed from philosophy.

The distinctions, discriminations, and classifications we make are the concepts, ideas, or notions we use. To have a particular concept, e.g., that of justice, recklessness, or mass, is to be able and disposed to assimilate or distinguish in certain ways whatever we encounter. Examining the relations between the various ways we classify things, and consequently between the characteristics which things necessarily have in virtue of being what they are, is examining the concepts we use. We can use the traditional word 'analysis' for this examination of concepts without in any way committing ourselves to the assumption that what is being examined is a complex whose component parts are to be revealed in the way that a chemist might analyze a substance or a politician might analyze a situation. What is complex about the concept is its relations.

In thinking of something in one way, e.g., as a motive, a cause, an example of knowledge, or a piece of recklessness, we necessarily connect it with some of our other ways of thinking about things and disconnect it from still others, somewhat as in taking up a physical position in regard to anything we face parts of our surroundings, turn our backs on other parts, and leave a flank exposed to still others; or in describing one point in space we necessarily link it to some points and separate it from others. Somewhat as the examination of a physical position shows us what other spatial positions it is near to or distant from, included in or excluded from, overlooks or is hidden from, is open to or closed by, so examination of a position in thought shows what other positions are contained in or excluded from it, support or rebut it, are relevant or irrelevant to it. As the relations of physical positions are spatial and of Euclidean points are mathematical, so the relations of concepts are 'logical'. Just as to discover the spatial or mathematical relations of a point is to discover the identity of that point, so to discover the logical relations of a concept is to discover the nature of that concept. For concepts are, in this respect, like points; they have no quality except position. Just as the identity of a point is given by its coordinates, that is, its position relative to other points and ultimately to a set of axes, so the identity of a concept is given by its position relative to other concepts and ultimately to the kind of material to which it is ostensively applicable. Naming a concept by mentioning the word which in a given language is used to express it merely identifies it in the way that a chalk mark on a blackboard identifies a point or a flag on a map identifies a position. While the different words for two concepts, the chalk mark for two points, or the flags for two positions can easily be interchanged, neither the concepts, the points, nor the positions could be interchanged without becoming different concepts, points, or positions. A concept is that which is logically related to others just as a point is that which is spatially related to others.

For conceptual analysis, as for pure mathematics, it does not matter whether what we analyze is true of or false of the world; but if it is true, then anything which our analysis shows to be conceptually derivable from it will also be true. Thus if Euclid's axioms are true of physical space, his theorems are also true. Similarly, if it is true that young people are interested only in what affects themselves, then, if an analysis of *interest* in terms of an *inclination to pay attention* is correct, it would be true that young people are inclined to pay attention only to what affects themselves.

This connection between conceptual and factual truths explains two important methods in philosophy. First, it explains a contemporary technique which the beginner is likely to think inconsistent with the philosopher's protestations that he is only analyzing concepts and not trying to make ontological discoveries. When, for example, Ryle wishes to refute an analysis of *knowing how to do* something in terms of first *knowing what* the rules or principles for doing it are and then putting them into practice, he draws our attention to a well-known nonconceptual fact of human behavior, namely that many people can make and appreciate jokes, but perhaps no one can propound principles of doing so. What Ryle is doing here is to argue that since it is true that we know how to make jokes, then what, according to the criticized analysis, should follow from this must also be true; but what follows, namely that we know the principles of joke making, is in fact false. Therefore, either we do not know how to make jokes—which is contrary to what we admitted and what we all know to be true—or this analysis is mistaken. If the critic is right in his argument of what does follow from the analysis, then the analyst can save his analysis only by disputing these well-known facts about the world. Philosophers of a metaphysical turn of mind have not hesitated to prefer their analyses to these facts. And it was against this preference that Moore protested in the present century when he begged philosophers to respect what common sense believes to be true.

Contrariwise, the claims of metaphysics typically arise from combining a factual and a conceptual premise to give an ontological conclusion. Thus Plato combined the undoubted fact that there are instances of justice with the conceptual principle that instances of something cannot exist unless there also separately exists that of which these are instances, to reach the metaphysical conclusion that the universe contains the form of justice as well as instances of it. In a famous passage Descartes argued from the undoubted fact that the same piece of wax remained before him despite the complete change in all its perceptual properties, brought about by being heated, to the view that there must be something nonperceptible in the wax which remained the same and which, therefore, required a special mental method of detection. Later, Berkeley used the fact that many things exist unseen by us, together with his conceptual principle that to be is to be perceived, in order to derive the existence of an all-seeing God. The method of these metaphysical arguments is no different from that of the scientist who combines the factual details of the path of Uranus and his theory of gravity to posit the existence of the unobserved, and at the time unobservable, planet Neptune; or of the mathematician who uses the principles of arithmetic to show that if one man is filling a 100-gallon tank at 80 gallons an hour and another is filling it at 60 gallons an hour, while a third is emptying it at 40 gallons an hour, then the tank will be full in one hour. The difference lies in the falsity of the metaphysician's conceptual principle.

Both the nature and the philosophical examination of a concept can be best exemplified by considering some of the ways in which we discover its logical features.

One way is to discover what is implied and what is ruled out by it. If one cannot both have one's cake and eat it, then it follows that if we eat it, we cannot have it and that our choice is between not having it and having but not eating it, and neither having nor eating it. Such is the nature of *if . . . then . . .* and *either . . . or. . . .* Similarly, one important difference between, e.g., *beautiful* and *young* is that if two things are identical in every other respect, they must be equal in beauty, but they could be identical in every other respect without being equal in age.

Another way is to discover the respects in which the concept under examination can and cannot be qualified. It is because *nobody* and *somebody* are logically different that we can sensibly ask for a description when told that somebody is outside the door, but only laughably, as Homer and Lewis Carroll realized, ask for a description when told that nobody is there. Similarly, it is appropriate to ask a man when he first *realized* that he had for years *felt jealous* of his sister and she of him; but whereas we can ask when he first *realized* that his sister had for years *felt great pains* in her back, we cannot ask him when he first *realized* that he himself had for years *felt great pains* in his back. In our attempts to understand the notion of an *electron*, we may ask whether tracks in cloud chambers are related to electrons in the same kind of way as vapor trails in the sky are related to jet planes. The difference between *thinking about* a problem and *thinking that* Hume was a greater philosopher than Locke partly consists in the fact that the former, but not the latter, is something one can be engaged in, be interrupted at, be tired out by, or do to no purpose. *Belief*, unlike *knowledge*, can be passionate, sincere, hastily formed, and erroneous.

Hypotheses about the nature of a concept can be tested like hypotheses about any other matter. For instance, if the traditional theory that the *meaning* of an expression is the object to which it refers were true, then the phrases 'the Prime Minister of Great Britain during most of the 1939–45 war' and 'the famous descendant of Marlborough known for his large cigars and his V-sign', which both refer to the late Winston Churchill, would have the same meaning. But they clearly don't. You would translate them differently; you could understand one without understanding the other; there would be no contradiction in maintaining that one says something true about Churchill, while the other does not.

Finally, we may ask for examples either of the kind of situation and conditions to which the concept under examination is applicable or of the ways in which it is applicable to them. A good example of the former is Austin's story about the two donkeys. If, in aiming at my donkey, I shoot your donkey because I, being shortsighted, think that it is mine, I shoot yours *by mistake*; whereas if I shoot your donkey because it suddenly moves into the line of my firing at mine, then I shoot yours *by accident*.

As regards the ways in which concepts are applicable, we have to ask whether *game* and *real* indicate a set of common characteristics in the way that, perhaps, *triangle* does; whether *mind* picks out an entity as *body* does; whether *know* and *believe* are like *walk* and *talk* in signifying what people do; whether *think, attend*, and *work* refer to a specific activity as *count* and *dig* do; and whether *proposition* has the same kind of role as *sentence*.

This is a convenient place to explain a feature of the analysis of concepts which is sometimes thought to be peculiar to contemporary English-speaking philosophers, namely, the examination of the linguistic forms in which our concepts are expressed. There is nothing new about this. When Socrates sought, in the *Theaetetus*, to discover the nature of *knowledge*, he examined the meanings of the Greek words for 'knowledge', 'opinion', 'truth', 'falsity', and 'error' in order to see how what is meant by one of these words is related to what is meant by the others. When Aristotle was looking for the difference between *choice* and *wish*, he pointed out, in Greek, that we could speak of someone's 'wishing', but not of his 'choosing', another's success, the impossible, or to be happy. Berkeley tells us that he wrote his *Theory of Vision* to discover what is meant by saying 'we see things at a distance or without [i.e., outside] the mind'. Kant pointed out that 'searching in our daily cognition for concepts' amounts to 'detecting in a language the rules of the actual use of words'.

Not only is there nothing new about analyzing concepts *via* an examination of their linguistic expression; there are reasons for thinking this is the only practicable way. Though there are distinctions and classifications which have never been made as there are prime numbers which have not yet been discovered and generations yet unborn, a distinction cannot be made or a classification employed without using some means to do it. Though babies, animals, and machines are capable of some discrimination and classification, perhaps of a sensory kind, it is difficult to see how the majority of the distinctions which men make in language or symbols could be made by any other means. As Wittgenstein remarked, "We say a dog is afraid his master will beat him; but not, he is afraid his master will beat him tomorrow." At any rate, it is quite certain that whether or not we have to make our distinctions by verbal means, this is our usual way of doing so. Usually we deploy our concepts by using words. We do not, of course, have to use the words we actually do use. My grasp of the concept of *motive* is displayed by my use of the English word 'motive' and of certain syntactical constructions of 'why'. But someone else may make the same distinctions in Greek or German. What makes the philosopher different from the linguist is his interest in *what* we say rather than in *how* we say it, in our *use* of words rather than in our use of *words*. For instance, the difference between *taking care to do something* and *doing something in a careful manner* can be expressed in English either in the way that I have just expressed it or by the phrases 'taking care *by* doing so and so' and 'taking care *in* doing so and so' or by positioning the adverb 'carefully' either before or after its verb, as in 'carefully arriving at the last moment' as contrasted with 'walking slowly and carefully'. Whether these ways of expressing the difference are peculiar to English and not shared by French and Japanese is a linguistic question. What differences are expressed by these English or some French or Japanese expressions is a conceptual question. It is easy to show that there is a conceptual as well as a linguistic difference between, e.g., 'purposefully' and 'purposely', between 'careless' and 'carefree', but probably only a linguistic difference between the prefixes in 'unimportant' and 'inadmissible'. Admittedly, a philosopher may become so interested in the minutiae of linguistic differences as to forget that what he should be looking for are conceptual differences, so interested in *how* we make distinctions as to forget *what* distinctions we are making. He may confuse points of idiom with points of logic. But such a lapse is not necessary. And it is always worth asking whether our language has such and such features because its users wish to make a certain distinction or whether its source is simply stylistic or philological. It is because we usually make distinctions and employ classifications through the medium of language that we can express our aim of discovering the logical features of concepts as, in Austin's words, "an attempt to discover what we would say when" or as, in Wittgenstein's words, "what the situations are in which we use this expression, what sentences would precede it and follow it (what kind of conversation it is part of)." And it is because the class-membership characteristics of anything are those in virtue of which it is what it is that we can do our philosophy either in the *material* or the *formal* mode, that is, either by talking of things or by talking of concepts and words. Indeed, we might use the much earlier language of Locke to show the underlying unity of our various ways of explaining the nature of our study: "Since nothing can be a man, or have a right to the name 'man', but what has a conformity to the abstract idea the name 'man' stands for, nor anything be a man, or have a right to the species man, but what has the essence of the species; it follows that the abstract idea for which the name stands and the essence of the species is one and the same."

For the same reason we can put questions like 'What is *knowledge*?' and 'What is *truth*?' and 'What is *inadvertence*?' either as 'What is it for something to be known, to be true, or to be done inadvertently?' or as 'What does it mean to say that something is "known," is "true," or is "inadvertent"?' The last form of the question is no more a question in linguistics than any of the others and is no more intended than they to be confined to English philosophers. To study being *qua* being or the *idea* of existence is to seek for those features of anything in virtue of which it is said in English 'to be', in French 'être', or in Latin 'esse'.

One danger in characterizing philosophy as the examination of concepts is that of overlooking the difference between using a concept and stating its use. As a result, clarification of the latter is confused with clarification of the former and the propriety of correcting philosophical errors in the latter is confused with the impropriety of finding fault with the former. Certainly, people can be confused in their use of concepts as they can be unidiomatic or ungrammatical in their use of a language. But this is not a failing of many of us in our use of our everyday concepts or of experts in their use of technical concepts. Nor, if it were, would it be the job of philosophers to correct it. But philosophers do try to correct the views of other philosophers and nonphilosophers about what this use of theirs actually is.

There is nothing mysterious in the distinction between being able to do something, e.g., use concepts or words, perfectly well and being able (or unable) to state how we do it, a distinction which G. E. Moore characterized as that between 'knowing what one means by a certain expression' and 'knowing the correct analysis of the meaning of that expression'. Most of us can speak grammatically, argue logically, and make and appreciate jokes without knowing or being able to say exactly how we do it. "God has not been so sparing to men," said Locke, "to make them barely two-legged creatures and left it to Aristotle to make them rational." What Aristotle did, as a logician, was to discover and formulate the rules which intelligent and logical people implicitly employ, just as Berkeley and Zeno attempted, though with only partial success, to discover the ways in which we use the ideas of *existence* and *infinite divisibility*. So, Augustine remarked, "What is Time? If no one asks me, I know; if someone does ask and I wish to explain, I no longer know." Socrates considered philosophy to be getting to know something which in another way we know already. Philosophers are to the users of ideas, including themselves, like preachers to practitioners, critics to poets, grammarians to native speakers, map makers to explorers of the unmapped, and Molière's philosopher to M. Jourdain who had been speaking prose all his life without knowing it.

There is no reason, for example, to suppose that Plato, Descartes, the logical positivists, and Ryle employed different concepts of *knowledge*. Where they did differ was in their theories about the nature of the concept which they, like you and me, all employ. Plato and the logical positivists, for example, confined knowledge to what is necessarily so, which for Plato meant his heavenly forms and for the logical positivists the analytical truths of logic and mathematics. But theories about the nature of a concept cannot be used to suggest that there is something wrong with the concept— that, for example, we should not say, as we all do, that we *know* various things about the world, about other people, and about the future. Furthermore, it is a short step from concluding that we should not use our concepts in the way we do, that we should not say what we do, to concluding that the things we express with the help of these concepts are false. It was against the former conclusion that Moore appealed to "ordinary language" and against the latter that he appealed to "common sense." The actual behavior of the concept is itself the test of the rightness or wrongness of theories about it, just as the properties of a chemical substance furnish the criterion of scientific theories about it. One can be pretty sure that a philosopher who concludes from his study of a concept that there is something wrong with it has made a mistake about it. Plato and the logical positivists, for instance, probably concluded that knowledge can only be of what is necessarily so because they incorrectly interpreted the fact that if something is known to be so it must be so as the supposition that if something is known to be so it is something which is necessarily so, instead of correctly as the fact that if something is known to be so it necessarily follows that it is so.

One reason for this important confusion between getting clear and correct about our use of a concept and allegedly clearing up and correcting this use may lie in the double use of the word 'concept', partly to signify, as we have been doing, a way of classifying something, e.g., as *knowledge, justice, human*, and partly to signify a view or theory about something, whether it be knowledge, justice, or mankind. The latter, but not the former, can be a conception; it can be true or false. We can have misconceptions, but not misconcepts. Thus, though Plato used the same concept of *knowledge*, of *justice*, and of *man* as Ryle, he had quite different conceptions about them.

Another reason for the supposition that it is legitimate for philosophers to criticize and change the ideas they are analyzing is a false analogy sometimes drawn between the work of philosophers and that of scientists. Hence those metaphysicians who have thought of themselves in the role of superscientists have indulged in much revision of our ideas. It is pointed out, correctly, that scientists frequently change their ideas to cope with new situations. The physicist's ideas of *force*, *matter*, and *causality*, the chemist's idea of *distinguishability*, and the psychologist's ideas of *intelligence* and *motivation* sometimes differ from the ordinary man's; Einstein's idea of *space* differs from Newton's, Rutherford's idea of the *atom* from Dalton's. Scientists also often reject the concepts of their predecessors, as *phlogiston*, *coronium*, or *animal spirits*. But this analogy between scientist and philosopher has been drawn in the wrong place. Just as a scientist is at liberty to change his ways of studying the objects, whether chemical, physical, or zoological, of his study, but not to change these objects themselves, a philosopher may change the ideas he or his fellow philosophers use, but not the ideas that he or they examine. To reject Plato's concept of *reminiscence* is not to reject the concept of *learning* for whose explanation he introduced the former concept; to attack the technical philosophical concept of *volition* is not to attack the ordinary concept of *will*. We must distinguish (1) the concepts that the philosopher is examining, whether they be the concepts of everyday or technical use, (2) the concepts, perhaps of a technical nature, which he may invent to help his examination, (3) the ideas, theories, concepts, or conceptions that a philosopher may have about the nature of the concepts he examines, and (4) the further theories he may be led to about, e.g., the soul or fate, as a result of his theories in (3). The philosopher is entitled to change, criticize, improve, or evaluate (2), (3), and (4), but not (1). His job is to discover the properties of (1). Scientists and ordinary people change the ideas they *use* in order to cope with new situations, whereas these philosophers would be attempting to change the ideas they *examine* because of supposed faults in them. Whether an idea is unsuitable for the job it is supposed to tackle is a question for the people who have to use that idea to tackle that job, and not for people who wish to discover what, and how, ideas are used to tackle what jobs.

Because, as we saw earlier, recent philosophers have emphasized the truth long familiar in philosophy that an examination of the ideas we employ must be through an examination of the uses of the words we employ, the question of the philosopher's right or duty to tamper with the ideas he examines is nowadays often raised as the question of his right or duty to change language. Heated arguments rage between those, like Moore and some contemporary Oxford philosophers, who make an "appeal to ordinary language" and those, like Russell, who heap abuse on the "cult of common usage" and sometimes advocate an "ideal" language. Now the phrase 'ordinary language' is usually used by contemporary philosophers either to mean the language of ordinary or everyday life, as opposed to that of specialized and technical activities like the sciences, or to mean the ordinary or standard ways in which an expression occurs in either the everyday or the technical field, or most commonly to mean the standard ways in which expressions of everyday use are used. The question whether a philosopher should disturb ordinary language is, therefore, largely the question whether the investigator of the nontechnical ideas we all use should try to change these ideas or their expressions; and to this I have already answered no. This is not, of course, to object to the invention or use of technical terms—like 'synthetic a priori', 'sense-data', or 'mongrel-categorical' —as part of the tools of the philosopher's trade. A philosopher's job is not to clarify, change, criticize, or improve the language in which we ordinarily express our concepts, though he may well have to do this to the language in which theorists express their analyses of such concepts. This is what Moore had in mind when he distinguished between an attempt to analyze the meanings of the words of ordinary language which we all perfectly well understand and an attempt to understand the words, ordinary and technical, which philosophers have used.

Advocates of an "ideal" language sometimes have a motive other than a desire to change our ideas. Linguistic analogies can mistakenly lead us to believe in logical analogies; e.g., 'Lions are hunted' and 'Tigers are thought of'; 'Bears are savage' and 'Centaurs are fictitious'; 'Snakes exist' and 'Snakes bite'; 'Tea is pleasant' and 'Milk is white'; 'The lines meet at infinity' and 'The roads meet at Doncaster.' Since apparently "language disguises the thought; so that from the external form of the clothes one cannot infer the form of the thought they clothe" (Wittgenstein), some philosophers have advocated a new language whose linguistic differences would be exactly correlated with logical differences. But this plan is both undesirable and impossible. It is impossible, for, in addition to the fact that we never know what new differences will appear between ideas which are in many respects similar, the new language, untested as it is in comparison with the great age of natural languages, would probably give rise to fresh problems of its own. Even if it were possible, it would be undesirable because not only can we better avoid our difficulties by becoming aware of them, but we become aware of them in the first place by closer attention to the very language in which they occur. We can see, for example, that *existence*, unlike *biting*, does not mark a characteristic. For while it might be said that most snakes bite, but some do not, it would be nonsense to suggest that most snakes exist, but some do not. Furthermore, the ambiguities which an artificial language tries to banish are one source of a natural language's wealth. Philosophers who propose an artificial language are like people who, on discovering minefields in a beautiful garden, go to live in a snake-infested desert instead of marking the mines.

If, then, philosophy—in the sense in which we talk of 'philosophy' as contrasted with 'a', 'my', 'your', 'the American', or 'communist' philosophy—is conceptual analysis, what is its value? Primarily, to discover certain important features which no other study can discover, namely, the necessary characteristics of anything, the characteristics in virtue of which it is what it is and is what it is called. How important this discovery will be depends on how important the things it studies are. The analysis of *concluding, deducing, inferring,* and *assuming* is, no doubt, more important than that of *muttering, mumbling, whispering,* and *groaning,* just as counting the stars in the heavens is, no doubt, more important than counting the sands on the sea shore. It is not surprising that more effort has been spent on investigating the *beautiful* and the *sublime* than on investigating the *dainty* and the *dumpy.* On the other hand, since philosophy investigates only necessary characteristics, it cannot tell us what things are good or right or known or voluntary or reckless, but only what it is to be any of these.

Philosophy is chiefly valued by some either for its therapeutic powers—for curing "the bumps that the understanding has got by running its head up against the limits of language"—or for its crux-disentangling capacity—for "showing the fly the way out of the fly-bottle." One may, for example, embark on an analysis of *emotion*—and hence of *grief, pity,* and *fear*—in order to understand the distinction between tear-shedding and weeping or between cackling and chuckling at a joke. It is no doubt when we are baffled by the mysteriousness of time, torn between free will and determinism, or puzzled by probability that we begin to philosophize. It is also true that many of our beliefs in areas where investigation and experiment cannot prove them right or wrong are due to conceptual assumptions or inferences, as when we believe in fatalism because we confuse logical necessity with physical inevitability, or when we are persuaded either to materialism or to spiritualism by conceptual arguments about the nature of mind and matter.

Others value philosophy as an ancillary to their own primary interests—as when it shows the psychologist that his experiments into the nature of thought are vitiated by his mistaken conceptual assumption that thinking is a specific kind of, perhaps inner, activity like talking or gazing at images, or when it shows the jurisprudent that his doctrine of negligence confuses it with recklessness, or when it shows the educationalist that indulging a pupil's wants is not necessarily catering to his needs.

SIX

PHILOSOPHY AS I SEE IT TODAY

Gabriel Marcel

First, I would like to spell out, as much as this is possible, the terms of the question which I plan to answer to some degree. It seems clear that in our time, as in previous times, it is possible and even necessary to consider or even to define the philosopher in relation to his history; this would imply, of course, the prior obligation to rethink this history. In my view, it would be not only absurd but scandalous to imagine that this history no longer concerns us, that it is somehow rendered irrelevant by the new conditions under which humanity might be called upon to live. It would be no less scandalous, of course, to choose a particular doctrine—here I am thinking principally of Marxism—in order to "canonize" it somehow by undertaking a sweeping devaluation of the systems which preceded it.

But the question which I wish to treat pertains, as I see it, to the situation of both the philosopher and philosophy in this constantly changing world of ours, where thought runs the very serious risk of yielding to the fascination that techniques, in all forms, are bound to exert on it. In the final analysis these techniques seem to lead more or less directly, all in the same way, to

NOTE: This English version of Gabriel Marcel's paper was prepared as a joint effort by Dr. Claire Gilbert of the University of Maryland, Messrs. Jacques Gilly and Matthew Perriens, and Mr. Bontempo. This version was approved by Gabriel Marcel.

the rearrangement of the planet (or even, in the more or less distant future, of interplanetary relations); they also tend to bring about a rationalized insertion of man into his own social group, and a further insertion of this group itself into some as yet undefined confederation, which, in the end, may be coextensive with the planet itself.

I would not hesitate to say that in facing this undertaking the philosopher is bound to perform a type of questioning rather similar to the questioning performed by Socrates. This certainly is *not* to say that philosophy today should once again embrace the directive of "Gnothi seauton" ("Know thyself") in the literal sense. We know only too well the illusions to which one is exposed when he abandons himself purely and simply to introspection: this is a vital point which I for one will take care not to forget. (Moreover, the knowledge of oneself as Socrates understood it was surely not "psychological" in the modern sense of the word.) Instead, the questioning that is called for today actually tends to discover, or if one prefers, to bring to light, the *fundamental neglect* of which technocrats and, I might add, ideologists at all levels are guilty.

I readily acknowledge that in the extreme this basic neglect is doubtless not very different from the neglect of Being so stigmatized by Heidegger. However, I would rather not use his terminology, and I would particularly avoid use of the distinction he has instituted between *Sein*, or *Etre-Being*, and *Dasein*, or *Etant-Existence*. For this seems to me, in spite of everything, to spring from a unique grammatical system.

Moreover, does the word "neglect" really suit our context perfectly? I shall clarify my thinking by asking if ingratitude is reducible to neglect, and I shall answer this question negatively. But isn't this really a matter of ingratitude at the metaphysical level that is involved here? Let us observe that ingratitude is the opposite of what is expressed by the French word *reconnaissance*. Let us further note that this French word should be understood in its double significance as "discovery," "exploration," or "looking ahead" *and* as "acknowledgment": In the war, for example, men could be ordered to go out on reconnaissance, or to reconnoiter, that is, to advance to some ground to see whether or not it was occupied by the enemy. But we also say that someone who has been loaned money is obligated to recognize or acknowledge (*reconnaître*) his debt. I realize that these dual senses are much more evident in French than in English or in German.

Now, I would propose that the major function of philosophy in our world today may well consist in an act of reconnaissance considered in its dual aspect. But, one might ask first, what is this term to which commitment should be made carefully? It appears to represent, in fact, the future as it presents itself to us, in the light of these same techniques whose influence and force seem to assert themselves more and more each day. We should not, however, fail to affirm that what is called for on our part is not so much a matter of *knowledge* as it is of *acceptance*, whose approval can be given or withheld, depending on whether this acceptance or rejection implies a definite reference to a system of values.

Here again, I confess, I hit upon a terminology to which I myself am inclined to object. The way in which the notion of value has been abused, particularly at the end of the last century and at the beginning of this one, would prompt me to seek a term less worn thin, less watered down. To set the background which must be invoked, I would willingly employ the adjective "experiential" (*expérientiel*), which Henry Bugbee introduced to great effect in his *Inward Morning*. This would serve to capture and highlight the first sense of *reconnaissance* we have noted—as "exploration," "looking ahead." But by so doing we then see the other meaning of *reconnaître* disclosing itself immediately, for indeed it is a certain debt which we are obliged to recognize.

But here, as always, I am not content to deal with colorless abstractions. How could we fail to see that pollution, which today has thrown all of the civilized powers into a state of panic, is but the thoroughly *impious slight*, ingratitude, the *misrecognition* (*méconnaissance*) of what man owes to nature? This is certainly a violation of what I have formerly called the *nuptial bond* between man and life.

Such remarks seem at first very simple, but they have an indefinite power of application. They permit us, I think, to recognize in our day that the heart of philosophy so conceived is nothing else but what I have called a *secondary reflection* or rethinking. That is, a recuperative reflection aimed at reascending that slope which has just barely been descended over these last decades—a descent marked by an approach centered on analysis and on the possible uses of methodically separated elements.

SEVEN

MATERIAL CONSTRUCTIVISM

Paul Lorenzen

I.

I deal with our topic by presenting answers to the following questions:

1. What is the nature of philosophy, i.e., what are its ends and means?

2. To what extent and in what way should philosophy be related to human needs?

3. Is there (and if so, where) a certain narrowness of modern analytic philosophy, especially concerning its relation to human needs?

Questions 1 and 2 are what are called 'systematic' questions, while the third is 'historical', a part of contemporary history. I do not propose to say much about question 3, because the answer might amount to quibbling on the term 'analytic'. What I shall present as 'materially constructive' in my systematic answers will possibly be recognized by some readers as 'analytic'. It might then be preferable to forget about these terms.

It is, actually, a kind of a joke to present a systematic statement about the nature of philosophy nowadays as an *ism,* as if traditional words could provide a solution. Moreover, the new *ism* is trivial. Who would deny that one should not be merely 'formal' (when 'material' is used as the opposite)? Who would deny that one should not be 'merely destructive' ('constructive' being taken as the opposite)? Nevertheless—after all we have heard since Carnap and the later Wittgenstein—why not propose to leave the formal languages to the *mathematicians*, the 'destruction' (the scientific 'analysis') of natural languages to the *linguists*, and to look for other tasks, which by division of labor could then be given to the philosophers? (This task will be the construction of the basic part of all scientific languages. See Part IV.0.)

II.

Let us look—*as if* nothing had happened since Socrates—for a special task, for some activity with some specific end, which we will then call 'philosophy'. The common starting point of both Socrates and of ordinary language philosophy is what we have in common: our common life, ordinary life, not the rather special forms of life such as theoretical thinking. We have to talk, to argue —or to use a mental term, to think—in ordinary life. We have to decide on ends, and we have to choose means for our ends.

This ordinary thinking is always concerned with particular situations of our lives. Whether our decisions on ends will lead to 'reasonable' decisions, whether our choices of means will lead to 'reasonable' choices, depends on ordinary thinking. The term 'reasonable' here indicates that we can be more or less "good" in our ordinary thinking, i.e., talking and arguing. In order to become "better," we attempt a *methodical training* in schools and universities in making decisions on ends and choices of means. Scientific thinking (in the broad sense of the German term *Wissenschaft*) is the result of methodically trained ordinary thinking. Scientific thinking is not concerned with particular situations of our lives. In school we talk and argue only about situations in general and—as exercises—about particular situations of the past. The scientifically educated person has to apply what he has learned at school to the particular situations of his life. *These particular applications cannot be learned in advance, but scientific education is the best preparation we have for the decisions and choices in our lives.*

All this is still far away from anything that ought to be called 'philosophical'.

1. The program for a methodical training of choosing means

for given ends leads first to science proper, to the *technical* sciences in a broad, modern sense of the term (Aristotle would have spoken of poiēsis). The most advanced disciplines are the natural sciences, but also the empirical social sciences, including empirical psychology, belong to the technical sciences in this sense.

For the technical sciences the ends are given. In other words a situation is *described in general*, and the task is to change the given situation so that the desired state of affairs comes about. This means that first we have to learn how to describe given situations. We have to acquire *knowledge* of the relevant *facts*. Then we have to hypothetically invent *laws* according to which situations change. With such laws we *explain* changes. But the point is that only with the help of such laws can we *predict* the effects of our actions. Only through technical knowledge can we *reasonably* choose means for our ends.

As auxiliary disciplines for the technical sciences we develop mathematics and the fundamental part of physics, general mechanics, i.e., the theory of the measurements which are used by the physicists to describe situations.

2. The program for a methodical training of deciding on ends leads to the *practical* sciences. Here we have to learn to judge whether desired ends serve human needs—or whether they are merely products of wishful thinking.

In ordinary life all along we pursue some nonarbitrary ends. But the range of ends is rather limited. We have to learn first how to *interpret* actions of others, to interpret them as means for ends in order to enrich our stock of possible ends. And ends may be means for other ends, subends for superends. We have to invent hypothetical *norms* for the purpose of interpretation. An action is interpreted by assuming that the actor acts according to a norm, i.e., that the actor acts *as if* he had accepted a general imperative of the form 'If you are in situation S, realize end A!' Only with such norms can we *understand* people, including ourselves. Unless we *understand* (in the sense of the German term *Verstehen* as introduced by Hegel, Droysen, Dilthey)—especially unless we understand our cultural institutions by interpreting them with the help of systems of norms— we have no chance to obtain *reasonable* decisions on ends.

3. But even if we presuppose a sufficiently educated *understanding* of our cultural institutions, e.g., in economics, law, politics, and all elaborate forms of our work and leisure, the problem has yet to be solved of how reasonably to decide on the plurality of norms still available.

The program for a methodical training in deciding on ends requires that we learn *justification* of norms. We have to learn to argue about the question whether alleged norms serve human needs, whether they may be called 'just' or must be called 'unjust'.

III.

The exposition given thus far of the development of scientific thinking as a methodical structuring of ordinary thinking does not provide a special task for philosophy—everything, so it seems, is taken care of by the technical or practical sciences. This would be correct—and we would not need philosophy at all—if the sciences had in fact this program of a methodical training of our technical and practical thinking. But this is a rather controversial point.

1. For Wittgenstein (and many of the *analytic* philosophers) at least the technical sciences know what they are doing. In accordance with the general trend of our times to be fascinated by the success of modern technology, it is taken for granted that the technical sciences, especially modern physics, yield paradigmatic cases of methodically built-up sciences.

But a second look at the basic theoretical principles of the natural sciences shows a quite different picture. In logic we have the uncertainty about the consistency of the *tertium non datur* (law of excluded middle), though it is normally ignored; in mathematics we have the more familiar difficulties with the inconsistencies of impredicative set-theoretical principles of comprehension. When we come to general mechanics (with geometry and kinetics as its first parts, but without empirical theories of gravitation), we get into a kind of chaos. Nevertheless, it is considered as heresy to doubt that the theory of relativity has supplied an *empirical* foundation for this fundamental part of physics.

Here we see a first task, different from those which are taken care of in the sciences: to perform methodically *the first steps* which have to be done *before* science proper can begin. *Logic* as a methodical introduction to the logical particles, negation, the junctors, the quantifiers, and the modalities would be an obvious case in point. A constructive underpinning of the *axiomatic* mathematical or fundamental physical theories (as set theory or geometry) would be another. We should *analyze,* take apart, what scientists factually do when they logically draw conclusions from premises. After having taken apart what is factually done, we should *construct,* put together, the parts in a critical step-by-step reconstruction to get the logical and mathematical-physical vocabulary for scientific languages.

2. When we turn to the practical sciences, the situation is distinctively more controversial. Following the precedent of Max Weber (and in the English tradition of the empiricism of Hume), one flatly denies that there could be reasonable arguments about ultimate ends. (I take 'ultimate' in the simple sense of not subordinated as means to another end—as in ordinary life we often do not eat in order to become fit for the work of the next day, but just for its own sake, for the fun of it, i.e., as an ultimate end that satisfies "in itself.") Of course, systems of norms which under certain conditions prescribe certain ultimate ends can be investigated with respect to their realizability—but these are technical problems. It can be investigated whether they are factually accepted, but this leads us at best to an *understanding* of social phenomena, never to *reasonable* judgments on questions of *justice.*

The step from mere understanding to value judgements, from *Verstehen* (understanding) to *Begreifen* (comprehending) in the terminology of Hegel is not taken by the vast majority of the practical (social, cultural) scientists. If this step is taken at all, the suspicion prevails that the methodical paths of the sciences have been abandoned, that wishful thinking and ideology instead of reason have been at work.

Here again the task arises to provide a basic vocabulary (logic may be presupposed now) for getting the practical sciences on their way. Analyzing what is factually done in the social sciences is obviously not sufficient; there are no generally accepted norms for arguments about norms as just or unjust. But this state of affairs does not prevent a *critical reconstruction* of the language of the practical sciences (take economics, law, and politics as paradigmatic cases) by which we could come to *reasonable* standards for such arguments. 'Ethics' (or 'metaethics', if you like) would be a suitable word for the task to construct a basic vocabulary for all practical sciences. The analysis of English terms, starting with deontic modalities as 'shall' (ought) and 'may' and going via such terms as 'end', 'means', and 'action' to mental terms such as 'wanting', 'believing', 'deciding', and 'choosing' and evaluative terms such as 'need' and 'just' (I am using 'need' for 'justifiable wants'), will not be sufficient. After this analysis we have to propose a methodical reconstruction of a basic vocabulary which serves the purposes worked out by analysis.

IV.

Logic, ethics, and the theory of sciences, i.e., the basic steps taken for granted in the particular sciences—these tasks I propose to call '*philosophical'.

Thus I have answered the question concerning which ends philosophy should have: the construction of a professional language which can serve as the common part of all scientific languages, technical and practical. Instead of 'professional language' we could use 'conceptual framework', but then this should include basic syntactical instruments for scientific languages. (Also, the term 'concept' instead of 'term' would first have to be introduced.)

1. How can such a construction be achieved? The general answer is short: methodically. By this I mean the construction has to proceed step by step in a noncircular way. We begin—as children do—with no words. But we do have—as children do—needs (different needs, but needs). First *words* are introduced by examples and counterexamples in the context of our needs. They make predicates in ordinary language and are therefore called *predicators*. They are first used in one-word imperatives, as in English 'Apple!' or 'Eat!' Together with proper names (as 'Eve' and 'Adam') we get elementary sentences: 'Adam! eat apple' and in the indicative 'Adam eats apple'. Any convenient syntax (e.g., some copula) may be introduced here as a *reasonable* reconstruction of the English morphology of the verb (action predicator).

We do not propose merely to construct the syntax (form) of languages, but their semantics (content, material) too. This is the point of *material* constructivism. Even the logical particles have to be introduced in the context of (material) sentences. The method is to use dialogues: each logical particle is introduced by setting up *norms* for the attack and the defense of sentences composed with this particle. These norms have to be demonstrated as reasonable.

Though everything depends on the details of the methodical construction (and this applies to all later stages of the construction; see my *Normative Logic and Ethics*,[1] and more detailed treatment in Paul Lorenzen and Oswald Schwemmer's *Konstruktive Logik, Ethik, und Wissenschafts Theorie*.[2] Something can be said in general about the step-by-step introduction of linguistic norms. This will be done in the following sections, the term 'reasonable' being used as paradigm.

2. There is a general confusion: the term 'reasonable' does not specifically belong to any of the sciences; it belongs to all technical and practical sciences insofar as they have to arrive at judgments that some means are *reasonable* choices and that some ends are *reasonable* decisions. Consequently, the term belongs to *philosophy, to the vocabulary which makes up the basic part of all scientific languages. But this vocabulary—which, together with a reasonable syntax, may be called for short the *basic 'ortho-language'*—is not a ready-made language. Ordinary English is not at all suited to this purpose. Especially the term 'reasonable' should not be taken from ordinary English, but should be methodically introduced into 'Ortho'. Nevertheless, any textbook of philosophy, any essay—including this one—has to *begin* with ordinary English, perhaps refined by some specialized English taken from our learned traditions. The answer to the question "How can philosophy achieve its aim to construct an ortho-language?" is the following: Take (if you talk to people with English as their native language) English as a means to get these people to join your efforts to construct a

---

[1] Paul Lorenzen, *Normative Logic and Ethics*, Bibliographisches Institut, Mannheim, 1969.

[2] Paul Lorenzen and Oswald Schwemmer, *Konstruktive Logik, Ethik, und Wissenschafts Theorie*, Bibliographisches Institut, Mannheim, 1973.

basic *philosophical* language. As Aristotle would have said, the native languages have to be used for *protreptic* purposes, as a means to encourage philosophical studies, i.e., the methodical construction of a language basic for all sciences. In protreptic talk nothing is seriously asserted, no terminology is seriously proposed—everything is provisional. The only aim is to get the reader to the point where he is prepared to stop his usual modes of talking and to join the efforts toward a methodical construction of all the sciences, beginning with a methodical construction of a basic language common to all the sciences.

What is the best method for protreptic? I have almost no empirical evidence for an answer. My own guess is that in the long run the best method is to tell the truth—and nothing other than the truth. At least that's what I try: to talk protreptically in such a way that later, after the methodical reconstruction of a sufficient vocabulary, all assertions which have been made turn out to be interpretable with this vocabulary.

This voluntary restriction for protreptic means that the protreptic part could be read again after the philosophical part, though it need not be read twice.

3. Once this point has been reached, the introduction of first words in elementary sentences could begin—in the context of particular life situations. But in *writing* about philosophy these situations cannot be lived through, they can merely be *described* in general. Again we use the native language for the purpose of describing situations in which a *reasonable* use of some ortho-term or some ortho-syntax could be proposed and accepted. I shall say that the native language is now used as *para-language* for the construction of an *ortho-language.* In protreptic language everything is allowed as long as it serves its purpose: to get the reader to stop his ordinary ways of talking and to try a methodical construction of an ortho-language. But in para-language we have to be very careful not to carry over the confusions of the native languages into the ortho-language.

Para-linguistic descriptions should do no more than give instructions on how particular situations could be brought about. The reader is at once student and his own teacher. Para-linguistic instructions belong to the teacher's manual only.

4. Thus we are, hopefully, on our way. *The question concerning how *philosophy should be done has been answered: after due protreptic preparation we construct an ortho-language with ordinary language as para-language, i.e., as a pedagogical device to circumvent the repetition of living through the situations which are instead merely described.*

It is an especially long way to some ortho-term serviceable as methodical reconstruction of the English term 'reasonable'. Let us use '*reasonable' as the ortho-term. Only after having gone through logic and through the reconstruction of a basic vocabulary for talking about actions (this would be an ortho-terminology: *end, *mean, *norm, *dialogue, *argument . . . ; see *Normative Logic and Ethics*, Chapter 7, where the '*'s have been omitted), we could formulate a criterion for the *arguments which are admitted in *dialogues. This is a negative imperative: 'No *subjective *arguments!' (In plain English: it is not permissible to use merely subjective arguments—subjectivity being defined as claiming exemptions for some persons or group of persons from laws or norms instead of giving a general modification of the laws or norms.)

If this '*impersonality' or '*transsubjectivity' of *arguments is called *reasonable, the point is that though in ordinary English it could be asked "Why argue reasonably?" the term '*reasonable' in Ortho is introduced only *after* the methodical construction of Ortho has been going on for quite a while. And this exercise has been *reasonable (*transsubjective) from the beginning. To use *arguments which are not *reasonable in *dialogue means to drop out of *philosophy. We have, then, to start with protreptic talk again— or to give up. Only after having first exercised reason are we able to introduce the term '*reasonable' into Ortho.

The critical reconstruction of scientific languages with the help of analyzing the factually accepted linguistic norms provides us, moreover, with a paradigmatic case for a general method of arguing about systems of cultural norms, e.g., in economics, law, and politics.

The critical reconstruction of a language is nothing else than a construction of a **critical genesis* of a system of cultural norms. The general method proceeds in a spiral movement from analyzing *factual geneses (of norms) to constructing *critical geneses (of norms), to *factual geneses again, to *critical geneses again—as long as life permits.

Whether we introduce a particular term for this method (say, '*dialectical') or not, it is only by following this method that the historical dimension of the sciences (including the analysis of the factual geneses within the history of cultural institutions as well as the philological-historical disciplines themselves) is integrated into the unity of the scientific approach to life based on philosophy.

V.

1. Question 2 of Part I needs no special answer. *Philosophy starts in the context of our (human) *needs, and the *technical and *practical *sciences are to be introduced as nothing else than a methodical training of *decisions on *ends and *choices of *means. *Philosophy provides the basic *Ortho for all *sciences. Though it cannot immediately *satisfy human *needs, it serves them via the *sciences. *Philosophy is like a lame man who cannot move anything without his coworkers. But the *sciences are like people working in the dark, if they do not use the light of *philosophy to see how they are related to human *needs.

2. Question 3 too has been partially answered: as long as analytic philosophy fails to understand (comprehend) itself only as 'the first word' (Austin) which has to be completed by a methodical reconstruction, it isolates itself from human needs. Analysis of ordinary languages degenerates to a playful ultimate end. And this applies even more to the construction of merely formal languages. Paradigmatically represented by Carnap, the approach of the construction of formal languages (formalism) has to postulate "tolerance" as a guiding principle, because the constructions do not themselves provide a criterion of choosing between different formalisms. Carnap actually chose only such formalisms which are used in the contemporary sciences. So he (and others) constructed formalized naïvetés out of the contemporary naïvetés (e.g., naïve set theory). Following the later Wittgenstein the Oxford philosophy realized that the metalanguage by which formalisms are interpreted should not itself be a formal language.

Contemporary science uses natural languages as metalanguage.

This led to the destruction (analysis) of natural languages with the well-known variants of horseshoe analysis (e.g., Bergmann's analysis of the language of traditional metaphysics) versus soft-shoe analysis (e.g., Austin). Ordinary language as the last meta-language is no solution to the foundational problems of the sciences, because either 'ordinary' is taken in such a strict sense that ordinary language is utterly insufficient for expressing the needed distinctions (say between 'true' and 'provable', between 'action' and 'behavior', 'law' and 'rule', 'value' and 'good') or 'ordinary' is taken in a large sense so that ordinary language contains many watered-down muddles of scientific or pseudo-scientific languages from the past and present. Material constructivism (or without an *ism,* "constructive philosophy") tries a critical reconstruction of just those parts of the professional languages of the sciences which *precede* methodically the special sciences. All these theories (philosophy of biology, philosophy of economics, etc.) which provide the fundamental terms (from which the sciences then take off) are preceded themselves by logic and ethics. Starting with those parts of ordinary language which are (if one wants) at any time under control by their use in ordinary life (i.e., under "empragmatical" control), the construction proceeds, first, to some categories of a rational grammar so that some elementary sentences are critically reconstructed together with terms for their grammatical description, second to logical particles (junctors and quantifiers), third to modalities. This yields a basis for empirical linguistics as well as for formal logic. The controversy between "classical" and "intuitionist" logicians about the *tertium non datur* (A or not A) gets thereby a constructive solution which shows that both parties are partially right. The empragmatical basis of the constructed material language—ortho-language— contains imperative sentences methodically preceding indicative sentences. This allows us to justify the construction of norms and deontic modal logic. (The Kripke "semantics" is shown to be no justification, but a mathematical device for solving decision problems.) "Ethics" is the critical construction of a terminology to formulate the principle that transsubjective thinking should precede all our actions. In historical terms this turns out to be a critical reconstruction of the Platonic theory of virtues and of the Kantian categorical imperative. The ortho-terms reconstructing the current distinction between (human) 'action' and (animal) 'behavior' show that behaviorist psychology as an empirical science is justified *within* the constructed ethical framework.

Logical and ethical principles alone are not sufficient for arguing about what to do in particular situations, e.g., now. Practical arguments about ends require critical historical and social sciences, arguments about means require technologies on the basis of natural sciences and of empirical social sciences. Mathematics is required everywhere as an auxiliary instrument. The methodically disciplined construction of the sciences has been carried out in the books mentioned above up to a language of 456 ortho-terms for the beginnings of mathematics, physics, history, and the (normative) "cultural" sciences. At many places this construction leads to the proposal of "solutions" for controversial foundational problems of these sciences (after restating them in "Ortho"). For mathematics axiomatic set theory is replaced by constructive arithmetic and analysis. Physics is redefined as an empirical science on the basis of nonempirical "protophysics" (rational mechanics).

The critical reconstruction of the language of historical sciences dissolves the traditional problems of the origin of the world and of life (in contrast to the current reductionist theory of life). For the cultural sciences the hermeneutical circle becomes a spiral, so that the interpretation of texts becomes an activity which proceeds in a methodical order as all other scientific activities. Which texts are to be interpreted—and for which ends—is determined by the higher ends of cultural critique and cultural reform. Here a critical reconstruction is given of the dialectical method of Hegel, Feuerbach, and Marx, using a critical reconstruction of the methodology of Max Weber.

But, of course, constructive philosophy does not claim that its constructions are *final* solutions. The whole framework (of 456 ortho-terms) may be doubted at every step. But mere doubt is of no help; only an alternative construction of roughly the same size would be helpful. "Put up or shut up"—because otherwise all discourse degenerates into verbal games.

EIGHT

THE CRITIC OF
INSTITUTIONS

Max H. Fisch

The Greek name of philosopher, so proudly worn and so humbly—
what besides the name have they had in common who in our western lands have worn it? We who sit here tonight as members of a
philosophical association—what have we in common besides the
association? To press the question would be to call up more ghosts
than could be laid again within the limits of your patience—
ghosts of particular and universal, existence and essence, member
and class, substance and attribute, subject and predicate, real and
nominal and persuasive definition. One or two only of these ghosts
I shall try to raise later, and let them haunt you if they still can,
but I want first to take our bearings.

We are all familiar in a general way with the series of episodes
in academic history by which the faculty of philosophy became a
very loose collection of departments of arts and sciences, philosophy
shrank to a single department within the collection, the arts and
sciences multiplied, and numerous other professional faculties were
added to those of law, medicine, and theology, so that philosophy is
now no longer one of four, but one of a hundred, and no longer a
prerequisite to the other three, but a competitor of the other ninety-
nine.

NOTE: Presidential Address delivered before the fifty-fourth annual meeting of
the Western Division of the American Philosophical Association at Indiana
University, Bloomington, Indiana, May 3, 4, and 5, 1956. [This paper appeared
originally in the *Proceedings of the American Philosophical Association*, 1955–
56. It is reprinted here with the permission of the author and the Association.]

When Locke wrote his *Essay,* he could look upon Boyle and Sydenham, Newton and Huyghens as the philosophers of the day, and profess himself to be only an under-laborer clearing the ground a little for such master-builders as these. Now it is Locke's *Essay* that is called philosophy, and nearly all that he called philosophy is science.

Since philosophy has shrunk from a faculty to a department, and diminished from a master-builder to an under-laborer, it might be expected, besides learning humility, to define for itself more clearly its now more limited task. Yet surely the diversity of what is now called, and of what calls itself, philosophy, is not less than it was in Locke's day, when he defined it as "nothing but the true knowledge of things." The questions we ask ourselves, or which, when addressed to us by others, we think properly addressed; the methods by which we seek our answers, or by which we justify them when found; and the tests to which we think it fair our answers should be put—have we philosophers as much in common in these respects as had those whom Locke called philosophers? Is there more than a family resemblance among us, bridging our extreme differences by likenesses of next to next, so that the extremes have in common only the series of which they are the opposite ends? Could we construct a definition of philosophy which, if it had authority, would not unchurch or unfrock many of the ablest among us?

Wittgenstein thought he had found a new subject or a new method which was different from what Plato and Berkeley had done, but which might be thought to take the place of what they had done, and might therefore be called philosophy. It is true that some of us now practice his method who might otherwise have practiced one or more of those already familiar and established. In any sense but that, however, his new method has not taken the place of any of the old ones, but has simply been added to them. The many have not become one, but have only been increased by one. So it has always been. Except for what has changed its name from philosophy to science, everything that has ever been called philosophy is still called philosophy, and, in spite of all changes of fashion, still survives in our midst.

May it all long survive! I have no wish to diminish the diversity or to make it seem less than it is. I am quite content that you should continue as diverse as you are, and yet all continue to bear the name I cherish for myself. If, therefore, I now proceed to recommend to you the oldest of all ways of thinking about philosophy, and to propose a new name for that old way of thinking, I ask you only to consider whether it includes what you are already doing and sets it in congenial relations with what other philosophers are doing. I shall be surprised and disappointed if it does not, but I ask no one to change his philosophic ways. If, however, there are younger members among us who have not yet found themselves philosophically, I suggest an arduous choice that will increase the diversity. And I have also a suggestion for departments of philosophy in our larger universities, which should have the same effect.

In spite of the vogue of analysis, perhaps the most familiar recent definition of philosophy is still that by Whitehead in *Science and the Modern World:*

> I hold that philosophy is the critic of abstractions. Its function is the double one, first of harmonising them by assigning to them their right relative status as abstractions, and secondly of completing them by direct comparison with more concrete intuitions of the universe, and thereby promoting the formation of more complete schemes of thought. . . . Philosophy is not one among the sciences with its own little scheme of abstractions which it works away at perfecting and improving. It is the survey of sciences, with the special objects of their harmony, and of their completion.

Now this suggests that the primary objects of philosophic study are the abstractions and perhaps also the methods and results of the special sciences, and that it aims at some kind of synthesis and completion of the sciences. It seems to me that this is, on the one hand, to assume an impossible burden, and, on the other, to restrict unduly the scope of philosophy. An impossible burden for the reason that we are asked to unify an indefinite plurality of sciences, no one of which is a unified whole in the first place, or has any prospect or need of becoming so. An undue restriction, because all the sciences together are only one set of institutions, and philosophy has no reason to confine itself to this set and ignore others, or even to give pre-eminence to this set. So I propose to describe philosophy as the critic, not of abstractions, but of institutions in general, of which the sciences and their abstractions are a quite special kind.

By institution, as a first approximation, I shall mean any provision or arrangement of means or conditions for subsequent activity, additional to or in modification of the means or conditions that are already present prior to the institution, whether present in nature prior to all institutions or present in nature only as modified by previous institutions.

And now I must crave your particular indulgence. In order to develop the notion of institution and the notion of criticism sufficiently for the purpose in hand, I must say some things that I cannot take time to justify, and some which I am not sure I could justify in any length of time. It is of course a retiring president's privilege to commit all the fallacies that have been exposed in the working sessions earlier in the day. Until further notice, I shall be reading as statements what are for the most part really queries, and I ask you therefore to keep supplying "Is it not true that . . .?", or "May it not be the case that . . .?", or "Will you permit me to suppose that . . .?". It is only to save time and to avoid the monotony of so long a series of questions, that I shall use the declarative form. I believe that, after making the corrections you would wish me to make, and inserting all the qualifications which a close scrutiny would find to be required, I would have enough left to warrant my later proposals. But that also I must submit to your judgment.

The notion of institution, in a closer approximation, involves those of purpose and choice, will and decision; that is, of the arbitrary. It is the notion of what would or might have been otherwise if the purpose had been different, but of what might also have been otherwise to the same purpose. It is the notion of what is subject to criticism in the light of the original purpose if that can be found, or in the light of any purpose that may have taken its place; and of what is alterable by subsequent decisions, but never so alterable as to cease to be arbitrary.[1]

---

[1] By "arbitrary" I mean not "unreasonable" but "dependent on will"; more exactly, I mean "residually arbitrary" in the sense that, when reason has done what it can, discretion remains and commitment is still required. The objectivity of value is not thereby impaired.

In a general way, the purpose is to supply the means for, or to give scope, opportunity, protection, assurance, effectiveness, direction, form or style to future activities of a certain description; or to prevent or discourage activities of other descriptions. When agriculture, industry and commerce have been instituted, we can work and we can supply ourselves with the necessaries and commodities of life. When games have been instituted, we can play. When the arts have been instituted, we can create and enjoy objects of beauty. When religion has been instituted, we can worship and pray and give solemnity to the great occasions of life. When schools have been instituted, we can learn and we can learn how to go on learning. When laboratories and libraries and museums and observatories and sciences have been instituted, we can engage in research. When government has been instituted, we can give some sort of working harmony to the other institutions, which we may call their constitution, or we can stabilize and protect a constitution which they already have, and adjudicate the conflicts that threaten it. These and all other institutions depend upon the two basic ones of family and speech. The length of human infancy makes obvious the primacy of the family. When instituted signs have been added to natural signs, we can speak and write, read and think; when the arts of rhetoric and literature, and learned societies and occasions for ceremonial speech have been instituted—we can make and suffer presidential addresses.

Every value is conditioned in one way or another by institutions, and all valuing tends to take on institutional form, to strengthen or to weaken or otherwise to modify existing institutions, or to give rise to new ones. To paraphrase Aristotle, the basic institutions come into being in order that men may live, and they continue in being, and others are added, in order that men may live well. The institutions of a society, in their order or constitution, are the conditions and means of those activities in which the good life consists in that society. They are also the matrix out of which the conception of the good life is developed. Every institution has its particular value or values, and develops its own rationale, and perhaps even a distinctive type of rationality. Out of the conflicts of institutions, the strains upon individuals that result from them, and the efforts at adjudication and reconciliation, there develops a general theory of the good life, and a generalized rationality, which is instituted as the continuing critic both of other institutions and of itself. It constructs the theory in terms of which the institutions of a society are justified to itself and to its neighbors, in terms of which internal conflicts are adjusted and dissatisfactions quieted, but also in terms of which the existing institutions are weighed and found wanting, and alternatives are conceived, advocated, and instituted. This continuing critic is philosophy.

Already in the eighteenth century Vico had derived the logic, metaphysics and ethics of Socrates, Plato and Aristotle from the disputations of the market-place, the public assembly and the law courts of Athens. We have since learned to suspect behind the earliest philosophical speculations in the Greek world the desire to make or to resist innovations in the institutions of the city states of Asia Minor and of Southern Italy and Sicily. We shall not much exaggerate the prevalent view if we say that philosophy began not in cosmic but in civic wonder; that its cosmogonies and cosmologies were politically inspired and had political applications; and that it conceived the world order in the image of the order of institutions in society before it began to use the former as a standard by which to criticize the latter.

In any case, the critic of institutions needed a metaphysics as well as a general theory of value or of the good life. Eventually it needed all the philosophic disciplines so far instituted, and it will need others still to come. But philosophy has moved during most of its history between the poles of politics on the one hand and metaphysics on the other; between the life of reason and the realms of being. I have no doubt that it will continue to do so.

The most general distinction in the history of philosophy has been that between nature and institution, and the basic problems of metaphysics turn on the relation between the two. Most of the other recurring distinctions are variations on this one, such as nature and culture, fact and value, matter and form, particular and universal, body and mind. Whatever we mean by mind, our best approach to it is not by introspection but through institutions. But though most of the concepts and distinctions of philosophy have been developed out of the theory of institutions, we forget their origin unless a traditional label reminds us, as in the distinctions between natural and instituted signs, law by nature and law by institution, or law by divine institution and law by human institution. We subject our concepts and distinctions to dialectical refinements apart from the theory of institutions, and we seldom subject them to the final test of being brought back home.

Let me illustrate the institutional setting of the problem of universals. An institution that is to survive must be so set up and set going as to become a unit in a system which includes other units of the same kind, and includes other kinds as well. A family must take its place in the family structure of society, in which it sustains certain relations to the families of groom and bride, which reproduce themselves in and through it, and other relations to other families in the neighborhood, the church, the P.T.A. A bank must find its place in the banking system, a school in the school system.

A new university, for example, will conform in most respects to a university type or pattern already exemplified in other universities. But this need not mean merely that its founders are fashioning their university after the idea of a university, whether Newman's or Plato's or any other. Peirce, for instance, defined a university for the *Century Dictionary* as a research institution. The editors asked if it was not a teaching institution. Peirce replied that it was not and never had been, and that we would have no universities in this country until we learned better. But it is less the attractiveness of Peirce's idea than the demands of government, industry, business, and agriculture that are gradually producing an overwhelming preponderance of the research over the teaching function in our universities. Meanwhile, a university has to fit into a system of higher education, to receive students who are graduated from high schools and transferred from other universities and colleges, to exchange credits, to have its graduates accepted on an equality with those of other universities. The idea may prevail in the long run, by repeated appeal to it as a standard of criticism, but in the short run the authoritative universal is less the Platonic idea, less the eternal object or the ideal limit or the abstract universal, and more the Hegelian concrete universal, the institutional system.

Was there a first institution? If so, it will not be the historian, the archaeologist or the anthropologist who can take us back to it. Was there a first family, a first church, a first school, a first bank? If not, we have only to extend the list, and we are sure to come to an institution of which there was a first, but it will not have been the first institution. Every act of instituting presupposes an existing set or matrix of institutions. We make use of old institutions in creating a new one, and the new must have from the start some continuities with the old, and is bound to acquire others, until its roots are sunk in most or all of them. Institutions have institutions for their parts, and are parts of institutions; institutions become reciprocally parts of each other; and there is no all-embracing institution which has all others for its parts but is no part of them.

Universalia ante rem, in re, and *post rem.* If I have not quite clearly illustrated all three, it is apparent that it would not be impossible to do so.

Or try matter and form, body and mind. Institutions cannot be pointed to in the sense in which we can point to physical objects or to human beings, or to certain of their details or qualities or movements. We cannot even point to parts of institutions, because the parts of institutions are also institutions. But there would be no institutions without human beings, and physical conditions, and perhaps there are none without some embodiment in physical objects as well. In some institutions the material embodiment is so prominent that in moments of absentmindedness we may come close to identifying the institution with it. The supermarket then becomes a stock of goods, the country club a golf course, the court a court house, the utility corporation becomes the utility, the church a building with altar and pews, and similarly with banks, schools, and research institutions. That is, we tend to identify what cannot be pointed out with what can. This is not always an unfortunate tendency. To redesign the material embodiment is the most obvious and often the most effective way of changing the institution. If we wish to have discussion instead of lectures in certain courses, the first step may well be not a directive to the teacher but an operation on the classroom, taking out the fixed seats that face forward, and putting in a large oval table with moveable chairs around it. That may suffice without the directive. We change our minds, or may change them, by changing the circumstances in which we act.

Yet the institutions cannot be analyzed into the human beings and the physical objects, or even into the behavior of the former and the shapes and movements of the latter. They are not sensible, but intelligible forms; forms we cannot perceive, but cannot think away without thinking the institutions away; forms, indeed, without which we can scarcely think at all.

We cannot adequately criticize institutions without conceiving alternatives. For purposes of criticism, the scope of an institution includes that to which, taken as a whole, an imagined alternative whole is preferred which is like the given whole in some respects and unlike it in others. Institutions are in this sense relative to our powers of comprehension. But our powers of comprehension have developed by experience of the way in which, within a whole, change at one point brings change at others, so that the question of the desirability of the first change becomes the question of the desirability of a whole which includes all the changes, as compared with a given whole in which none of these changes has as yet taken place. Furthermore, comprehension is not ordinarily immediate or direct. We do not grasp an institution as we do a visual work of art which may be taken in as a whole from any of several points of view. Institutions are comprehended by the help of maps and charts and models and complex theoretical descriptions and historical narratives. The techniques of comprehension may become so specialized to particular institutions or sets or types or aspects of institutions, and so focused on description without reference to the purposes of criticism, that an institutional or social science detaches itself from the critic of institutions. All the present social sciences have in this way detached themselves in the nineteenth and twentieth centuries, as the natural sciences already had in the seventeenth and eighteenth. And the critic is left without command of the apparatus and techniques of comprehension.

INTERLUDE

As an interlude at this point, I should like to read the scenario for a three-act skit called "The Progress of Philosophy."

Act I

The world is back stage and back drop. The philosophers are studying and criticizing. After prolonged study of a part of it, one of them addresses the others, and they stop and listen. As they listen, they do not look at him, but at the part of the world he is talking about. Now and then they interrupt, point at something, and correct him. This is repeated for other parts of the world. All the philosophers move freely from part to part, and there is not much deference to the authority of those who have lingered longest over a particular part. But off to the right a group of them are constructing some very complicated apparatus and building a fence around it and bringing in pieces of the world through a gate. They have stopped calling themselves philosophers and they paint a sign on the fence, saying, in big letters, PHYSICS, and in smaller letters underneath, "PHILOSOPHERS NOT WANTED."

Act II

The world is completely blocked off from view by a row of inclosures, with such further labels as CHEMISTRY, BIOLOGY, PSYCHOLOGY, ECONOMICS, SOCIOLOGY. A few philosophers wander back and forth complaining about the inclosures and recalling the good old days when this was known as "The Philosophers' Common." One of them gives another a boost to look over an inclosure at the world beyond. The philosopher on top reports that there are gates on the farther side through which the scientists go out into the world and return. Meanwhile other philosophers have stationed themselves at knotholes in the fences. Now and then they take peeps to see what the scientists are doing, but for the most part they hold their ears to the holes and listen to what the scientists say, and exchange reports with each other, and critical comments. One philosopher suddenly shouts through his knothole, "Oh! Mind your language!" A few moments later he whispers, "Would you like to have me mind it for you?" The philosophers form a chorus and sing the philosophers' theme song. When they come to the refrain, each of them approaches his knothole. The refrain is, "Mind your language! Or would you like to have us mind it for you?"

Act III

We hear more bustle than ever in the inclosures, and the banging of the gates suggests much traffic with the world. But the philosophers have not only forgotten the world but have turned their backs on the sciences and are sitting in two huddles down front. Those at the left are playing a game of cards which is supposed to settle the pecking order in philosophy. As they lay down their last cards, one says, "Object!"; the second, "Meta-!"; the third, "Meta-meta-!"; and the fourth, "Meta-meta-meta-!" But before proceeding to peck, they are distracted by a speech which has begun in the huddle at the right, and they straggle over to hear it. The speech is to the following effect. "Since the scientists won't let us mind the world, or *them*, and they don't much care whether their *language* is minded or not, and we can't mind it very well through the knot-holes anyway, why not start minding *ordinary* language? That's something they can't deprive us of, and we always have it with us, so we needn't budge from where we are." After some discussion, they decide that that is what they should have been doing all the while, so that what seemed like a forced retreat from the world and from science was really an advance to the rear, and this is what progress in philosophy consists in. So they take out notebooks and start scribbling, and then they read each other short papers on such subjects as, "Am I now dreaming?" "Can I feel your pain?" "Can we witness or observe what goes on 'in our heads'?" "Can a man witness his own funeral?" At the end they stand and sing their second song: "Doesn't it strike you / And greatly surprise you / That ordinary language / Is so very extr'ordin'ry?" (*Curtain.*)

Now, if my conception of philosophy as the critic of institutions is sound, philosophy must stand in a relation to the social sciences very different from that in which it stands to the natural sciences. Philosophy needs the social sciences, and they need it, a great deal more than it needs the natural sciences, or they it. For philosophy, the natural sciences are primarily a set of institutions, institutions of research and teaching, intimately linked with agriculture, engineering, industry, medicine and other technological institutions. Philosophy, as the critic of institutions, is concerned with all of these primarily as objects of value; that is, with reference to the activities to which they give form and direction, and the value of those activities in the good life as a whole. The objects of the natural sciences themselves are not the philosopher's primary objects. They belong to that side of the nature-institution couplement which concerns him only secondarily. He needs to revise his metaphysics from time to time in the light of general developments in the natural sciences, but he seldom needs a detailed knowledge of their findings. On the other hand, while philosophers of science have doubtless contributed in the past to the understanding the natural scientists have of their own procedures, and have perhaps even contributed some refinements to the procedures themselves, these are now well established and it does not seem probable that in future the natural scientists will greatly need philosophy in their own proper business, though certainly they will need it whenever they attempt to turn science into metaphysics or to erect a metaphysics on the conclusions of science, with an imperfect realization of the institutional character of science, and of the necessity of bringing institutions other than scientific into the metaphysical scheme.

With the social sciences the case is quite different. We cannot content ourselves with considering them as institutions among others, for their objects are our objects too in a way in which those of the natural sciences are not. Our chief purpose here must be not to study the social sciences but to study, with their help, what they study. Every institution, including language, is the concern of one or more social sciences, and the social sciences are continually making discoveries in ignorance of which we cannot continue or resume our traditional function. If we resign ourselves to ignorance of the social sciences, we must resign ourselves to being critics of only one institution, namely language, and very ignorant critics of that.

On the other hand, the social scientists need us. There is great confusion among them as to their functions, methods, and concepts. Some of them, aspiring to the condition of natural science, would turn the social sciences into behavioral sciences, values into observable natural facts or events, and institutions into behavioral patterns. Yet these same scientists may be employed as experts to evaluate alternative institutional arrangements, and may irresponsibly assume the values of those who employ them, or assert their own values, without any attempt at the objectivity they profess in their research. Other social scientists are convinced that values are of the essence of what they study, but that neither institutions nor values are data of the natural science kind. They would like to deal with them scientifically, but they do not know how. Finally, there are social scientists who, often without knowing it, are really philosophers, interpreters and critics of institutions, who view the industrious value-free researches of their colleagues with a disdain which few professed philosophers would permit themselves. Now, as Peirce said to Royce, "I wish you would study logic—you need it so much," so we might fairly say to all three groups of social scientists, "We wish you would study philosophy—you need it so much." In all three groups, however, and in the many intermediate groups as well, there is already a minority of social scientists who have some sense of the relevance to philosophy of what they are doing, and who are willing to believe that philosophy might help them toward a more rational ordering of their own endeavors. They would welcome us to their counsels, and would be glad to be welcomed to ours. They would accept our services as friendly critics, and even invite our collaboration.

I have now finished the part of my paper for which I begged your particular indulgence, and I come to my proposals. Let me repeat that they do not include a proposal that any of you should practice philosophy in any other way than that in which you are now practicing it. I believe that you are all philosophers as I understand philosophy, and that, if it does not seem so to you, that must be because I have failed to make myself clear. I do think, however, that a series of developments in academic history has led to concentration on the institution of language, and comparative neglect of many others; and I think that another development in academic history now offers us an opportunity to redress the balance. That new development is the great increase in college and university enrolments which is already well begun. I base my proposals on the premise that, within a future for which we may reasonably plan, there may be twice as many persons making a career of philosophy as there are now, and that the intellectual and cultural vitality of philosophy may be recovered by a distribution of effort among those who join our ranks different from that which now obtains among us. I have two sets of proposals.

The first set is addressed to all of us as advisers of individual students. It is that we be on the alert for students who seem to have some aptitude for one or another of the social sciences, and who have not already given hostages to fortune, and that we urge them, after a thorough grounding in the more technical philosophic disciplines, to obtain a similar discipline in a social science of their choice. They should carry their studies far enough to have had first-hand experience of the research methods of the science in question, and, if possible, be admitted to membership in the profession. They should subscribe to at least one representative journal, and cultivate the friendship of at least one outstanding young scientist in the field, through whom they may hope to be kept informed of current developments as from within the science. They should attend its departmental seminars and professional meetings, and in due time offer papers of their own. They should turn their growing scientific knowledge to philosophic account, and make it available to their fellow philosophers so far as that is desired.

For purposes of such advice, I think we should include history among the social sciences, and I think we should encourage some students to turn instead to law, public administration, business management, labor union organization, social work, and even to supplement professional training by practical experience in these fields.

My second set of proposals is addressed to the philosophy departments in our larger universities. Without diminishing, and perhaps while even increasing, the absolute numbers of persons with strength in mathematics, natural science, languages and literature, and the other arts, I suggest that they seek to increase greatly their relative strength in the social sciences. If my conception of philosophy is sound, a department with twelve members, for example, might reasonably have an expert in each of the major social sciences and in law. These men should be encouraged to spend part of their time in cultivating their several sciences, and in maintaining good communications with the respective departments. We should not expect them to begin publishing as soon, or to publish as often, as their colleagues in logic, the philosophy of the natural sciences, semantics, or analysis. They would of course be writing, and they would present papers in our meetings as well as in social science meetings. Many of these would never be published, or would be published only after many metamorphoses. If philosophy becomes again the general critic of institutions, the expertness required for useful publication will demand a greater maturity and a wider experience of life, in addition to the logical, analytical, and dialectical skills we already prize.

If there are really able young men and women who are willing to extend their preparation for philosophy in the way I propose, and if college and university departments of philosophy are ready to add persons so trained to their staffs, and promote them on evidence other than print, I do not doubt that the foundations will supply the necessary scholarship funds for a trial period, until the universities themselves can make suitable provision.

We might also ask the foundations to support for several years a summer session in which leaders in the social sciences would conduct seminars at an advanced level for philosophers. I think the foundations can be persuaded that philosophers are worth educating in this and other ways. For example, another project that would require foundation support would be the preparation of a classified bibliography of social science literature carefully selected and critically annotated for the particular purposes of the general theory and critic of institutions. The continuation of such a bibliography in periodic supplements might then be undertaken by one of our university departments which had expanded its staff to include a corps of experts in the social sciences. Such a department might also enlist foundation help in launching a journal which, along with *Ethics*, would lead the way in the kind of recovery of philosophy toward which all my proposals are directed.

Two concluding words.

1. It may turn out in fifty or seventy-five years that the social sciences have been a mistake. That is, it may turn out that their effort to approximate the mind-free value-free concepts and meth-

ods of the natural sciences, and their search for generalizations of the natural science kind, have been a mistake. The social sciences may then return to the condition of philosophy, each functioning as critic of institutions from the base of a particular institution or set of institutions. This would be unobjectionable, and it may perhaps be necessary. All institutions are implied by any one, and working out as it were from a particular one may yield as adequate an understanding as attempting to survey them all without focusing sharply on any. More exactly, a just survey is possible only after working out from each to the others.

Meanwhile, however, we must live with the social sciences as they are, and on their terms as well as ours. If we do not, they will be driven by the pressure of rapid social changes to create their own value-orientation, their own synthesis, their own general theory and critic of institutions. If God did not exist, it would be necessary to invent Him; and if the critic of institutions no longer lives, and cannot be resurrected, in departments of philosophy, it will be necessary to create it outside of them.

2. Fortunately for most of us here tonight, philosophy has other resources besides the social sciences and besides its own more technical disciplines. It draws nourishment from all the humanities as well, and in the end it performs its critical function in the humanistic rather than in any scientific way. Thus the history of philosophy has an importance which the history of science cannot have. The history of philosophy is philosophy itself taking its time, and its way of taking its time includes not merely a continual bringing forth of things new, but a continual review of the old. It continually re-sifts, re-selects, and re-orders its past creations, re-edits, re-translates, re-reads, re-interprets, and criticizes afresh. Its great classics do not diminish but grow in power. The art of teaching is itself often the art of bringing the thoughts of our students back again and again to a sentence of one or another of the great philosophers, until our students grasp the significance which only the entire history of philosophy before and since packs into that sentence, and until they bring to bear upon it all the critical resources which that history affords. Thus the institution

which is eminently the critic of all others is also that which, more than any other, is critical of itself.

University of Illinois

POSTSCRIPT

Though this paper has the local color of its place and time in a period of rapid expansion in American higher education, the conception of philosophy it proposes, if valid at all, is valid for all times and places, and a reader willing to try it out in a time of retrenchment will readily supply the local color of that time.

NINE

PHILOSOPHY AS I SEE IT

Frederick C. Copleston

When looked at from one point of view, philosophy is clearly parasitic. I am not using the word 'parasitic' in a depreciatory or abusive sense. I mean simply that philosophy as it actually exists can be seen as feeding on something else. The philosophy of science, for example, presupposes the development of science and feeds on it by reflecting on its presuppositions and its methodology or logic. Similarly, the moral philosopher assumes man's moral life as a phenomenon or set of phenomena, turns it into an intentional object and examines, for instance, basic concepts such as right, good, and obligation, the role of moral principles, and the nature of moral argument. Again, the philosopher of religion presupposes the historical existence of religion and reflects, say, on features of religious language. As for the philosopher of art, it is obvious that he does not, as a philosopher, paint pictures or compose symphonies. Nor, if he is wise, does he usurp the functions of an art critic. He inquires, for example, into the nature of the aesthetic judgment. Whether we choose to emphasize critical inquiry into presuppositions or examination of different language games, it remains true that philosophy presupposes and draws its nutriment from certain first-order activities or types of experience. And as long as these different types of human activity or experience persist, so long will the relevant philosophical disciplines continue in existence.

The development of empirical science has obviously excluded the attempt to solve scientific problems by nonscientific methods. But it is patently false that the development of science has rendered philosophy superfluous. It has given rise to the philosophy of science. And as long as religion exists, so long will there be room for the philosophy of religion.

It does not necessarily follow that philosophy consists simply of a set of unrelated disciplines. Suppose, for example, that we focus attention on its function as a critical inquiry into presuppositions. The philosopher can of course confine his inquiry to a given area, to the presuppositions of science, for example. But there seems to be no *a priori* reason why he should not inquire into the ultimate presuppositions, if any, of human thought in its intentional activity in general. Or suppose that we emphasize the role of philosophical reflection in regard to different language games, to use a Wittgensteinian phrase. We are not entitled to assume that the different types of language—descriptive, evaluative, religious, and so on—are cut off from one another by a hatchet. It may be reasonable to say with Wittgenstein that we should not simply assume that they must have something in common. But it is equally reasonable to claim that we should not assume the opposite. We have to look and see, as Wittgenstein himself remarks. In any case, as a language, such as the language of morals, cannot be understood except in terms of its function or functions in human life, it is reasonable to suggest that reflection on the complex of language games leads on naturally to a philosophical anthropology of some sort. And reflection on philosophical anthropology opens up still wider vistas.

Let me put the matter in another way. In a novel by William Golding one of the characters asserts that between the world of science and technology on the one hand and the sphere of moral and religious experience on the other there is an unbridgeable gulf. Well, this may sometimes seem to be the case. But that it is the case should not be assumed without having explored the possibility of a synthesis which at the same time respects differentiating factors. Kant, to name only one famous philosopher, attempted to construct a coordinating synthesis which would not blur or overlook differences. And whatever one may think of his actual procedure and views, he was dealing with genuine problems, consideration of which is quite properly expected of philosophy. It would indeed be absurd to claim that all philosophers should set about constructing comprehensive syntheses or world views or metaphysical systems.

For philosophers, like other men, differ in their interests, bents of mind, and particular gifts. If a philosopher wishes to confine his attention to a very limited field, he is obviously free to do so. But he is equally free to pursue the task of constructing a general categorial scheme or system of general ideas in terms of which different types of human experience or different aspects of reality as experienced by us can be coordinated and their interrelations exhibited. If we are entitled to seek such conceptual mastery in a very limited area, we are equally entitled to seek it in a much wider field. As Professor P. F. Strawson has well remarked, no further justification of descriptive metaphysics is required than that required by theoretical inquiry in general.

It can be objected that the relevant issue is not one of freedom at all. If a philosopher wishes to pursue ambitious projects of synthesis or to construct a world view, he is obviously free to do so. And this sort of activity certainly falls within the range of meaning of the word 'philosophy' as commonly used. The relevant issue is what constitutes scientific philosophy, when scientific philosophy is understood not as implying any particular reference to empirical science, but as referring to philosophical activity which yields definite and assured results. The plain fact of the matter is, it may be said, that the succession of systems has got us nowhere, so far as definite knowledge is concerned. We have therefore come to see the need for an analytic approach and for breaking up wide complex questions into precisely stated and sharply defined questions which can be tackled successively. The mania for system making has done a disservice to philosophy by producing general impressions which have little cognitive value.

Objections to "inductive metaphysics" can of course be raised by metaphysicians themselves, on the ground, for example, that attempts at synthesizing the world of common sense, the world of science, the world of values, and so on inevitably rest on unexamined presuppositions. The metaphysician, it may be said, should work back to an unquestionable point of departure and then proceed deductively. Only in this way can he hope to make metaphysics a genuine science. While I have no intention of condemning the attempt to construct a presuppositionless philosophy (even if the attempt turns out to be unsuccessful, there is no reason why it should not be made), I do not propose to pursue the theme here. I simply indicate that I am not unaware of the point of view mentioned.

We can grant at once that ambitious projects of synthesis increase the danger, or indeed likelihood, of blurring differences, jumping to conclusions, indulging prejudice and wishful thinking, overlooking inconsistencies, and so forth. Further, it seems to me foolish to suppose that there can be any final, definitive, and completely adequate world view. A man swimming in a river cannot see the whole river. He can of course make some statements about the river as a whole which must be true if it is proper to speak of a river at all. And what he sees is doubtless there to be seen. But his vision is limited. Analogously, a philosopher can make statements which must be true, for instance, of all material things, inasmuch as their truth is entailed by the nature or concept of a material thing. But the more he tries to go beyond the skeletonic framework of such statements and to paint a fuller picture of the totality, the more likely is the picture to express a certain perspective.

Not that such pictures are useless. In my opinion at any rate Schopenhauer focused his attention on the evil and suffering in the world to such an extent that he interpreted happiness in an untenable way, namely in negative terms, as a temporary cessation of pain. And in his interpretation of human history in general Marx exaggerated the role and determining influence of man's economic life. At the same time Schopenhauer drew attention, precisely by his overemphasis, to aspects of human life and history which had been slurred over in some other systems. And Marx made a signal contribution to altering our reading of history by forcibly drawing attention to factors which are certainly present, even if there are other factors to take into account. World views may not be final and completely adequate, but this does not entail the conclusion that they are valueless or ineffective.

In any case, whatever the defects of comprehensive world views and metaphysical systems may be, it is open to doubt whether philosophy can be appropriately represented as a process of answering separate questions successively. It is indeed obviously true that questions should be stated as clearly and precisely as possible. Trading in vagueness and obscurity is something to be avoided. But the picture of philosophy as a process of arriving at definite results or conclusions which can be filed away for future reference is an odd one. It may be said that it seems odd only if we compare it with what philosophy has often been in the past, and that it represents what philosophy ought to be. But this view of philosophy presupposes that it can be broken up into entirely separate or atomic questions. And this notion is open to challenge. If one simply asks for a list of conclusions which have been universally accepted up to date, it is indeed difficult to supply such a list. But it can be objected of course that there is an important difference between proof and persuasion, and that a question may in fact have been definitely answered, even though some philosophers fail to see this. Hence discussion of any proffered list of definite results is apt to be both lengthy and inconclusive.

It seems to me, however, that the interlocking of philosophical questions can be exhibited fairly easily. The question of human freedom (in a psychological sense) has formed a recurrent theme for philosophical discussion. But it is not a question which arises in a vacuum. It arises in a context or, rather, in a series of contexts. And reflection on it leads naturally to consideration of other questions or themes. As I have said, it is quite legitimate for a philosopher to confine his attention to certain questions or to a limited field. But his mind can also be led to further topics and to a process of unification or synthesis, not arbitrarily but under the guidance of interrelations.

A good many philosophers have taken it that a sharp dichotomy between factual assertions and judgments of value has been definitely established. And the same has been assumed in regard to the distinction between analytic and synthetic propositions. But both views have in fact been challenged. Without, however, arguing the case for any particular thesis in these discussions, I think that whatever view one holds has implications which open up wider vistas. In fact, I do not suppose that anyone would seriously deny this. For it is obvious that what one holds in regard to the distinction between factual assertions and judgments of value has implications in ethical theory. In fine, I find any sharp dichotomy between "unscientific" speculation and "scientific" solving of separate questions one by one an unacceptable interpretation of philosophical activity. We cannot profitably dispense with either analysis or synthesis.

What I have been saying probably sounds like some reflections, perhaps rather trite reflections, by a historian of philosophy who, by the very nature of his subject, is inclined to historical relativism and who is not disposed to regard as final any particular philosophical system of philosophy or any particular current of thought. As this is supposed to be a personal statement, perhaps I should refer to the sympathy which I feel with Maurice Blondel's transcendental reflection on the dynamism of the human spirit and also with Karl Jaspers' conception of philosophy as drawing attention to the possibilities of human "existence." With both men philosophy is self-limiting—limited, that is to say, not by external authority, but by internal self-criticism and reflection. And with both men philosophical reflection opens the human spirit to the Transcendent, without claiming to transform the Transcendent into an object of exploration. While I have a profound admiration for the genius of Hegel, whom in some respects I regard as the greatest of modern philosophers, I cannot avoid the conviction that Kierkegaard's criticism was largely justified, even if he sometimes tended to caricature the philosophy of Hegel. But I have no intention of turning my personal preferences into criteria for deciding what is and what is not "genuine" philosophy. Some philosophers would claim that the thought of Karl Jaspers is not "real" philosophy. I think that it is. But it by no means follows that I do not regard "Oxford philosophy" as genuine philosophy.

The accusation has been brought against Oxford philosophers that they regard philosophy as a kind of in-game, a purely academic pursuit which has little relevance to life outside departments of philosophy. And Hegel believed, notoriously, that it was the job of philosophers to understand historical development, whereas Marx maintained that it was time for them to change the world. I am not concerned here with discussing accusations against any given philosopher or group of philosophers. But I wish to ask in general whether it can be justifiably expected or demanded of philosophers that they should contribute to changing the world or to solving our social and political problems. My remarks on this subject will be inevitably brief and sketchy.

There is one fairly obvious way in which the philosopher can contribute to political discussion, namely by drawing attention to examples of fallacious arguments, the emotive use of language for propaganda purposes, the procedure whereby, for instance, an un-democratic regime is commended by describing it as 'genuine' or 'true' democracy, and so on. Clarification of this sort is not, how-ever, precisely what people generally have in mind when they de-mand that the philosopher should descend out of his ivory tower and enter the social and political arena. What they are demanding is that he should take sides or commit himself. And the question arises whether such self-commitment can reasonably be regarded as being in some assignable sense a consequence of his philosophy. As a man, the philosopher is as much entitled as anyone else to make political judgments and to participate in campaigns for causes. But he is entitled to do a lot of other things, such as driving a car, which can hardly be regarded as being the philosopher's actions as a philosopher. When people demand that philosophers should com-mit themselves in this or that way, are they simply expressing the value judgment that social or political self-commitment is of greater worth than philosophical reflection?

It seems to me that no one simple answer can be given to the question at issue. Bertrand Russell was a notable campaigner for causes. But he maintained that there was no intrinsic relation be-tween his philosophy on the one hand and his political campaigns on the other. And he was quite right. For it would be absurd to suggest that his participation in the ban-the-bomb campaign was a logical consequence of his reductive analysis. And as for ethics, in his view it was concerned not with making actual judgments of value, but with determining the nature of the value judgment as such. If he claimed the right to make value judgments and to express them vehemently, this was logically consistent with his ethical theory.

But the judgments which he made did not follow from his philosophy, if we understand 'philosophy' in the stricter sense which he gave to the term.

Russell was well aware, however, that the term 'philosophy' was commonly used in a wider sense than the one recommended by himself when he was concerned with defining the limits of scientific philosophy. He did not need to be told that with a good many philosophers actual judgments of value formed part of their thought as this is outlined in histories of philosophy. Nietzsche is a case in point. When value judgments are incorporated into a philosophy, they may obviously constitute a ground for recommending or defending certain social and political states of affairs or projects and for condemning others. Actual self-commitment obviously does not follow as a logical consequence, for this depends on personal decision and will. But if it takes place, it can be in accordance with a philosophy, in a stronger sense than simply being compatible with it. Suppose that I defend a personalist philosophy in which value is attached to the human person, defined in a certain way. It is then perfectly reasonable for me to apply my philosophical position in the social-political area and condemn any political system which seems to me to deny, belittle, or threaten the value of the person. Whether or not I participate in a campaign to overthrow such a system or to prevent its introduction is another question. But if I do so, my action is in accordance with my philosophy. There is not that gap between philosophy and self-commitment which there would be if, for instance, I confined philosophy simply to logical or linguistic analysis.

The matter is obviously more complicated than this. For one thing, someone may claim not to make value judgments in his philosophy, when it appears to an external observer pretty clear that he does. For another thing, the sort of value judgments which a man makes outside philosophy as he understands the term may seem to demand a revision of the philosophy in question. Refinements apart, however, we can perhaps draw the unexciting conclusion that when people demand that philosophers should descend out of their ivory towers and enter the social-political arena, they are in effect demanding a broader concept of philosophy which would point the way to certain lines of action, in accordance with values and ideals embodied in the philosophy, unless of course they are to be understood as maintaining that committed action is more valuable and more desirable than philosophizing. As for political decisions which do not involve important differences in the field of moral judgments and judgments of value, one can no more expect a philosopher to do the politician's work for him than one can expect the philosopher to do the work of the scientist or artist.

A philosopher can of course try to alter our way of seeing the world by developing what P. F. Strawson has described as a revisionary metaphysics. Such an attempt obviously presupposes the judgment that our way of seeing the world ought to be altered or that another way of seeing it would be truer or more valuable. (But all philosophical inquiry, of any kind, presupposes a judgment of value.) And "the world" can be understood as including human life and history and the social-political sphere. If people complain that philosophers offer no "visions," this may be empirically true in a great many instances; but it is obviously not necessarily true, even if we are none too enthusiastic about the effects of apocalyptic thinkers such as Nietzsche and Marx. Philosophers can be "prophets." They can be, because they have been. It is indeed understandable if a good many philosophers turn with relief to a rather dry conception of philosophy and studiously avoid what they regard as wild and uncontrolled speculation, disguised poetic visions, religious edification, social-political propaganda, and what not. I sometimes feel that way myself. At the same time it is none too clear that value judgments can in fact be excluded from philosophy, even if its scope is narrowed. And it seems to me that while philosophy, reflecting on its history, wisely limits itself in certain ways, the interlocking or interrelations of philosophical problems effectively prevents the permanence of the degree of self-limitation to which many people object. I find myself unable to believe that we have now arrived at the final concept of philosophy, when 'we' means the representatives of a currently fashionable line of thought. There are recurrent philosophical problems, and philosophy itself provides one of them, a basic one.

TEN

THE PHILOSOPHIC ENTERPRISE

Brand Blanshard

I

Philosophy is best understood, I think, as part of an older and wider enterprise, the enterprise of understanding the world. We may well look first at this understanding in the large. I shall ask, to begin with, what is its goal, then what are its chief stages, then what are the ways in which philosophy enters into it.

The enterprise, we have just said, is that of understanding the world. What do we mean by understanding—understanding anything at all? We mean, I suppose, explaining it to ourselves. Very well; what does explaining anything mean? We stumble upon some fact or event that is unintelligible to us; what would make it intelligible? The first step in the answer is, seeing it as an instance of some rule. You suffer some evening from an excruciating headache and despondently wonder why. You remember that you just ate two large pieces of chocolate cake and that you are allergic to chocolate; the headache seems then to be explained. It is no longer a mere demonic visitor intruding on you from nowhere; you have domesticated it, assimilated it to your knowledge, by bringing it under a known rule.

What sort of rules are these that serve to render facts intelligible?

NOTE: This paper is a revised form of a Mahlon Powell Lecture delivered at the University of Indiana in 1961. It is now printed for the first time and with the University's permission.

They are always rules of connection, rules relating the fact to be explained to something else. You explain the headache by bringing it under a law relating it *causally* to something else. In like manner, you explain the fact that a figure on the board has angles equal to two right angles by relating it *logically* to something else; by pointing out that it is a triangle, and that it belongs to the triangles as such to have this property.

Such bringing of a case under a rule explains admirably so far as it goes. But suppose someone asks for a further explanation. When you explain your headache by reference to the chocolate or the angle sum of the figure by referring to its triangularity, he says: "Yes, yes, I know this, but what I don't understand is why the rule itself holds. How do you explain *that*?" We can only give the same answer as before. To explain a rule is to connect it with some other rule from which it follows, just as to explain a fact or event is to connect it with some other fact or event. When you can so connect it, you can explain it; when you cannot, you can't. You can explain why a triangle should have angles equal to a straight line because you can show that this must be true if certain other propositions are true that you normally accept without question. Can you show similarly that the rule about chocolate producing headaches follows from some further rule? No doubt an expert allergist could. He would show that in trying to assimilate the protein molecules of the chocolate, certain of your body cells break down; and the rule that eating chocolate produces a headache follows from the further and more precise rule that a certain kind of cell deterioration produces a certain kind of headache. But then why should *this* hold? Why should a change in body cells produce a conscious ache? All explanations so far offered here run into a stone wall. We can see that certain changes in the body are in fact followed by changes in consciousness; we have not the slightest idea why.

At this point two courses are open to one who is trying to explain his world. He has come—or if he has not, he soon will—to a generalization that he cannot now explain by bringing it under anything more general. Is he to continue in his attempt or not? The likelihood of his doing so may well depend on what he takes the ideal of explanation to be. Present-day empiricists are quite content to end their inquiries with rules or laws that are merely statements of general conjunction. Certain changes in the body are always accompanied by certain changes in consciousness. Why? That is a foolish question. If they are always in fact so connected, what more could a sensible person ask? One explains a falling snowflake or raindrop or meteor by bringing it under the law of gravitation, and if that law has been made precise, if one can show that the earth and the snowflake are so connected that each pulls the other with a force varying directly with its mass and inversely with the square of its distance, what more could one want? One might, to be sure, find some still wider generalization from which the law of gravitation itself followed; this was a leading interest of Einstein's toward the end of his life, and it made sense. But if further explanation means more than this, the empiricist holds, it is a will-o'-the-wisp. Every explanation of fact must come sooner or later to a dead end. It must halt somewhere with a generalization that is a pure statement of *de facto* togetherness, itself opaque to reason.

But there is another ideal of explanation open to us, that of the rationalists, of whom I am one. They hold that when you end with any law whatever that is a mere statement of conjunction, your explanation is incomplete and you are bound to *try* at least to go beyond it. What leads them to say this? It is their sense of the goal that understanding is seeking, of what would bring the attempt to explain finally to rest. When you ask the question "Why?" you are seeking an answer of some kind; but of what kind? We can see with regard to some answers that we can raise the same question again, of others that we cannot because we have already reached the end of the line. Suppose you remark that two straight lines do not enclose a space, or that whatever is colored is extended, or that a thing cannot at once have a property and not have it, and suppose now some bright skeptic asks you why. Could you give him an answer? I do not think you could, not because there is an answer that you don't know, but because anyone who understood your remark would know the answer already and would be asking a silly question. When you have a law that connects things by a self-evident necessity, the question "Why?" has no point, for the kind of insight you have is just the kind you are asking for. If you see

that, being what it is, A *must* be B, the further question "Why?"
is meaningless.

*What understanding is seeking, then, what would bring the search
to rest, is seen necessity.* Where it is present, we have what we
wanted; where it is absent, we have not yet fully understood.

Now a rationalist is a person who assumes that behind every *is*
there is a *must,* that if snow is white or fire burns or John has a
cold, the question "Why?" has an answer, and that this answer
would disclose a necessity. You may protest: "Can you prove this?
Do you really think that because we are seeking necessity, it must
be there to be found, that things must be intelligible because it
would be so satisfactory to us if they were?" The answer, of course,
is "No." The philosopher who takes something to be true because
he wants it to be true betrays his calling. But unless the philosopher
could assume that there was some answer to his questions, he
would have no motive for pressing them. For the critical rationalist
the intelligibility of things is neither a necessary conclusion nor an
arbitrary assumption, but a postulate, that is, a proposition which
for practical purposes he must assume and which experience progressively confirms, but which is incapable of present proof.

Thus the rationalist is, if you will, a man of faith. His faith is that
there is to be found in the universe the kind of intelligibility that
would satisfy his intellect, that there is a coincidence between
reality and his intellectual ideal, that at every point there is an
answer to his question "Why?" This faith is the mainspring of his
endeavor. He is ready to discard it if he has to, but not until he
has to; and he will regard an apparent defeat as only a temporary
setback if he can. After all, if there is no answer, why seek it? One
may say indeed with George Saintsbury that "the end of all things
is bafflement, but it is good not to be baffled too soon." But if we
expect nature at any moment to set a roadblock to our reason, we
shall almost surely be baffled too soon.

My own faith as a rationalist goes further still. If you ask me
why snow is white or why you are reading these lines, I am inclined, as I admitted, to say that there is an intelligible, that is, a
necessary, answer to the question, whether we know it or not. Some
people would agree with this but would be reluctant to take the

next long step with the rationalist. That step is to say that this necessity holds not only between the event of your reading these lines, for example, and some event just before it, but between your so doing and *all* other events. I am inclined to think that if you had not at this moment been reading these lines, the *Mona Lisa* would not be hanging in the Louvre. The argument is in principle this. Start with the supposition that a present event had not happened, and ask what it commits you to. If you deny the consequent, you must deny the antecedent, which means that if you deny the present event, you must deny the whole succession of necessary causes which led to this event, no matter how long the string. Very well, take some remote bead on that string and deny it; what then? All the events that follow from it as necessary effects will presumably have been different, and since the causal lines diverge in many directions, much of the present world will inevitably have been different.

Make the argument concrete. Is there any remote event in history to which your reading these lines can be traced back? There are indefinitely many; I shall name just one. In the year 490 B.C. a council of war was held on a hill overlooking the Greek coast. The council consisted of eleven commanders of a small Greek force, who were considering what to do about a huge Persian army that was disembarking below them. They knew the intention of that army. It was to wipe out Athens. The presiding general, Callimachus, took the vote of the council on whether they should give battle or not. The vote was five to five, and it fell to him to cast the deciding ballot. He voted for immediate attack and shortly paid for it with his life on the plain of Marathon, not realizing that by his vote he had decided the fate of the Western world. The historian Sir Edward Creasy argues convincingly that if Athens had gone under, so would Greece; and that with the fall of Greece, the science, philosophy, and art of the West would all have been smothered in their cradle. Plato, Archimedes, Leonardo would probably never have been heard of.

In short, deny that you are reading these lines, follow the stream of causation backward, then follow its diverging lines forward again, and you cannot with any confidence say that Leonardo would have lived or painted at all, let alone that his masterpiece would be hanging in the Louvre. Indeed, I suspect that every event in the universe is thus connected, directly or indirectly, with every other. And since in my view, which must here remain unargued, causality involves necessity, the universe must be assumed to be both a causal and an intelligible system in which every part is necessarily linked to every other. The complete explanation of anything would in the end involve everything. The world is a whole in which there are no accidents and no loose ends.

II

Now the career of reason, of which philosophy is one part, is a slow persistent climb toward the vision of that whole. On its way it passes through four levels—those of infancy, common sense, science, and philosophy. We shall see more clearly the part of philosophy in this enterprise if we briefly retrace our steps through the earlier levels.

For each of us the adventure of the mind begins in a swamp so far below where we now stand that we cannot see it or clearly imagine it. We begin with sensation, "a booming, buzzing confusion" of sensations, signifying nothing. What takes us out of the primitive swamp is the formation of solid little islands in the swamp, nodules of qualities that stick together and behave in settled ways. It is a triumph of tender reason when the child can grasp one stable cluster of qualities as a bottle and another as a rattle. He is breaking through to the level of common sense where we chiefly live.

By the commonsense world I mean the world of things and persons. The transition into this world the child makes in those years that Bertrand Russell called the most decisive in one's life, the years from one to two. About this most familiar of all realms I want to make two observations, first that it is an intellectual construction, and second that it is no permanent home.

First, it is a construction. Things as a whole are never given in sensation; when we perceive a red ball, what we see must be pieced out by interpretation based on our past experience of its having another side. Common sense believes that some of the things I see moving about are persons with feelings and ideas like my own, though this is a metaphysical flight that it can never directly verify. Further, it believes that when you and I look at the ball, we are seeing the same thing—a daring and highly dubious theory. Indeed the head of the plain man is full of theories about men, women, foreigners, artists, and communists, and his religious beliefs are brimming over with metaphysics.

The second remark to be made is that much of this theory is bad theory. The plain man's theory of knowledge, his religious beliefs, and his generalizations about things and people, recorded often in his proverbs, are riddled with inconsistencies. "Be not pennywise," he says, and adds, "Take care of the pence and the pounds will take care of themselves." He accepts both quite serenely.

In the commonsense world, then, reason can find no permanent home or halting place. It must move forward into science. This advance is not an abrupt leap into a new order or dimension. Science, as T. H. Huxley said, *is* common sense refined and organized. The commonsense world is a theoretical construction that has been built up by roughly fifty thousand centuries of trial and error, and much of it comes as a legacy acquired without effort. The scientific order is a superstructure most of which has been built in the last three centuries. But the two structures are continuous, and the newly built upper story will perhaps be occupied by our descendants as effortlessly as we have acquired the lower ones. To pass from the lower to the higher, however, requires the ascent of two flights of stairs, the first of which takes us to a new level of abstraction and the second to a new level of exactness.

First, abstraction. The physicist as a man may have much interest in Jane Doe as a person, but as a scientist he has little or none. He breaks her up into a set of properties and studies these singly. In point of mass, she is indiscriminable from a sack of potatoes, and if dropped from the leaning tower, she would accelerate at the same rate. For science, the interest held by a law is proportioned to its generality, and the more general it is, the more abstract are the qualities that are related by its laws.

Secondly, exactness. The scientist is never satisfied until the characters he correlates are measured and their variations can be stated as functions of each other. Anyone may notice an apple falling from a tree or the increasing pressure in the pot when it boils, but it takes a Newton with his law of the inverse squares to describe exactly what the apple is doing, and Boyle with his inverse variation of volume and pressure to describe exactly what is happening in the kettle.

III

The passage from common sense to science is not a passage to a new kind of thinking, but a refining of processes already at work. So is the passage from science to philosophy. It is a grave mistake to set up science and philosophy as rivals of each other; they are continuous with each other. A philosophy that ignores science will probably build castles in the air, and a science that ignores philosophy will be dogmatic or myopic or both. Philosophy, as I view it, is so bound up with science, so integral a part of the same enterprise, that I have here insisted on winding into it through the avenue of science.

Is there any need for going further? Many people in these days say no. "What is knowledge is science," Russell remarked, "and what is not science is not knowledge." It used to be said that to the English had been given the realm of the sea, to the French the domain of the land, and to the Germans the kingdom of the air; this meant of course the stratosphere, where philosophers are supposed to live, and indeed have been living ever since Thales wandered abroad with his head in the clouds and fell into a well. With these critics I must confess that I have much sympathy. The philosopher who pontificates about being and nonbeing in a prose that follows Dr. Johnson's alleged rule of never using a word of one syllable if he could find one of six seems to me rather worse than a bore. He is supposed to be a specialist in clear thinking and therefore clear speaking, and if he appears in public in a state of logical and linguistic unbuttonedness, groping for words for what are themselves mere gropings for ideas, he does neither philosophy nor education any good. But that is not philosophy as practiced by those who have known their craft—by McTaggart and Moore, by Broad and Price and Lovejoy. Surely no one who has understood these philosophers could regard as anything but important what they were trying to do. Well, what have they been trying to do?

They have tried to supplement the work of science in at least two respects. In both of these respects science has to be extended if our thirst for understanding is to be satisfied, but in neither of them do scientists take much interest. The fact is that, logically speaking, philosophy begins before science does, and goes on after science has completed its work. In the broad spectrum of knowledge, science occupies the central band. But we know that there is more to the spectrum than this conspicuous part. On one side, beyond the red end of the spectrum, there is a broad band of infrared rays; and on the other side, beyond the violet end, are the ultraviolet rays. Philosophy deals with the infrareds and the ultraviolets of science, continuous with the central band but more delicate and difficult of discernment.

Take the red end first. Consider the sense in which philosophy comes before science. Many of the concepts the scientist uses and many of his working assumptions he prefers to take for granted. He can examine them if he wishes, and some scientists do. Most do not, because if they waited till they were clear on these difficult basic ideas, they might never get to what most interests them at all. But it would be absurd to leave these basic ideas unexamined altogether. This somewhat thankless preliminary work is the task of the philosopher.

We referred to these unexamined ideas as concepts and assumptions. Let us illustrate the concepts first.

Common sense and science are constantly using certain little words of one syllable that seem too familiar and perhaps unimportant to call for definition. We say, "What time is it?" "There is less space in a compact car," "There was no cause for his taking offense," "He must be out of his mind," "I think these strikes are unjust to the public." Consider the words we have used: 'time', 'space', 'cause', 'good', 'truth', 'mind', just', 'I'. If someone said to us, "What do you mean, *I*?" or, when we asked what time it was, "What do you mean by 'time'?" we should probably say, "Oh, don't be an idiot," or perhaps with St. Augustine, "I know perfectly well what time means until you ask me, and then I don't know." I suspect this last is the sound answer regarding all these words. We know what they mean well enough for everyday purposes, but to think about them is to reveal depth after depth of unsuspected meaning. This fact suggests both the strength and the weakness of present-day linguistic philosophy. It is surely true, as this school contends, that a main business of philosophy is to define words. The first great outburst of philosophy in the talk of Socrates was largely an attempt at defining certain key words of the practical life— 'justice', 'piety', 'temperance', 'courage'. But their meanings proved bafflingly elusive; he chased the ghost of justice through ten books of the *Republic* and barely got his hands on it in the end. Socrates saw that to grasp the meaning even of these simple and common terms would solve many of the deepest problems in ethics and metaphysics. But we must add that Socrates was no ordinary language philosopher. He was not an Athenian Noah Webster, collecting the shopworn coins that were current in the marketplace; on the contrary, he took special pleasure in showing that at the level of ordinary usage our meanings were muddled and incoherent. Only by refining and revising them could we arrive at meanings that would stand.

Now the scientist who is trying to find the truth about the cause of flu cannot discontinue his experiments till he has reached clearness on the nature of truth or the concept of causality. The political scientist who holds that democracy is in certain respects better than communism cannot remain dumb till all his colleagues have agreed as to the definition of 'good'. These people must get on with their work, and they are right not to stop and moon about ultimates. But these ideas are ultimates after all; we must use them hourly in our thinking; and it would be absurd if, while researchers were trying to be clear about relatively unimportant matters, no one tried to get clear about the most important things of all. And the right persons to make that effort are surely the philosophers. A philosopher friend of mine sat down in a railway car beside a salesman who, recognizing a kindred spirit, poured out a stream of talk about his line. "And what's your line?" he concluded. "Notions," replied the philosopher. That seemed all right to the salesman, and it should be so to us. Notions are the line of the philosopher, such key notions as truth, validity, value, knowledge, without which scientific thought could not get under way, but which the scientist himself has neither the time nor the inclination to examine.

We suggested that it is not only his ultimate concepts but also his ultimate assumptions that the scientist prefers to turn over to others for inspection. Let me list a few and ask whether there is any natural scientist who does not take them for granted. That we can learn the facts of the physical order through perception. That the laws of our logic are valid of this physical order. That there is a public space and a public time in which things happen and to which we all have access. That every event has a cause. That under like conditions the same sort of thing has always happened, and always will. That we ought to adjust the degree of our assent to any proposition to the strength of the evidence for it. These are all propositions of vast importance, which the scientist makes use of every day of his life. If any one of them were false, his entire program would be jeopardized. But they are not scientific propositions. They are assumed by all sciences equally; they are continuous with the thought of all; yet they are the property of none. It would be absurd to leave these unexamined, for some or all of them may be untrue. But the scientist would be aghast if, before he used a microscope or a telescope, he had to settle the question whether knowledge was possible through perception, or whether there could be a logic without ontology. Scientists have at times discussed these matters, and their views are always welcome, but they generally and sensibly prefer to turn them over to specialists. And the specialists in these problems are philosophers.

I have now, I hope, made clear what was meant by saying that philosophy comes before science. It comes before it in the sense of taking for examination the main concepts and assumptions with which scientists begin their work. Science is logically dependent on philosophy. If philosophy succeeded in showing, as Hume and Carnap thought it had, that any reference to a nonsensible existent was meaningless, the physics that talks of electrons and photons would either have to go out of business or revise its meanings radically. If philosophy succeeded, as James, Schiller, and Freud thought it had, in showing that our thinking is inescapably chained to our impulses and emotions, then the scientific enterprise, as an attempt at impartial and objective truth, would be defeated before it started. Philosophy does not merely put a bit of filigree on the mansion of science; it provides its foundation stones.

IV

If philosophy begins before science does, it also continues after the scientist has finished his work. Each science may be conceived as a prolonged effort to answer one large question. Physics asks, "What are the laws of matter in motion?" Biology asks, "What kinds of structure and behavior are exhibited by living things?" Each science takes a field of nature for its own and tries to keep within its own fences. But nature has no fences; the movement of electrons is somehow continuous with the writing of *Hamlet* and the rise of Lenin. Who is to study this continuity? Who is to reflect on whether the physicist, burrowing industriously in his hole, can break a tunnel through to the theologian, mining anxiously in his? Surely here again is a task that only the philosopher can perform. One way of performing it, which I do not say is the right way, is suggested by the definition of philosophy as the search by a blind man in a dark room for a black hat that isn't there, with the addendum that if he finds it, that is theology. It may be thought that since no two true propositions can contradict each other, the results of independent scientific search could not conflict, and that there is no problem in harmonizing them. On the contrary, when we examine even the most general results of the several sciences, we see that they clash scandalously and that the task of harmonizing them is gigantic. Indeed the most acute and fascinating of metaphysical problems arise in the attempt to reconcile the results of major disciplines with each other.

How are you to reconcile physics with psychology, for example? The physicist holds that every physical event has a physical cause, which seems innocent enough. To say that a material thing could start moving, or, once started, could have its motion accelerated or changed in direction without any physical cause, would seem absurd. If you say that a motion occurs with no cause at all, that is to the physicist irresponsible; if you say that it represents interference from outside the spatial order, it is superstitious. Now is not the psychologist committed to saying that this interference in fact occurs daily? If my lips and vocal cords now move as they do, it is because I am thinking certain thoughts and want to communicate them to you. And the only way in which a thought or desire can produce such results is through affecting the physical motions of waves or particles in my head. It will not do to say that only the nervous correlates of my thought are involved in producing these results, for those physical changes are not my thoughts, and if my thoughts themselves can make no difference to what I do, then rational living becomes a mummery. My action is never in fact guided by conscious choice, nor anything I say determined by what I think or feel. Common sense would not accept that, nor can a sane psychology afford to; the evidence against it is too massive. And what this evidence shows is that conscious choice, which is not a physical event at all, does make a difference to the behavior of tongue and lips, of arms and legs. Behavior may be consciously guided. But how are you to put that together with the physicist's conviction that all such behavior is caused physically? That is the lively philosophical problem of body and mind.

Conflicts of this kind may occur not only between natural sciences but between a natural and a normative science. Take physics and ethics. For the physicist all events—at least all macroscopic events —are caused; that is, they follow in accordance with some law from events immediately preceding them. This too seems innocent enough. But now apply the principle in ethics. A choice of yours is an event, even if not a physical event, and thus falls under the rule that all events are caused. That means that every choice you make follows in accordance with law from some event or events just preceding it. But if so, given the events that just preceded any of my choices, I had to do what I did do; I could not have done otherwise. But if that is true, does it not make nonsense to say in any case that I ought to have done otherwise, since I did the only thing that I could have done? But then what becomes of ethics as ordinarily conceived? If the scientific principle is true, one will have to rethink the ethical ground for remorse and reward and punishment and praise and blame. This is the ancient problem of free will, which was discussed with fascination by Milton's angels while off duty from their trumpets, and is discussed with equal fascination by undergraduates today.

To be sure, there are people nowadays who say that these old metaphysical issues are really only linguistic and disappear with a due regard to common usage. Thus when we see a man making something happen and know that he is not acting under coercion or some special inducement, we say he is acting freely; that is standard usage and hence correct usage; hence when we say that the man is acting freely, we are speaking correctly; hence we *are* acting freely; and hence there is no problem. I am not convinced. No doubt the man *is* acting freely in the sense chosen. Unfortunately this sense is irrelevant to the metaphysical issue. For what the determinist is saying is that even when we are *not* under any sort of coercion in the ordinary sense, our choices still follow from causes; and whether *that* is true is not to be settled by studying the plain man's language, for the chances are that he has never thought about it; nor would he necessarily be right if he had.

There are many other conflicts like the two we have mentioned. They fall in no one of the disciplines, but between them, and they must be arbitrated by an agency committed to nonpartisanship. The only plausible nominee for this post is philosophy. Philosophy is the interdepartmental conciliation agency, the National Labor Relations Board, or if you prefer, the World Court, of the intellectual community. Like these other agencies, it has no means of enforcing its verdicts. Its reliance is on the reasonableness of its decisions.

We are now in a position to see the place of philosophy in the intellectual enterprise as a whole. Intelligence has shown from the beginning a drive to understand. To understand anything means to grasp it in the light of other things or events that make it intelligible. The first great breakthrough of this drive was the system of common sense, which was molded into form by millennia of trial and error. This system is being superseded by science, whose network of explanation is far more precise and comprehensive. Philosophy is the continuation of this enterprise into regions that science leaves unexplored. It is an attempt to carry understanding to its furthest possible limits. It brings into the picture the foundations on which science builds and the arches and vaultings that hold its structures together. Philosophy is at once the criticism and the completion of science. That, as I understand it, is what all the great philosophers have been engaged upon, from Plato to Whitehead.

They may never wholly succeed. It is quite possible that men will use such understanding as they have achieved to blow themselves and their enterprise off the planet. But while they do allow themselves further life, the enterprise is bound to go on. For the effort to understand is not a passing whim or foible; it is no game for a leisure hour or "lyric cry in the midst of business." It is central to the very nature and existence of man; it is what has carried him from somewhere in the slime to the lofty but precarious perch where he now rests. The drive of his intelligence has constructed his world for him and slowly modified it into conformity with the mysterious world without. To anyone who sees this, philosophy needs no defense. It may help in practical ways, and of course it does. But that is not the prime reason why men philosophize. They philosophize because they cannot help it, because the enterprise of understanding, ancient as man himself, has made him what he is, and alone can make him what he might be.

ELEVEN

WHAT PHILOSOPHERS DO

Adam Schaff

The editors of the present anthology have asked us to discuss the nature and the goals of philosophy. This writer prefers to approach the topic indirectly by asking what it is that philosophers do, or perhaps more precisely, what it is that they *should* do. In this writer's opinion this approach will bring us closer to our goal.

The first impulse would be to point to persons who engage in philosophy professionally, in an institutionalized manner, and to their activities within the appropriate institutions, such as universities and research institutes, which employ them *qua* philosophers.

Such an approach would certainly be correct, but a little reflection reveals that it does not help us *explain what philosophy is*. Superficial observations of the activities of those who aspire to the name of 'philosopher' can only strengthen our conviction that the variety of their doings, and sometimes even the incompatibility of such doings and opinions, is so great it is often difficult to comprehend why they all bear the same name. The question concerning what is common to all those varied activities and what can be extrapolated as the common subject matter and goal of what is termed 'philosophizing' thus reappears—just as a result of those observations which have been suggested as an *ersatz* answer to the question posed at the beginning. The motley impressions evoked by observing the variety of their activities apparently give rise to the search for some common characteristic they might share. This is why the answer must be in depth and must strive to extrapolate that which is common to the activities of those various people who are called 'philosophers', regardless of any other differences between them.

Perhaps the simplest solution would be to do what is done when we wish to single out the various disciplines within the specialized (or "positive," to use the traditional terminology) sciences. When we single out various disciplines, we use as the criterion the distinct nature of the subject matter, and usually the distinct nature of research methods. (The term 'subject matter' covers not only objects but also their various aspects and properties, relations between them, etc.) What then is the distinct subject matter of the reflections which we term 'philosophical', and what are the distinct methods of such reflections?

We disregard here—although it should certainly be acknowledged—the opinion of all those who reject the above reasoning because they refuse to admit that philosophy *belongs* in the sphere of science. By treating philosophy as being in the 'sphere of science', in the broad sense of the latter term, we make a certain choice. We adopt a certain attitude which will affect our further reasoning and must therefore be mentioned explicitly. Although we defend this attitude, we do not at the same time claim that philosophy can be separated from other disciplines on the basis of subject matter *in the same way* in which we proceed to single out specialized disciplines by defining *their* respective subject matters as, for instance, we do in the case of physics or medicine. If philosophy is to be treated as a distinct branch of science (so that those who are active in that field may be termed 'philosophers'), then it must have its own subject matter. Yet it does not follow therefrom that the distinct nature of its subject matter must be reflected in any specific set of material objects as, for example, all material bodies in the case of physics and all human organisms in the case of medicine; or in any specific aspects or properties of such objects. (Note that the various branches of medicine, which have the status of distinct disciplines, all have the totality of human organisms as the subject matter of research, but each discipline is concerned with one part or property of the human body, as is the case with anatomy, cardiology, gastrology, etc.) That which distinguishes the activities of philosophers from those of representatives of other disciplines reduces to *what* philosophers do and *how* they do it.

The *what* which accounts for the difference between the pursuit of philosophy, on one hand, and research in, e.g., chemistry or psychology, on the other, consists above all in the *level of generality of those statements which we consider to be specifically philosophical in nature*. It is true that every science generalizes and formulates laws that cover a class of elements, but philosophical statements are still more general in nature, since they formulate laws that cover all phenomena.[1] This is not done by any specialized discipline, even if, as is the case with gravitation theory, the discipline claims its laws to be maximally general in nature. Also, philosophical statements are on the metatheoretical level as compared with the various branches of science or studies of facts. In this connection it is not necessary that such philosophical statements develop as reflections on a given discipline as it were *externally* (i.e., whether they are formulated by philosophers who do not themselves professionally engage in the pursuit of a given branch of science) or *internally* (i.e., as methodological or metatheoretical reflections by representatives of that specialized discipline who feel the need of broader generalizations, as is typically the case of the philosophy of biology, the philosophy of physics, etc.).

Since *no* branch of science (or everyday thinking either) can do without such concepts as truth and falsehood, cause and effect, necessity and chance, *none* can do without its specific philosophy. As has been mentioned above, the source of such reflections is unimportant. Thus they may issue from professional philosophers or from philosophizing representatives of the specialized discipline in question (as is recently the case of the biologist Jacques Monod, author of *Le Hasard et la Nécessité*). This fact, among other things, has suggested the idea, common as the various forms of analytic philosophy, that the task of philosophy consists in an analysis of the language of science and is confined to such an analysis—which obviously greatly restricts the concept of philosophy.

Thus the specific domain of philosophy consists of those general

---

[1] The historical disciplines do not fit well the picture given for these other areas, but in the present writer's opinion, the assertion that they are entirely idiographic in nature is wrong.

theoretical and metatheoretical statements which go beyond the framework of any specialized science and thus form or contribute to the formation of our *Weltanschauung*. But, as has been mentioned above, the *differentia specifica* of philosophy cannot be reduced to the issue of the universal and/or metatheoretical nature of philosophical statements. There is more to this task: its *what* must be linked with its *how*. The question here is *how* we arrive at those most general statements of a philosophical nature when we have a definite body of knowledge provided by the specialized disciplines. In other words, the question is that of the deducibility (or nondeducibility) of philosophical statements from the existing body of positive knowledge provided by the specialized disciplines at a given stage of their development.

I am afraid that I will now say something which young philosophers will find shocking: philosophical statements are usually not arrived at in a way that complies with the requirements of the specialized disciplines. Whenever a philosophical issue or a branch of philosophy, following the general development of science, attains that degree of precision which complies with the requirements of the specialized sciences, then that issue or branch loses its philosophical nature. Moreover, that branch of philosophy which deals with the issue becomes a separate discipline or an integral part of a specialized science. The expected shock for young philosophers to which I allude would probably be due to the fact that the above statement could be interpreted as the declaration that philosophy is speculative in nature and hence scientific philosophy is essentially impossible. Now that would be an erroneous impression, for the reader will find below that I agree with the postulate that philosophy is to be pursued in a *scientific* manner, that agreement being accompanied by an appropriate explanation. Nonetheless, philosophical statements usually are not formulated as a result of a procedure dictated by the rigor which is characteristic of specialized sciences. Thus nothing more has been said than that philosophical statements are arrived at as a result of a different procedure—one which is not identical with the procedure dictated by the rigor which is characteristic of specialized sciences. Nevertheless the procedure of philosophy does not thereby become counterscientific in the sense of being speculative, or at least it *need not* become such.

The procedures valid in specialized sciences may be classed as deductive and inductive. In the case of the former, we adopt a set of axioms and a set of transformation rules, which provide the foundation of strict reasoning in which each step follows rigorously and univocally from the preceding one. This yields a model of precision which is specific to the deductive disciplines and which can be imitated in any hypothetical deductive system. Of course a philosophical system also can be constructed in this way if we adopt a certain hypothesis as the set of axioms. However, it can easily be noted that the precision of philosophical systems so constructed is merely apparent, because of the difficulty related to the substantiation of the choice of a given hypothesis as the set of axioms of the calculus. This is why this procedure may be eliminated from our considerations.

The other procedure is associated with those sciences in which laws are formulated through generalization of data obtained by observations and experiments. The rigors and requirements vary according to the subject matter of research, but one element is common to the whole class of those disciplines: as they can never attain the absolute precision of the deductive sciences, they must indicate the methods of verification or refutation of their statements so that these may attain the status of scientific statements.

Now philosophical statements usually are generalizations which do not lend themselves to such a procedure. Hence no crucial experiment can be devised to verify or to refute such statements. (When this becomes possible following the development of science, then such statements cease to be philosophical.) Thus it is possible to defend statements which not only differ from one another, but even stand for outright opposite attitudes. The final stage of a discussion of them consists in formulating difference of opinions and not in proving that the opponent's opinions are erroneous, since such a proof is not possible. This fact accounts for the "eternal nature" of the fundamental problems in philosophy, and of the philosophical schools which advance their own solutions of those problems. Such schools in the course of history often change their respective terminologies and phraseologies, but they stick to their *essential* viewpoints. This fact also accounts for the conviction, common among many philosophers, that philosophy reduces to its own history.

Thus when a comparison is drawn with statements of the specialized disciplines, the position of philosophical statements is in a sense weaker. Are, then, such statements needed at all in science? Yes, they are, as far as a *Weltanschauung* is needed, or as far as general heuristic hypotheses are needed, such hypotheses being in the last analysis a hinterland of various scientific inquiries, even if those who make such inquiries do not realize that they are so needed. This is so because the Messrs. Jourdains, who are astonished to learn that they talk in prose, abound not only among people in the street, who realize neither *that* they philosophize nor *what* are the far-reaching philosophical implications of such casual but well-understood statements as "This is true," "This is false," "That was the cause of the accident," "It was by chance that I returned home," etc. For they are to be found also among those representatives of natural and social science who believe that they refer to "pure" facts without any philosophical admixtures, and who fail to realize how much that construct which is "fact" and allegedly free from philosophical contaminations is burdened with philosophy. Engels used to say about the positivistically minded natural scientists of his time who were vigorously dissociating themselves from philosophy that their attitude resulted not in any liberation from philosophy, which is impossible, but in falling victims to the worst kind of philosophy, namely eclectic conglomerations of high school philosophy and current opinions, which are adopted by these philosophers without being recognized for what they really are. If philosophy is an inseparable comrade-in-arms of all scientific pursuits (which, obviously, greatly increases the importance of philosophy), then it is better to adopt a philosophical position consciously and with an expert knowledge of it than to succumb to it spontaneously, which makes it impossible to identify and to select appropriate opinions.

Let us agree then that philosophy cannot be dismissed. But does this mean that we are resigned to the fact that our thinking includes counterscientific speculations? No, because, as has been said above, although philosophical generalizations are arrived at in a different manner than are those in the specialized disciplines, this results in their being different in nature, but it need not result in their being counterscientific. The point is that in the case of those generalizations which, by their very nature, skip over certain stages in the processes of generalization that are necessary for a hypothetical (and always hypothetical only) *Weltanschauung,* the labels 'scientific' and 'nonscientific' must be used differently than in the case of the specialized disciplines. A philosophy which is not in conflict with scientific statements (i.e., statements of the specialized disciplines), and which strives to generalize them in accordance with the general laws of logic and methodology, can aspire to a scientific status. The demarcation line between scientific philosophies and nonscientific philosophies is not drawn very sharply, but it is clear enough to allow for a distinction which is important for all those who want to include philosophy in a unified scientific image of the world, and who are not willing to adopt the doctrine of two truths—a doctrine which imposes a *sui generis* split personality on those who adopt it (although it cannot be denied that the strange doctrine of two truths is being adopted by scientists who are eminent experts in their respective fields).

This answers the question concerning what philosophers do by pointing to the peculiar nature of philosophical statements, both with respect to the kind of generalization they are and with respect to the way of arriving at such generalization as compared with the specialized disciplines. Since what has been said above may prove shocking and distressing to the various lovers of philosophy, let it be said once again that this opinion results from the standpoint I have adopted on the question, and as such it is my personal opinion that shares the fortunes and misfortunes of all philosophical statements: it can be rejected by the adoption of a different philosophical standpoint. This takes us to the second sphere of problems which must be raised if the question about the nature and the goals of philosophy is to be answered.

Observation of the activities of philosophers, which we earlier characterized as an *ersatz* approach to the main question, shows beyond doubt that their activities are differentiated based both on their fields of interest and on the schools of thought which determine their standpoints, and hence also based on the answers to the question discussed here. Their activities are somehow interconnected (in particular, membership in a given school often determines the field of one's philosophical interests), but the relation is certainly not one-to-one.

Let us begin with the differentiation of fields of interest, since this is the simpler matter. The fact that one philosopher specializes in the history of philosophy while another specializes in epistemology, that some of them spend their lives studying ethics while others concentrate on aesthetics, the philosophy of language, or the methodology of natural science, is trivial and can be explained above all by psychological factors. The problem becomes more complicated when one's links with a certain philosophical school result in one's claiming that only certain philosophical interests make sense, whereas all others should be dismissed as meaningless. Thus, for instance, the Vienna Circle positivists were convinced that the analysis of the language of science was the only legitimate subject matter of all philosophizing, and they therefore rejected as meaningless all the traditional problems of philosophy. (This, however, did not prevent them from engaging in an immanent empiricism that inevitably led them to the metaphysics of subjective idealism.) Likewise, though in a somewhat different way, some representatives of philosophical anthropology assert that the problems of man are the only problems which the philosophers may study, whereas the methodology of natural science should be the *chasse gardée* of natural scientists and should be barred to philosophers. Now all such bans do not make sense and, in fact, are broken in practice. As has been said at the outset, all analyses of a specified type are philosophical in nature, and all fields of study are open in that respect.

The differentiation of philosophers according to membership in different schools of philosophical thought is, however, a more important matter. One and the same issue may be offered various and even mutually incompatible solutions. Moreover, if we assume that the views of representatives of the various schools are logically consistent, we can only comprehend the differences in the points of departure and in the assumptions adopted, without being able to prove which school is right (with the proviso that, obviously, one is always right on the strength of one's own assumptions). These facts result in a striking situation which, however, is understandable in view of the nature of philosophical reasoning which I have previously described.

But this yields significant conclusions, with which beginners in philosophical thinking, especially, should become familiar (although more experienced philosophers also may derive some profit from recalling them). Since the issue at stake is always tinged with the personal opinions of a given philosopher, and especially since these contributions to the anthology are to some extent personal declarations of philosophical faith, I will refer to my own case. Being a Marxist by conviction, I am—as far as my philosophical opinions are concerned—a member of the Marxist school of philosophy. What does this mean?

This means that since I believe the fundamental principles of Marxist philosophy to be correct (i.e., in my opinion, the best out of all those which are offered by the current schools of philosophy), I try to apply them in my philosophical research, and I try to convince others that those principles are the right ones. This results from my realizing the importance of adopting a definite philosophical standpoint for man's theoretical and practical activities, and hence from my concept of a philosopher's moral responsibility to advocate those views which he deems right. Thus, as I see it, I am a philosopher engaged and inspired by the party spirit—in the sense of being a member of a definite school, a definite party in philosophy. This is, of course, not to be confused with membership in any political party, for these may coincide, but they need not. And they are certainly not identical. This is mentioned here because a Marxist term (in itself not a very accurate rendering of the term which in German and several other languages means something like "partyhood") is involved, and it is often misinterpreted, even by some adherents of Marxism.

Now, following the fundamental theoretical and methodological principles of the school of which I am a member, I strive to make my philosophy scientific: my generalizing philosophical statements should be in agreement with the data provided by the specialized disciplines at a given stage of their development, as has been said; such statements should not be at variance with theorems formulated in the specialized disciplines; and they should generalize such theorems methodologically in the light of the assumptions made.

While declaring my membership in a definite philosophical school and my commitment to specified philosophical conceptions, which aspire to be scientific in nature, I realize that my principles are philosophical, and hence I also realize the difference between them and those principles which are valid in the specialized disciplines. This fact compels me to accept several consequences:

(a) The falsehood of rival doctrines cannot be demonstrated ultimately in the light of the criteria current in the specialized disciplines.

(b) It cannot be denied that, just because of their different viewpoints, rival doctrines may notice problems which remain outside the field of vision of one's school (such facts are confirmed fully by the history of philosophical investigations), so that it is not possible to claim that one's doctrine is the only true one, whereas all rival doctrines are false.

(c) One's philosophy must be an open system, ready to incorporate new questions, if such are raised by the general development of science (the development of scientific philosophy included), and to accept the principle of Cartesian scepticism, which states that all problems, including philosophical ones, must be reconsidered whenever there are sufficient scientific reasons to question the traditional solutions—which is just synonymous with antidogmatism.

The attitude based on the acceptance of these principles might be termed that of toleration, as opposed to the concept of closed philosophical systems. In this writer's opinion the attitude of toleration, interpreted as above, is the foundation of progress in philosophy, and hence it is *the* attitude which philosophers should strive to develop in young students of philosophy by their activities as teachers. This is one more contribution and a very important contribution to the answer to the question "What is it that philosophers *should* do?"

The attitude of toleration thus understood is—despite current opinions to the contrary—fully compatible with reasonable engagement and the "party spirit" (in the sense explained above) of philosophy. The fact that it is impossible to demonstrate, by using methods valid in the specialized disciplines, that rival doctrines are erroneous shows only that philosophy differs from those disciplines, which has been accepted at the outset. This fact, however, cannot be used as an argument against the possibility of making choices, of choosing one of the many doctrines which vie with one another. On the contrary, philosophers do make such choices and are then free to evaluate doctrines other than their own, even though they may not use, in such evaluations, the qualifiers 'true' and 'false' in the same senses in which these terms are used in ordinary scientific controversies. This is so because, as has been said earlier, such choices are made on the level of generalizations, with disregard of certain missing links in scientific reasoning. This is also why in such choices social and individual emotional conditioning plays a much greater role than it usually does in the case of specialized disciplines. Yet, from the point of view of its effect on human activities, scientific activities included, this does not reduce the role of philosophy, but on the contrary makes its role even greater. It is from this fact that philosophers derive their conviction not only of the correctness of their opinions but also of the importance of the struggle for the victory of those opinions in the minds of other men. Thus a true philosopher is an active, engaged one. He ought to preserve his engaged attitude, inspired by the "party spirit," when he carries into effect the principles of open philosophy and the attitude of toleration, without which scientific philosophy cannot be pursued. In my opinion, it is one of the teaching duties of the philosopher to shape that sense of moral responsibility, we might say the sense of moral mission, which underlies engaged philosophy. I accept this duty as a Marxist philosopher, but in my opinion this is an issue which concerns all philosophers. This is why I point to this duty in concluding my reflections on what it is that philosophers *should* do.

TWELVE

PHILOSOPHY BEYOND WORDS

Alan Watts

"Of that whereof one cannot speak, thereof one should remain silent." With these words, published in 1921, Ludwig Wittgenstein concluded his *Tractatus Logico-Philosophicus* and brought Western philosophy, as it had been known, to an end. Thereafter all schools of philosophy should have become centers of silent contemplation, as in Yoga or Buddhist meditation. But, on the principle of "publish or perish," even Wittgenstein had to keep on talking and writing, for if the philsopher remains silent we cannot tell whether he is really working or simply goofing off. But with Wittgenstein intellectually respectable and academic Western philosophy became trivial. He showed that it could not discuss metaphysics—that the exciting questions of ontology and epistemology were meaningless, and that thereafter the philosopher must content himself with being simply a sophisticated grammarian or specialist in mathematical logic. William Earle in his witty essay "Notes on the Death of a Culture"[1] described the new academic philosopher as a pragmatic nine-to-five businessman, going to his office with a briefcase to "do philosophy" in the same spirit as an accountant or research chemist. He would not dream of wandering out at night to contemplate the stars or to ponder such matters as the destiny of man and the final significance of the universe. If he thought he could get away with

---

[1] William Earle, "Notes on the Death of a Culture," in Maurice R. Stein (ed.), *Identity and Anxiety*, The Free Press of Glencoe, Inc., New York, 1960.

it, he would go about campus in the scientist's white coat.

As an adolescent I used to frequent an area in London, near the British Museum, where certain shops advertised themselves as purveyors of "philosophical instruments." Imagining that philosophers confined themselves to abstract thinking and required no other instruments than pen and paper, I was surprised to find that these shops sold slide rules, chronometers, microscopes, telescopes, and other scientific appliances, and that they were old-fashioned and venerable shops surviving from an age when science was called "natural philosophy." Thinking it over, this made sense. For philosophy, as Aristotle had said, begins with wonder—so that the true philosopher is a person who is naturally curious, who finds that existence is a marvelous puzzle, and who would like to find out (in Clark Maxwell's childhood phrase) "the particular go of it." Thus if philosophy is an attempt to describe and explain the world, to discover the order of nature, it must obviously go on into physics and chemistry, astronomy and biology, not to mention mathematics and metamathematics.

But what is the sense of wonder? On the one hand, it is a sort of aesthetic or mystical thrill, like being in love, or as Whitman felt of the planets and stars that "the drift of them is grand." On the other hand, it is an attempt to solve the puzzle of translating the pattern of the world into the linear orders of words and numbers which can be scanned and controlled by the faculty of conscious attention. For there are many of us who do not feel that we know anything, or are humanly competent, unless we can make this translation. The difficulty is that, from the standpoint of linear thinking and scanning, the natural world comprises innumerable variables. Using conscious attention, most people cannot keep track of more than three variables at once without using a pencil. A skilled organist, using both hands and feet, could manage a six-part fugue. But the practical problems of life—of politics, law, ethics, economics, and ecology—involve hundreds of thousands of variables with which the scanning pace of conscious attention simply cannot keep up, even when aided by computers. What scholar, except perhaps an authority on the manufacture of Japanese swords in the sixteenth century, can really keep abreast of the literature in his field? How can the President of the United States possibly be informed of all that he needs to know? There simply isn't time to pass one's eyes along the miles of letters and figures required, much less to absorb and make sense of them.

This is likewise the problem of philosophy, considered as a verbal and conceptual discipline. As natural philosophy, as a discipline which must always keep in mind the findings of the sciences, it cannot keep track of ever more complex descriptions of the world's pattern. It cannot give us a *Weltanschauung*, a total and orderly view of the world, based on masses of intellectually indigestible information. As an attempt to describe or define the nature of being, of consciousness, of knowledge, or even of energy or electricity, we find that this can no more be done in language than one can obtain an answer by spelling out theological questions on the dial of a telephone. Whether spoken or written the word W-A-T-E-R neither quenches thirst nor floats a boat, and, in a somewhat similar way, verbal efforts to describe existence give no understanding of it because you can't say anything about everything. It would be absurd to say that the universe, as a whole, is moving in a certain direction, for this would require some external point of reference which would, by definition, have to be included in the idea of universe. In fact, we cannot even imagine what kind of verbal or mathematical answer would satisfy such a question as "What is reality?"

But does all this mean that philosophy, or basic wondering, has come to a dead end? A philosopher, a wondering individual, retains an urgent interest in, say, problems of ethics and aesthetics and is not going to stop thinking about them. And a metaphysician, even though he knows that he cannot even formulate his ontological and epistemological questions, will not easily abandon his amazement at being and knowing. He feels incomplete, intellectually and emotionally hungry, unless he has somehow made sense of being an "is" in imminently painful transition to being an "isn't," of experiencing himself as a complex system of vibrations, as a multiplicity of sensitive tubes, tissues, and nerves inevitably doomed to dissolve with the greatest reluctance. He asks, "How and why am I in this delectable-horrible situation?" Above all, he wants to penetrate whatever it is that is the substantial referent of the word 'I.' No amount of sophistry will persuade him to set aside these questions of feeling and devote himself exclusively to symbolic logic or collecting postage stamps.

I have said that in the West the preoccupations of most academic philosophers have become trivial. In the university, departments of philosophy are usually underpopulated and removed to obscure offices, and the coveted degree *Philosophiae Doctor* is awarded to people who experiment with rats, devise computers, or concoct new drugs. This is not without reason, for I am suggesting that, in the West, *real* philosophy turned into science. To answer the question "What is reality?" we had to go beyond talking and thinking to empirical experiment, to the use of "philosophical instruments." But marvelous as the development of science has been, those almost ineffable questions are still unanswered, and the technologies based on science are seriously threatening the continuance of life on this planet. They have amplified—turned up the volume on—human behavior, and we are not at all sure that we like ourselves.

For this reason alone there is still an important place for the philosopher as a sort of ombudsman or critic of the applied sciences, and in this sense people like Arthur Koestler, Lewis Mumford, Jacques Ellul, Noam Chomsky, and Buckminster Fuller must be considered more relevant philosophers than Carnap, Ayer, Reichenbach, and Anscombe—to mention but a few of the hard-core academicians. But to any *young* reader (as of 1972) who has the philosophical spirit, the wonder at being, all these names are in the past. I don't want to say obsolete or *passé*, for they are in the same eternal past as Voltaire and Hegel. But today young and philosophically enthusiastic people are reading Herman Hesse, Krishnamurti, D. T. Suzuki, Theodore Roszak, Spencer Brown, Fritz Perls, Gurdjieff, Thomas Merton, and Baba Ram Dass, or, to go back a long way, Meister Eckhart, Lao-tzu, the *I Ching*, the *Tibetan Book of the Dead*, the *Upanishads*, Patanjali, and the *Bhagavad Gītā*. (This is just a sample. For verification, consult your local paperback bookstore or *The Last Whole Earth Catalog*.)

This odd miscellany of names and titles indicates that the trend of serious philosophy in the West is going in the direction of contemplative mysticism, that is, to an interior empiricism which may require such "philosophical instruments" as LSD-25, the control of breath (*pranayama*), or the practice of Zen meditation for the direct exploration of consciousness and its varying states. The problem is that if man, as amplified by technology, is a self-contradictory, suicidal, and nonviable organism, some way must be found of changing or getting beyond whatever it is that we mean by the word 'I.' It is already clear from the sciences of biology and ecology that every living organism is a single process or field with its environment. But this situation is not ordinarily reflected or experienced in our normal self-consciousness or sense of identity, wherein we still seem to be isolated centers of sensitivity and activity inside bags of skin. But if one were to feel one's existence as the organism-environment process which the biologists and ecologists describe, one would be having an experience of "cosmic consciousness" or of identity with the total energy of the universe as described by the mystics. The "peak experiences" of an Eckhart, Ramakrishna, Hakuin, or (interestingly enough) Schrödinger[2] and all the accounts of these changes of consciousness given by James,[3] Bucke,[4] and Johnson[5] would seem to be vividly sensuous apprehensions of our existence as the biologists and ecologists describe it in their theoretical languages. The mystic is therefore *feeling* himself-and-the-world as it is accurately *described* by scientists, in somewhat the same way as, by informed use of a telescope, one can get the feel of one's place in the solar system and the galaxy, or as by frequent air travel one really knows that the earth is a globe.

Now the mystic tells us things that really do not make sense when put into words: that what we do and what happens to us are actually the same process, as are also something and nothing, solid and space; that as the stars shine out of space the world emerges immediately from the Void in an eternal now of which the past is

---

[2] Erwin Schrödinger, *My View of the World*, Cambridge University Press, New York, 1964.

[3] William James, *Varieties of Religious Experience*, Modern Library, New York, 1936.

[4] Richard M. Bucke, *Cosmic Consciousness*, E. P. Dutton & Co., Inc., New York, 1959.

[5] Raynor C. Johnson, *Watcher on the Hills*, Harper & Row, Publishers, Incorporated, New York, 1959.

merely the wake or echo, not the cause; that this Void is in fact one's basic self, but is felt as emptiness in the same way as the head is a blank to the eyes; that each one of us is therefore an aperture through which the universe knows itself, but not all of itself, from a particular point of view; that death is the same total blankness (i.e., our self) from which we emerged at birth, and that what happened once can always happen again. And so on. All this means nothing to a literate intellectual of a Western industrial culture in the same way that descriptions of color, light, and darkness are meaningless to the congenitally blind, or that the most ingenious comments of a music critic give no impression of the sound of a concert.

But this literate intellectual is "blind" only because of the *idée fixe* that the intelligible is only what can be said. Surely I *know* how to breathe even if I cannot describe the full physiology of the process. Furthermore, I learned how to swim not by reading about it in a book but by getting into the water and following certain instructions. Thus, as Spencer Brown has pointed out,[6] one may go beyond Wittgenstein's limit by analogy with music and mathematics. We cannot say (describe in words) the sounds of music, but by a convenient notation we can instruct a person what to do with a certain instrument—instruction of the same kind as "drop a perpendicular" or "describe a circle" in geometry.

Thus in the pursuit of philosophy as a purely verbal discipline Wittgenstein made it clear that because there is no way of answering such questions as "What is reality?" one must regard them as false problems and consign them to silence. But he did not follow his own advice. By 'silence' he seemed to mean ignoring or dismissing, and changing the subject of discourse. But if the philosopher, still agog in his heart with the metaphysical question which he cannot formulate in meaningful words, were to follow Wittgenstein's instruction more literally, what then? He would actually *be* silent. He would not only (at least for a time) stop talking, but also stop thinking, by which I mean talking and figuring to oneself

---

[6] G. Spencer Brown, *Laws of Form*, George Allen & Unwin, Ltd., London, 1969, pp. 77–78.

sub voce. He would hear, see, touch, taste, and smell without comment or judgment, without any attempt to translate the experience into words. If words came into his mind automatically and compulsively, he would listen to them as mere noise, or get rid of them by humming the meaningless sound "Ah!" He would then be in a state to know reality directly so that he would no longer need to ask *what* it is—i.e., into what verbally labeled class it should be put.

Remaining in this state, he might marvel at how many things there are that aren't so. He would have no sensation of himself as an ego or observer separate from the whole field of his experience. He would have no perception of anything that is past or future—only of a vibrant eternal now which, when felt with the ears alone, would be heard as emerging immediately from silence and nothingness. Discussing it later with colleagues who had made the same experiment, he might agree that our normal view of life is backward: that the present does not follow from the past, but the past from the present, streaming away like a contrail. Having really felt what it is to breathe, he might realize that the distinction between the voluntary and the involuntary is arbitrary—to the evaporation of the problems of free will and determinism. But he would genuinely have had to come to the state where verbal thinking has stopped, and consciousness remains bright and clear. He would then be practicing what in Sanskrit is called *dhyana*, in Chinese *ch'an*, and in Japanese *zen*, and which may approximately be translated "idealess contemplation."

Characteristically, when the professional philosopher hears about this he begins to think up objections without trying the experiment. For he may be sure that not-thinking is a vacuous, anti-intellectual mindlessness from which no good can come, not realizing that if one thinks all the time, there is nothing to think about except thoughts—which is rather like incessant talking without listening. The health of the intellectual life requires precisely that there be pauses in it, and not merely such diversions as sleep, physical exercise, or carousal. Academic philosophers tend to be scholastics like the theologians who refused to look through Galileo's telescope. As natural philosophy developed instruments to explore the external world, theoretical philosophy needs instruments, or at least experiments, to explore and feel the nonverbal world—if for nothing else than to stop confusing the world as it *is* with the world as it is *represented* in common language. W. Pagel[7] and Joseph Needham[8] have documented the collaboration of natural philosophers (scientists) and mystics in the sixteenth and seventeenth centuries in their common opposition to scholastic rationalism and their common interest in the empirical approach, for the mystic wants to go beyond doctrine and dogma, beyond belief, to the actual experience of the Ground of Being—to us Paul Tillich's decontaminated phrase for God.

This means, then, that philosophy in and of the schools must turn (and in some places is turning) to what have been called spiritual disciplines, though (and I think properly) without commitment to any doctrinal system. In fact, beliefs are obstacles to *dhyana* because consciousness must be clear of thoughts. American and British philosophers, with characteristic pragmatism, will of course ask what good this will do, and whether it will provide directives for behavior. But the apparent paradox of *dhyana* is that if one is doing it for a result, one is not doing it, since its essential attitude is to be aware of what is, not what should or might be. In the same way, a musical performer becomes self-conscious and awkward if he worries about what effect he is having on his audience, and thus the results of *dhyana* are always unintentional. Egocentricity, for example, diminishes without any self-frustrating egocentric intention to get rid of it. Furthermore, the temporary suspension of conscious thought acts in somewhat the same way as "sleeping on" a problem, for it frees the brain as a whole to analyze it, replacing the linear scanning of conscious attention. As is well known, the brain, below the level of consciousness, regulates the myriad variables of our organic processes without thinking. Brain operation, unhindered by conscious effort, is obviously the source of the astonishing performances of lightning calculators, and there seems no reason why

---

[7] Walter Pagel, "Religious Motives in the Medical Biology of the Seventeenth Century," *Bulletin of the [Johns Hopkins] Institute of the History of Medicine,* 3 (1935), 97.

[8] Joseph Needham, *Science and Civilization in China,* Cambridge University Press, New York, 1956, vol. 2, pp. 89–98.

such subliminal cogitation should not be effective in being addressed to highly complex social, ethical, and legal questions. After all, it is well recognized in the legal profession that a good judge must not only know the law as written; he must also have a sense of equity—that is, a mysterious sense of fair play which no one has ever been able to define, although we recognize it at once when we see it. Such a judge cannot *teach* equity because, like even the greatest neurologists, he does not understand his own brain, for the order of the brain is so much more complex than what Northrop Frye has called the order of words.[9]

But I think it must be understood that the order of the brain is complicated because, and only because, we are trying to translate it into words. If I may invent a verb, the more we try to "precise" the world, to discern its clearly cut structure, the more precise we compel ourselves to be. The world retreats into ever greater complexity by analogy with the whirlings of a dog chasing its own tail, and, as Spencer Brown has put it, "In this sense, in respect of its own information, the universe *must* expand to escape the telescopes through which we, who are it, are trying to capture it, which is us."[10] In this game of trying to control the controller and guard the guards, the philosophers and scientists, the lawyers and generals, are compulsively locked. Make almost any statement to a logical positivist or scientific empiricist, and he will say, of the first word or phrase in your statement, that he does not know what you mean. He forces you to define it more precisely, and then pulls the same stunt on whatever definition you give him . . . *ad infinitum.* In the same way, the law complicates itself out of manageability

---

[9] Put simply—by J. Z. Young (J. Z. Young, *Doubt and Certainty in Science,* Oxford University Press, New York, 1960) and in a highly sophisticated way by Karl Pribram (Karl Pribram, *Languages of the Brain,* Prentice-Hall, Inc., Englewood Cliffs, N.J., 1971)—it is amazing to see how what really amounts to subjective idealism can be stated in neurophysical terms. The structure of the nervous system (which we do not really understand) determines our view of the world and yet is itself, presumably, something in that world. Which comes the first, egg or hen? And what do I mean by 'I' in saying "I do not understand my nervous system," which is presumably what I really and truly am? The limitation of philosophy is that you can't kiss your own lips, which is another way of saying, with the *Upanishads,* TAT TVAM ASI, or "You're IT."
[10] Brown, op cit., p. 106.

by trying to define itself, and security systems become hopelessly paranoid in trying to secure themselves. To the degree that you make an object of the subject, the subject becomes objectionable. The end is suicide.

To the extent, then, that professional philosophers have locked themselves into a word game, to define definition, they cannot be said to be lovers of wisdom. They will reason, endlessly, about reasoning; calculate about calculating; talk about talking until no one can keep track of it. This does not mean that no more philosophical books can be written or discussions held. There must simply be something to write and talk about, other than writing and talking, and we can write and talk meaningfully only of shared experiences. Thus to have anything to discuss among themselves philosophers must become contemplatives, and mystics in the strict sense (Greek *muein*) of those who, at least sometimes, keep silent —not only vocally but also in their heads. Every so often the philosopher must become again as a child, and contemplate the world as if he knew nothing about it, had no names for it and no idea of what is happening. This is an essential cathartic for the intellectual: to listen directly to the universe as one listens to classical music, without asking what it means. This is Yoga (Sanskrit *yuj*=Latin *jungere*) in the sense of being joined to or one with what is going on. Patanjali's definition, *yogas chitta vrtti nirodha*, means approximately that Yoga is silence of the mind, and this is the way that Western philosophy must go if we are to take Wittgenstein's aphorism as a positive direction.

THIRTEEN

LET'S MAKE MORE MOVIES

Paul Feyerabend

I

In the first scene of Brecht's *Life of Galileo*, Galileo uses a short demonstration to convince the boy Andrea of the relativity of motion. In Scene 7 he repeats the point for a learned cardinal. In Scene 9 he refutes some of Aristotle's views on floating bodies by a simple and elegant experiment.

When realized on the stage these brief episodes make us acquainted with some features of a scientific debate. A few more examples, and we might know how to argue in similar cases. But they also show how people *behave* when engaged in argument; how their behavior influences the life of others, and what role such influence plays in society. Presented swiftly, concisely, and forcefully, the episodes impose upon us an interesting and uncomfortable conflict: having been trained by our teachers, by the pressure of professions, and by the general climate of a liberal-scientific age to "listen to reason," we quite automatically abstract from "external circumstances" and concentrate on the *logic* of a demonstration. A good play, on the other hand, does not permit us to overlook faces, gestures—or what one might call the *physiognomy* of an argument. A good play uses the *physical manifestations of reason* to irritate our senses and disturb our feelings so that they get in the way of a smooth and "objective" appraisal. It tempts us to judge an event by the interplay of *all* the agencies that cause its occurrence. Even better, a good play does not merely tempt us; it deflects us from our intention to use rational criteria only; it gives the material manifestations of the idea business a chance of making an impression, and it thus forces us to *judge reason* rather than use it as a basis for judging everything else. Let us see how this works in a special case.

II

Brecht s Galileo is not a professional. The fact that he has ideas and can support them by argument is the least important thing about him. What interests the writer is that Galileo is *a new type of thinker*, that he is a man rather than a "trained scientist" (48, 106).[1] He is virile, sensual, impetuous, aggressive, extremely curious, almost a voyeur, a glutton physically and intellectually (63), and a born showman (41). When the curtain rises we see him half naked, enjoying morning bath, breakfast, astronomical conversation —all at the same time. Thinking is for him a joyful and libidinous activity, the play of his hands in his pockets that accompanies it and expresses its emotional nature "approaches the limits of the obscene" (51). This is the man who explains Copernicus to Andrea "in an offhand manner" and without trying to drive the point home. He simply "leaves [the boy] alone with his thoughts" (51). He leaves him alone not because of lack of interest, for Andrea, despite his youth *and despite his ignorance* is treated as an equal ("as a result of our research, Signora Sarti, Andrea and I have found, after long debate, . . ." [1236]). Nor is the collaboration enforced; it is the natural result of a charming friendship between a vigorous scholar and an intelligent, inquisitive, and headstrong boy. Thought, so it seems, has left university and monastery and has become part of everyday life. This is the situation Brecht wants to discuss.

The situation is not unambiguous. We are not merely shown a new form of life, we are also shown some of its internal contradictions and the problems to which they lead.

For example, Galileo is fond of certain phrases, gestures; he uses them frequently and occasionally with an air of self-righteousness. Andrea repeats them, though less imaginatively and much more

---

[1] In what follows I am quoting or paraphrasing from *Materialien zu Brechts "Leben des Galilei,"* Suhrkamp Verlag K. G., Frankfurt, 1967, pp. 1–212, and *Gesammelte Werke 3*, Frankfurt, Suhrkamp Verlag K. G., 1967, pp. 1230 ff.

rigidly. When the situation seems to get out of control, when the discoveries of his master are in danger of being pushed aside, then all he can do is describe them with raised voice (1327). In the end he turns out to be a somewhat unintelligent and slightly unstable Puritan (Scene 14). Could it be that relaxed collaboration creates slaves more readily than does the usual teacher-pupil interaction with its emphasis on training and domination? Galileo's daughter who wants to participate in what seems to be such an entertaining life is cruelly rejected—"this is not a toy . . ." (1258)—so the new knowledge business that announces itself with the nude Galileo in Scene 1 is not accessible to everyone, nor is it free from stereotype. The distinction between those who play in the correct fashion and those who do not is driven home when Galileo confronts Mucius, who has gone his own way. He sees him "with his pupils crowded behind him" (1299) like a pack of unsure dogs. The dogs not only protect their master; they also want to be fed and amused; and Galileo, who does not always come up to their rather narrow moral expectations, resorts to tricks to keep them interested and loyal, to "suppress their discontent" (63). The tricks he produces are important scientific demonstrations, they are essential parts of what we call, in retrospect, the "scientific revolution," they are full of deep insight, and they are performed with an elegance and ease that make them veritable works of art (62). Yet their origin now almost seems to be the wish to dominate, not by physical power, not by fear, but by the much more subtle and vicious power of truth. And their function: to satisfy the intellectual greed of his followers and to tie them closer to him. (Politicians need new wars, and scientists new discoveries to prevent their soldiers from becoming discontented.)

It is quite true. Research *has* ceased to be a purely contemplative process; it *has* become part of the physical world; it *has* started to influence people in new ways; it *has* established new relations between them. But instead of becoming an instrument of liberation as well, it creates new needs which are as insatiable as the needs of a sexual pervert: "[Galileo] refers to his unsatisfied drive to do research in the very same manner in which an arrested sex maniac might refer to his glands" (60). Even the happiness of his daughter, her whole life, counts little when it conflicts with the urge to know (1312).

In the play this aspect of the new science is explained by Galileo's political failure. Research goes on afterward. The results are more splendid than ever. They are still revolutionary, from the point of view of mechanics and astronomy, but they have lost their chance to reform society for a long time to come. Knowledge is a secret for professionals again; the content has changed; the form remains. This is what the story *tells* us. In addition it *shows* that this particular aspect was present from the beginning and thus exhibits the contradictory nature of every historical event.

So far, a brief and very incomplete sketch of the working of a tiny part of a complex and colourful machinery. What can we learn from it?

III

The problem that appears in the play is one of the most important *philosophical problems*. It is the problem of the role of reason in society and in our private lives, and of the changes which reason undergoes in the course of history. What happens when a strange and ethereal entity such as thought that has "eternal" laws of its own and makes submission to these laws a condition of rationality, knowledge, progress, even of humanity, takes up residence in the physical universe and starts directing the lives of men? Are the consequences always desirable, and what changes should be carried out if they are not? On the stage the problem is not dealt with in a purely conceptual manner. It is *shown* as much as it is *explained.* This is anything but a disadvantage. Philosophical discussion has often been criticized for being too abstract, and one has demanded that the analysis of concepts such as *reason, thought, knowledge*, etc., be tied to concrete examples. Now concrete examples are circumstances which guide the application of a term and give content to the corresponding concept. The theatre not only provides such circumstances, it also arranges them in a way that *inhibits* the facile progression of abstractions and forces us to reconsider the most familiar conceptual connections. Also the business of speculation which occasionally seems to swallow everything else is here set off from a rich and changing visual background that reveals its limitations and helps us to judge it as a whole. (Today an interesting visual point arises from the fact that businessmen, philosophers, scientists, and hired killers all dress alike and have comparable professional standards. But the briefcase in the hands of these pillars of democracy may contain a contract, a thesis, a new calculation of the S-matrix, or a submachine gun.) It is of course possible to present the additional elements in words, but only at the expense of regarding our problem as solved before we have started examining it. For we now simply *assume* that everything can be translated into the medium of ideas. We have to conclude, then, that there are better ways of dealing with philosophical problems than verbal exchange, written discourse, and, *a fortiori*, scholarly research.

IV

This result was well known at a time when philosophy was still close enough to the arts and to myth to be able to avoid the trap of intellectualism. Plato's objections to writing (*Phaedrus* 275a ff.); his use of dialogue as a means of bringing in apparently extraneous material; his frequent changes of style (cf. *Philebus* 23b); his refusal to develop a precise and standardized language, a jargon (*Theaetetus* 184c); and, above all, his appeal to myth in places where a modern philosopher would expect a scintillating culmination of argumentative skill—all these features show that he was aware of the limitations of a purely conceptual approach. Earlier societies (and some nonindustrial cultures of today) have overcome these limitations in a different way, not by trying to *rebuild* emotions, gestures, physical phenomena in the medium of language, but by *making them part* of the basic ideology. This ideology represents the entire cosmos, and it uses all the resources of society—architecture, thought, dance, music, dreams, drama, medicine, education, even the most pedestrian activity in the process.[2] Philosophy, however, chose to restrict itself to the word.

[2] Cf. M. Griaule, *Conversations with Ogotemmeli,* Oxford University Press, Oxford, 1965.

V

This restriction was soon followed by others. Plato's attempt to create an art form that could be used to *talk* about reason *and* to *show* its clash with the "world of appearances" was not continued. Technical terminology, standardized arguments replaced his colorful and imprecise language; the treatise replaced the dialogue; the development of ideas became the only topic. For a while one tried to construct comprehensive conceptual systems and used them for evaluating the relative merits of institutions, professions, results. There was a hierarchy of professions; each individual subject received meaning from the total structure and provided a content for it. The hierarchy fell apart with the demand for autonomy that arose in the fifteenth and sixteenth centuries and became orthodoxy with the arrival of modern science. Even philosophy was broken up into various disciplines with special problems that had little relation to each other. Was its quality improved? It was not, as is shown by the history of one of its more desiccated parts, viz., the *philosophy of science*.

VI

The scientific revolution of the sixteenth and seventeenth centuries does not yet suffer from the effects of specialization. Science and philosophy are still closely related. Philosophy is used to expose and to remove the hardened dogmas of the schools and it plays a most important role in the arguments about the Copernican system, in the development of optics, and in the construction of a non-Aristotelian dynamics. Almost every work of Galileo—the real Galileo and not Brecht's invention—is a mixture of philosophical, mathematical, physical, psychological ideas which collaborate without giving the impression of incoherence. This is the *heroic time* of the philosophy of science. It is not content just to *mirror* a science that develops independently of it; nor is it so distant as to deal with alternative *philosophies* only. It *builds* science, and defends it against resistance and explains its consequences.

Now it is interesting to see how this active and critical enterprise is gradually replaced by a more conservative creed that has technical problems of its own, and how there arises a new subject that accompanies science and comments on it but refrains from interfering. The development is occasionally interrupted by a vigorous and irrepressible thinker such as Ernst Mach, who sets his ideas against the well-established mechanical world view of the nineteenth century and who wants to change science not just to increase its efficiency, but also to preserve freedom of thought.

His suggestions are taken up by scientists and philosophers. The former use them in the Galilean manner, to awaken science from its dogmatic slumber and to turn it upside down. The result in *philosophy* is a new conformism. In the beginning, this conformism has all the appearances of a Great Revolution: "metaphysical" philosophies are criticized, sneered at, or simply pushed aside; weak speculation in the sciences is triumphantly exposed (not without considerable help from the scientists themselves); advances in logic are turned into formidable machines of war. But now, after all this initial commotion has subsided, what remains?

There remains a subject whose professed aim is to "explicate" science, which means we are not supposed to change science, but to make it clearer. The call for clarity is raised without any attention to the problems of the scientist. Satisfaction of the demands of a particular school-philosophy, namely, logical empiricism, is deemed sufficient. What we have here is therefore a *double conformism*: *both* science *and* logical empiricism are to be preserved, and "explication" is the machinery that does the dirty work. Only this machinery soon gets entangled with itself (paradox of confirmation, counterfactuals, grue), so that the main problem is now its own survival and not the embalming of science and of positivism. That this struggle for survival is interesting to watch I am the last one to deny. What I do deny is that physics or biology or psychology or even philosophy can profit from participating in it. It is much more likely that they will be *retarded*.

They will be retarded because of the naïve simplicity of the philosophers' approach and because of its mistaken urge for precision. After all, we are not only interested in whether a given methodology solves problems that appear when certain simple logical models are used, or whether it agrees with the principles of a popular ideology such as logical empiricism. We also want to know whether it has a point of attack in the knowledge we possess—*and that means* in the imperfect, internally inconsistent, unfinished, vague, incoherent, ambiguous theories "facts" we happen to accept at a certain time— and how we can improve *this* knowledge in the complex physical, psychological, social conditions in which science finds itself. A logically perfect set of rules may have disastrous consequences when applied in practice (a logically perfect idea of dancing may cause recurrent cramps); or, what is more likely, it may turn out to be absolutely useless.

Such a judgment can of course be obtained only by putting philosophy in a wider context and by combining methodological speculation with historical inquiry. This was done not so long ago, and the results are amazing: science violates *all* the conditions which logical empiricists pretend to have abstracted from it, and the attempt to enforce the conditions would wipe it out without putting anything comparable in its place.[3] The separation of science and the philosophy of science has indeed become complete. What is the remedy?

VII

In the case of science versus the philosophy of science the remedy is obvious. What is needed is a philosophy that does not just comment from the outside, but participates in the process of science itself. There must not be any boundary line between science and philosophy. Nor should one be content with an increase in efficiency, truth content, empirical content, or what have you. All these things count little when compared with a happy and well-rounded life. We need a philosophy that gives man the power and the motivation to make science more civilized rather than permitting a superefficient, supertrue, but otherwise barbaric science to debase man. Such a philosophy must show and examine all the consequences of a par-

---

[3] Cf. Paul Feyerabend, "Against Method: Outline of an Anarchistic Theory of Knowledge," in M. Radner and S. Winokur, eds., *Minnesota Studies in the Philosophy of Science*, vol. IV, University of Minnesota Press, Minneapolis, 1970.

ticular form of life including those which cannot be presented in words. Thus there must not be any boundary between philosophy and the rest of human life either.

We must rid ourselves of the restriction to words, treatises, and scholarship that has shaped philosophy for now well over two thousand years. We must try to revive mythical ways of presentation and we must also try to adapt them to contemporary needs and resources. This brings us back to the problems at the beginning of the essay.

VIII

One of the characteristics of ancient myth is that the elements which it uses to represent the cosmos and the role of man in it are arranged to increase the stability of the whole. Each part is related to each other part in a way that guarantees the eternal survival of the society, and of the state of mind it represents. This is not always an advantage. We want to improve the quality of life and we want to be able to see where improvement is needed. Now discontent arises only where parts are in conflict with each other, for example, when one's wishes and emotions are found to conflict with external reality. New *ideas* arise when the possibility of such a conflict is not excluded. A comprehensive system of presentation is potentially progressive only when its parts can be set against each other. And parts can be set against each other only when they have first been *separated* from the whole and permitted to live their own lives. The separation of subjects that is such a pronounced characteristic of modern philosophy is therefore not altogether undesirable. It is a step on the way to a more satisfactory type of myth. What is needed to proceed further is not the return to harmony and stability as so many critics of the *status quo*, Marxists included, seem to think, but a form of life in which the constituents of older myths—theories, books, images, emotions, sounds, institutions— enter as interacting *but antagonistic* elements. Brecht's theatre was an attempt to create such a form of life. He did not entirely succeed. I suggest we try movies instead.

IX

One of the advantages of film is that the number of the elements which are at the disposal of the director and their degrees of freedom are vastly greater than in any other medium. On the stage it is impossible to separate color and object and to show their effects independently. The film can overcome this difficulty. On the stage it is impossible to separate expression from the presence of a human body. The film can overcome this impossibility. On the stage it is impossible to show how a character is put together piece by piece until a strong and vigorous individual stands before us. The film can overcome this impossibility. Of course, the impossibilities of the theatre I have just described are a matter of degree, and they are not absolute. I shall never forget how Ekkehard Schall, step by step, transformed the character of Arturo Ui. Each step was a superb exercise in slapstick, the intermediate results were utterly laughable until out of their mere accumulation there suddenly emerged a hideous shape of incredible political force. The theatre is much richer than the average critic is inclined to think. But the film still adds to it without losing its achievements. It can show the transformation of *faces* (operation; makeup; mimicking) in addition to the transformation of bodies. It can show the effects of distance in space, time, and context. It can move from stage or book into life and back again into stage and book. And so on. Of course, it will need a new generation of *thinking* directors to exploit all the possibilities of this medium. But their rise will be the beginning of mythologies that will continue the work of the older philosophers and put an end to the strange business that has lived off their results in the last few centuries.

FOURTEEN

PHILOSOPHY

A. J. Ayer

Philosophy must be of some use and we must take it seriously; it must clear our thoughts and so our actions. Or else it is a disposition we have to check, and an inquiry to see that this is so; i.e., the chief proposition of philosophy is that philosophy is nonsense. And again we must then take seriously that it is nonsense, and not pretend, as Wittgenstein does, that it is important nonsense.

In philosophy we take the propositions we make in science and in everyday life, and try to exhibit them in a logical system with primitive terms and definitions, etc. Essentially a philosophy is a system of definitions or, only too often, a system of descriptions of how definitions might be given.[1]

This quotation is taken from a paper of F. P. Ramsey's which was written in 1929, the year in which I came up to Oxford and began the systematic study of philosophy. It represents a view of the subject which was then coming into fashion and one that I adopted wholeheartedly. Of the alternatives that Ramsey offered I chose the one in which philosophy is required to furnish definitions. Though it was pleasant to fasten the charge of uttering nonsense onto other would-be philosophers, the idea that the chief proposition of philosophy is that philosophy is nonsense appeared to devalue the subject more than it deserved.

It might well have been thought that to represent philosophy as a system of definitions was also to devalue it unduly, but that was not how it seemed to many of us then. We realized that a great

---

[1] F. P. Ramsey, *The Foundations of Mathematics,* Littlefield Adams and Co., Totowa, N.J., 1960, p. 263.

deal of what had passed for philosophy would have to be sacrificed
—in a rather insensitive fashion we offered it the consolation prize
of being reclassified as poetry—but we thought that enough remained to justify our claim to the good will of the former establishment. There was after all a Socratic tradition of which we could
claim to be the heirs, and had not Locke declared himself content
"to be employed as an under-labourer in clearing the ground a little,
and removing some of the rubbish that lies in the way of knowledge"?

We were wrong. Socratic questions like "What is justice?" or
"What is knowledge?" are not requests for definitions, at least in a
straightforward sense, and even if they were, our conception of
philosophy would still have been unduly narrow. The interesting
point is how we came to adopt it.

I think that the main reason lay in the grant of autonomy which
we thought ourselves obliged to accord both to science and to common sense. For this G. E. Moore was largely responsible, not just
through his defense of common sense, which we accepted, but
because of what lay behind it. For if one could know, independently
of any philosophical argument, the truth of propositions of the
sorts that Moore listed, propositions about physical objects as common sense conceives of them, propositions about the past, propositions about one's own and other people's mental life, it followed
that the evidence which we had in favor of such propositions was
sufficient to establish them without their needing any license from
philosophy. And plainly this point could be generalized. If there
were adequate criteria for the truth of commonsense propositions,
so were there adequate criteria for the truth of propositions belong-
ing to the formal or the natural sciences, to literary scholarship, to
history, or to law. Perhaps inconsistently, we drew the line at
morals, aesthetics, and politics. Partly our reason was that there was
not enough general agreement on these topics to support the assumption that we were supplied with adequate criteria; partly, that
with metaphysics and theology in the offing we did not want to run
any risks of legitimizing appeals to intuition. So we did not go all
the way along the road which ends in admitting everything on its
own terms. But to the very considerable extent that we did go

along it, we drew the obvious conclusion that whether the appropriate criteria were satisfied was a matter of empirical or formal fact. The philosopher had nothing to say to it.

Not only did this put the sceptic out of court—for if we knew for certain the truth of what he professed to doubt, he could not possibly win, though there might be some sport in seeing how he lost—but it left the philosopher with nothing to justify and no occasion even to speculate. For what could he have to speculate about? All the places were already taken. In what way then could he advance knowledge except by sifting out nonsense? He could tell us what was meant by various types of statement. He could not criticize, but he could clarify.

But did we not already know what was meant? Was there any problem about the meaning of such statements as "This is an ink-stand" or "Hens lay eggs," to take two of Moore's examples? And in the cases where there might be a problem for many people, those of technical statements in the sciences or in other fields, would not the relevant specialist be the man to ask? Surely it would be a lawyer's rather than a philosopher's business to say what was meant by 'barratry', a physicist's rather than a philosopher's business to construe statements about mesons or neutrinos.

The official answer was that in a way we did know what was meant and in another way did not. And to the extent that we did not, it was not because the terms in question were obscure or technical. They could just as easily be terms in everyday use. "I know what time is," said St. Augustine, "so long as you do not ask me." But what was he hesitating about when they did ask him? What definition to give? Perhaps. But if we look at what philosophers like Kant or McTaggart or Bergson, who have concerned themselves with time, have said about it, they seem to be offering us theories rather than definitions. And to go back to Moore's examples, surely there is no difficulty about defining 'ink-stand' or 'hens' or 'eggs' or the verb 'to lay'. The dictionary does it quite adequately. It is not in that sense that we do not know what is meant by the sentences in which these words occur.

But in what sense then? We do not know how to analyze these sentences. We know what is meant by the English sentence 'This is an ink-stand', but we do not know what its correct analysis is. But how does "knowing the analysis" differ from "knowing the meaning"? The distinction is due to Moore, but he never properly explains it. In some cases there would seem to be no difference. Thus one example which is sometimes offered of a successful analysis is the proposition that brothers are male siblings, which one can certainly learn from a dictionary. It is, however, not a very good example, since the question what brothers are is not of any philosophical interest. What is of philosophical interest is the more general question how to interpret statements of identity, and how it comes about that they are not trivial. And here consulting the dictionary would not be helpful.

Neither would it be helpful when it comes to analyzing sentences like 'This is an ink-stand', and this not only because the ink-stand is not appearing in its own right but merely as a specimen of a physical object. For looking up the dictionary definition of a physical object would not be of any use either. The question which Moore raised when he asked for the analysis of sentences like 'This is an ink-stand' was, in general terms, the question how physical objects are related to the sense-data which he thought that the demonstratives in such sentences were used to designate.

But now we see that a gulf has opened up between knowing the meaning of the sentence and knowing its analysis. For how could reflection on the meaning of sentences like 'This is an ink-stand' ever lead one to formulate Moore's question. How do sense-data get into the picture?

The answer lies in there being another chink in the armor of Moore's position. Not only did he not know *what* he knew, in the sense of not knowing its analysis, but he also did not know *how* he knew it. And the answer to the first question was supposed to yield the answer to the second. What was going to count as a satisfactory analysis of sentences expressing perceptual judgments was a way of reformulating them which would show how these judgments could be known to be true. Thus sense-data were brought in because of Moore's assumption that it was only through being presented with some sense-datum that one could ever know of the existence of a physical object. And if one asks how he and Russell and so many other philosophers before them came by this assumption, the answer is that they were persuaded by a set of arguments, not about the meaning of words like 'see' and 'touch', but about the possibility of hallucinations, the variations of appearances under different conditions, the causal dependence of the way things look to us on the state of our nervous systems. These arguments bear on the meaning of sentences like 'This is an ink-stand' only insofar as they provide a motive for redescribing the situations which we take as warranting our acceptance of such sentences. The introduction of a term like 'sense-datum' helps to bring out the complexity of these situations, which but for those arguments we might have overlooked.

From Berkeley onward, the introduction of sense-data, or of anything that fulfilled roughly the same function, has fostered reductive analysis. The advantage of a phenomenalist as opposed, say, to a causal theory of perception is that if it works we do not have any problem about how we know that there are physical objects—or rather, we have only the general inductive problem of explaining how we can ever be justified in going beyond our data. We do not have any further problem because we are making what I call a 'horizontal inference'—extrapolating to entities of the same kind as those with which we started. On the other hand, if we regard ourselves as making a vertical inference, extrapolating to entities of a different kind, then we do have the further problem of supplying some proof that there are such external entities as our causal theory postulates, objects which according to the theory we do not and could not ever perceive.

But can it be doubtful whether there are physical objects? Must not an analysis of perceptual statements which allows this doubt be wrong? Not necessarily. The point which the champions of common sense overlooked is that there may be different sets of posits, as Quine called them, which might serve to account for our experiences; and that it depends upon contingent features of our experience that any such system works. It is a philosophical problem to make it intelligible how a system works, and the main objection to the causal theory of perception, at least in its classical form, is that it fails to do this. The difficulty is to see how we could possibly pick out any external objects as being the causes of our sense-data unless these objects could be independently identified. So long as the identification of these objects is made to depend exclusively on physical theories, it remains a mystery how the theories themselves can ever get going. This argument is not, however, an objection to the inclusion of a causal clause in an analysis which allows for the objects to be independently identified.

From this point of view phenomenalism is superior. But the trouble with classical phenomenalism is that it was too ambitious. It assumed that analysis had to consist in furnishing translations, or at least descriptions of how translations might run; and this seems not to be feasible. One has to fall back, I believe, on showing how the commonsense conception of the physical world can be viewed as a theory with respect to a neutral basis of sensory elements. This is achieved by a method of fictive construction. One shows how the elements could get "transformed" into enduring objects, and how the spatial and temporal relations found between them could be developed into a system. If this method is successful, it does, in a way, yield both an analysis and a justification. It shows *how* the theory works and *that* it works.

In this case a process of description seems to be enough. The positing of physical objects is not very hazardous, though it could conceivably go wrong. For example, in microscopic physics the ordinary criteria of identity through time break down, and one could imagine this happening on a larger scale. It might be the case that objects moved discontinuously or that many fewer things stayed put over any length of time, so that we were deprived of our traditional frames of reference. I think that I can imagine an everyday world in which the concepts of field theory would be more serviceable than the particle concepts with which we actually operate. But even then we could be philosophically content with description, a description of those features of our experience that favored the concepts of field theory. We should just be describing a rather different world.

There are, however, more troublesome cases where description does not seem to be enough. One of the worst of them is the other-mind's problem. Here we have no particular difficulty in describing the criteria that we actually use. "How do you know that he is depressed?" "He told me so." "Look at him." "He does not play with the children as he used to." "He tried to kill himself." There is no question but that these are acceptable answers, at least in the sense that we unhesitatingly accept them when we are not philosophizing. 'We can be wrong, of course.' He was not depressed at all. "He had fallen into a Byronic phase." This comes out when the psychiatrist gets on to him. But then it does come out. More often than not our attributions of mental states to others are settled beyond serious doubt.

Why then should there be any philosophical doubt? The reason is not so much that things sometimes go wrong as that our procedures seem logically unsatisfactory. It is not that the accepted criteria do not work, but that we cannot account for their working in the way they do. The stages of the argument are well known. Propositions about people's behavior do not entail propositions about their mental states. If mental and bodily states are connected inductively, it is an odd sort of inductive connection, in which one term of the relation is not observable. Of course it is observable in one's own case, and it is this that gives the theory that the connection is inductive what plausibility it has. But it is an uneasy position to hold. The empirical evidence does not seem strong enough for the weight which is put upon it.

This being so, why should the sceptic not prevail? Why do I not admit that I do not have any very good reason to attribute thoughts and feelings to anyone other than myself? I cannot in fact rid myself of the belief that other people do have a mental life, but I might be brought to admit that it was irrational. This seems to have been Hume's position in general, though he was surprisingly unconcerned with this particular problem. But it is not at all easy to hold a belief as firmly as I hold this one, and also think it irrational. So it is very tempting to fall back on saying that the evidence is *sui generis* but is nonetheless adequate for that. The trouble is that the sceptic's argument remains unmet.

In one way, indeed, the sceptic has prevailed. His victory is shown in the prevalence of physicalism. I cannot believe that the theory that sentences ascribing mental attributes to oneself or to others are equivalent to sentences ascribing physical attributes would ever have resulted from a dispassionate study of the way in which these sentences are used. If Carnap and, more hesitantly, Ryle made this suggestion, it was rather because they had become convinced that only by reducing the mental to the physical could they account for our ability to know about the mental states of others. The wildly implausible reduction of one's own mental states to physical ones was then forced on them by their acceptance of the valid argument that the analysis of statements about a person's experiences could not be radically different according as the statement was uttered by another person or by the person himself. I think that the same is true of the thesis that mental and physical states are factually identical, though here a metaphysical preference for materialism is also at work.

In any event, the assumption of factual identity does not get rid of the problem. For here it is conceded that what is in fact a state of the patient's brain is perceived by him as a feeling of pain, so that the belief that he does so perceive it has still to be justified And it surely cannot be deduced from our observations of his brain, even if we were equipped to make them. Consequently, even if we could be said to be witnessing his feeling when we examined his brain, it remains unclear how we could know that this was so. This difficulty would indeed be removed if we took the bold step, which some physicalists do recommend, of simply defining a mental state as whatever causes such and such behavior and then applying Ockham's razor. But this does seem an improper begging of the question.

The invocation of Ockham's razor, though surely unjustified in this instance, if only because of one's consciousness of one's own experiences, does, however, create a difficulty for the otherwise attractive suggestion that we are justified in attributing mental states to others because this makes better sense of the evidence than any other hypothesis. Perhaps the answer is that we do not in fact have the physiological theories which would enable us to explain such things as intelligent behavior without attributing conscious purposes to the agent, and that even if we did have them we could not make very much use of them. For instance, it would hardly be practicable to keep people's brains under constant observation. Even so, the theoretical difficulty remains that even if we did possess these theories and could use them, it does not seem likely that we should cease to attribute mental states to others, any more than we should cease to attribute them to ourselves.

We have come a long way from the conception of philosophy as a system of definitions and closer to the Wittgensteinian idea of it as an attempt to rid ourselves of intellectual cramps. There is something in this idea, at least with regard to the problems which I have been discussing. It trades on the fact that when we tackle these problems we do not at this time of day expect to come up with anything startling, as it might be, some fresh clue to the existence or nonexistence of physical objects, or other minds, which everyone had overlooked. Again, this is not a commitment to common sense, though it has sometimes been so taken. Even though we do not expect any new evidence to be forthcoming, it is still possible to offer a radically new interpretation of the evidence that we already have. And indeed this is just what Ryle and Wittgenstein did, rightly or wrongly, when they campaigned against inner processes.

If the idea that philosophy serves to remove intellectual cramps covers more of the ground than the idea that it provides a system of definitions, it still does not account for the whole range of philosophical activities. For instance, it has little if any bearing on the currently fashionable topics of reference and identity. I include under this heading such questions as "What is the distinction between subjects and predicates?" "Do proper names have a sense?" "Are identity statements necessarily true if they are true at all?" "Can indirect discourse be regimented in such a way that it comes to satisfy the criteria of extensionality?" In these cases we tend to proceed more scientifically. We advance hypotheses and test them by linguistic examples.

It may be thought improper to ask what is the interest of these questions, since it is surely legitimate to hold that they are interesting in themselves. To a certain extent, I share this attitude. For instance, I find identity statements puzzling and should like to see the puzzle resolved. But I am not quite content to leave it there.

I do not agree with Austin's epigram that importance is not important, but truth is. Not every truth is important, or at least not to me. In the case of philosophical grammar, I find that my interest flags unless it leads to speculation.

But what further point can there be to discussions about reference or about indirect discourse? My answer is that they can be seen as having a bearing on ontology. I have a Humean picture of the world as consisting in discrete observable episodes, with no room in it for modalities or intentional objects. These objects belong, if anywhere, to a secondary system, but the notes of the secondary system have to be cashed in primary coin. We are free to make various arrangements of our primary elements, but there are only these elements to be arranged. I am therefore interested in any interpretation of intentional discourse which will make it compatible with this position. I attach less importance to the Quinean program of eliminating singular terms, but I think that it has a value in doing justice to the fact, or what I take to be the fact, that we are presented not primarily with particulars, but with qualities or patterns out of which particulars can be constructed. In many ways, Quine follows Russell and there is an echo here of Russell's idea of making language reflect the structure of the world.

But what right have I to my Humean picture? For the answer I have to go back to the theory of knowledge. This is what I believe that I am given to build on. Or rather, it is a systematization of what I am given to build on, but one that is closer to the data than anything else I can think of, which would be sufficiently elaborate to deserve the appellation of a world picture. I do not want to say that this is what there really is, because I do not want to exclude other options. For instance, I do not want to rule out the possibility of opting for scientific realism. But if one did take this option, I think that the theory which one would then regard as supplying a description of the world would have to be justified at the Humean level, even though my primary facts will be explicable in terms of it.

One might indeed think that this was not a question of options but a question of fact. Scientific realism is true or it is false. But once you depart from the Russell-Frege treatment of existence, whereby to exist is just to satisfy some propositional function, you have to provide some other criteria. Russell himself made this departure when he talked about the ultimate furniture of the world. In terms of his own analysis of existence, his assertion that classes did not exist should have meant that no functions of any higher order than the first were satisfied; but of course this was not what he intended it to mean. He meant that classes were not part of the ultimate furniture of the world. He treated this as a question of fact, but gave no criteria for deciding it, and indeed it is hard to see what criterion he could have given other than that of the possibility of reduction to a selected basis. It is for this reason that I represent such a question as one of a choice of pictures. This is in line with Carnap's view of ontological questions as relating to a choice of languages, and perhaps also with Quine's doctrine of ontological relativity. The danger in any such view is that of opening the floodgates. We do not really want to legitimize the Homeric gods. It would seem that Quine has to legitimize them, if he is able to discover that anyone believes in them, so long as he can say nothing more than that they are excluded by his background theory. The question is whether his ontological relativity allows him to take the further step of saying that his background theory is superior to one in which the Homeric gods are accommodated. So far as I can see, one can take this further step only if one uses a theory to prove its own superiority, and I should in fact prefer to do this rather than succumb to total anthropological tolerance. It would indeed be more agreeable to have a noncircular proof. But in this case, as in that of the problem of induction, I fear that circularity may be inescapable.

FIFTEEN

HOW I SEE PHILOSOPHY

Paul Ziff

Sometimes as questions. What does the word mean? What does the phrase mean? What does the sentence mean? What do you mean? Do you mean what your words mean? Do your words mean what you mean? Do you mean what your words mean but not what your phrases mean? Or do you mean what your words mean and what your phrases mean but not what your sentences mean? Or do you mean what your sentences mean but not what your words mean but what your phrases mean? Or do you mean what your sentences mean but not what your phrases mean but what your words mean? Or do you mean you mean what your sentences mean but not what your words and not what your phrases mean? Or do you mean that you mean what some of your words and all of your phrases but not your sentences mean? Sometimes as questions. Is there more than garbage in talk about necessity contingency possibility? Other than garbage in talk of intentions motives wants aims goals purposes? All kinds of questions any kind. What times is it? Where's George? Do you have anything to drink? Was the resemblance between Ike and Daddy Warbucks an accident? Because it's not the questions but how one thinks about it how one handles what one makes of it? Are there other minds? Yes. So pried at with simian fingers nothing interesting results for theory of some sort is what's wanted.

Sometimes as writings waves of words piled up spilling over leaking out of libraries dribbling out of corners of mouths. Russell Bradley Cook Wilson Bosanquet Prichard Lewis Langford Whitehead Bergson Wittgenstein Hegel Carnap Methodius Hutcheson

Smith Shaftesbury Price Bentham Aquinas McTaggart Mctaggart Kant (thirty pages of whose pure reason ought to be enough to persuade even the reasonably well educated mentally deranged that it might be better not to turn to the past better not to dig up what is best left undug best not exhume the fetid remains of long ago postures) Dionysius the Pseudo-Areopagite Meister Eckhart Maimonides Gödel Peirce Little Orphan Annie Gregory Thaumaturgogo Herbrand Skolem the Green Hornet and the Shadow. Because it's not what one reads but what one makes of it? So we need and we gotta hab a deep hole foh to put in all de deep thinkers. Who we put in fust? It doan mattuh. Dump dem in! Der goes Kierkeebore. Bye Begel! So long Sartre! Dig dat Highdigger! Watchknow Will Durant? And dere's holy cow Playdough mould it ta any shape ya laks! C'mon gimme a paw ya pore ole clot ya doan b'long all de way down dere. Looka dat Weiss man! He fel on de haid o de Lip man drinkin Neerbeer. Christ man ya off ya rockuh? Pullin out Playdough an leavin an ole humean bean all Locked up! Yo is berkeleyin up de wrong.

Sometimes as resisting temptations. The temptation to commit history to mind. One doesn't read Plato Aristotle & Co. without profit. The temptation to commit nomination: Ura analyst! Ura behaviourist! Ura a positivist! A third to categorize. "But that is an empirical question!"—this brought forth with a smile of innocence a pale expression wide open blue clear blue eyes the confidence with which these weighty words bind feet and hands roll the stone before and blocking and filling closing any gaping mouth.

Sometimes as an academic enterprise. For there are temptations everywhere crawling in every departmental chair. So as feet marching in three directions forever at odds with heads screwed on backwards mouths caught *in flagrante delicto* bright pink-red amber edged tongues rolling round and round and round and round and round and round.

Sometimes squinteyed distinctly presbyopic gazing at truths and as samples of savory sage metaphysical such we have. The first truth. Things get worse. Comment: this first truth is an exact statement of what is imprecisely expressed as the second law of thermodynamics. Not all things all the time everywhere: there are apparent pockets of decreasing entropy but these are not closed systems etc. etc. etc. Things get worse. The second. For all x and for all y x is worse than y. Comment: it follows that x is worse itself. But that's the way it is. The third. For all x the only good x is a dead x. Comment: is the relevant phrase a referring expression? The fourth. Which has a curious logical form. To the tutored eye it would seem to be a blend of declarative and interrogative forms: For all x and for all y who was dat x I seen yo wid? dat was no x dat was a y. But it is a true statement comment on reality appearance too.

Sometimes and mainly and mostly and for the most part and the main part and so principally and even chiefly as a janitor tending a conceptual zoo. Sweeping out categories combing concepts fighting fuddles cauterizing confusions pulling out monkey wrenches turning cages into fields finding fodder grinding raw beef into edible articled patties polishing tools and implements and instruments sorting sifting counting sand. But it's so hard to get anywhere when you have a neat an' orderly mind. The first thing you have to do of course the very first is to make sure that the slops stay in the bucket. That you don't empty them everywhere. You keep them in the bucket. You don't have to stir it. You just keep them in the bucket. That's the thing. You keep the slops in the bucket. Don't tip the bucket over! No! Don't stir the bucket. Just keep it in the corner. *Sum ergo cogito.*

SIXTEEN

A LETTER TO MR. OSTERMANN

W. V. Quine

Dear Mr. Ostermann:

You have asked me about the philosopher's responsibility. I can perhaps best begin by contrasting it with the doctor's responsibility. The licensed physician, whatever his specialty, has had a basic training that renders him abler than most laymen in medical emergencies generally. Hence if he is present at an accident it is his

---

NOTE: Professor Quine's remarks concerning philosophy constitute his responses to the following questions addressed to him by Robert Ostermann in the course of Mr. Ostermann's preparation of his article on American philosophers for *The National Observer*. (See "How Today's Thinkers Serve Society," *The National Observer*, July 20, 1964, p. 18.)

The questions are:

1. What do you consider to be the business of philosophy and the responsibility of the philosopher?
2. To what matters, what kind of questions, do you find your attention most compellingly drawn? Why?
3. What about such questions as how a man orients himself to the world of his experience, what meanings he finds in events, what values he aspires to, what standards guide his choices in all he does? If the philosopher does not examine them, as well as other questions of broad human concern, who shall? Or is speculation on them without value?
4. How do you identify the problems you approach as properly yours?
5. How big a part does the examination and criticism of the work and methods of others play in your work?
6. Why did you choose philosophy for a career?

responsibility to step forward and help. The medical profession recognizes this responsibility, and this is much to their credit.

Is there a somehow analogous responsibility for philosophers? No, the case is utterly different. Philosophy is not a unified profession with a great core of shaped competence, as medicine is. 'Philosophy' is one of a number of blanket terms used by deans and librarians in their necessary task of grouping the myriad topics and problems of science and scholarship under a manageable number of headings. The fact that one man's topic and another's are grouped under 'philosophy' makes neither man responsible for the other's topic, nor for any substantial intervening topic.

I am not alluding to the fragmentation of specialties; I speak of the insignificance of a certain verbal grouping. The individuals who are engaged in disparate pursuits called philosophy can be as broad as you like in their concerns, but the spread of their concerns need be neither coextensive nor concentric with the spread of the administrative and bibliothecary term 'philosophy'.

Take my case. Part of what I treat in my books and classes is reckoned as philosophy. Part of it is reckoned as mathematics. In fact I give a graduate course in the mathematics department. But I recognize no responsibility for nine-tenths of what else may be grouped by deans and librarians under the head of 'mathematics'—*or* 'philosophy'. A professor's professional responsibility pertains to the topics that he professes: that he writes of, lectures on, advises on. Whether these happen to be listed under the broad heading of philosophy or under that of mathematics has no bearing on whether he is also responsible for other topics that happen to be listed under philosophy or mathematics.

The terms 'mathematics' and 'philosophy' are something like 'Middle Atlantic' and 'Northwest Central', where 'medicine' has more the organic connotation of 'Texas'.

The fact that medicine is organized around a common core of competence is to be explained in part by the fact that such competence can be markedly effective and vital to human welfare. If some philosopher were to arrive at results of comparable decisiveness on "such questions as how a man orients himself to the world of his experience, what meanings he finds in events, what values he aspires to, what standards guide his choices" (I quote you), and if these findings proved as vital as medicine to human welfare, then philosophy might indeed come to organize itself like medicine around a common core. But even this eventuality need not obligate any philosophers hitherto so called to cultivate that core; it could as well cause their topics to be relisted under another name than 'philosophy'. Actually I should have thought psychology an equally likely region for the topics you mention; but no matter.

Any of us of course might have engaged in topics more beneficial to humanity than those we actually are in. You and I might have been more useful as medical men or spiritual leaders than as editor and logician. If you and I were today to find a way of allaying a major political or social evil—a way as real as what Enders and Salk found for polio—then I think we would be duty-bound even now to quit our respective posts and join in the good new cause. But this responsibility would hinge no more on the nature of my present work than on that of yours. Nor, I venture to say, does the nature of my present work make me any likelier to discover that social remedy than the nature of your present work makes you. The fact that mine is partly allocated under a corner of that blanket word 'philosophy' is neither here nor there.

It crossed my mind at one time of national crisis that I could increase my usefulness by shelving my theoretical interests and serving in the navy. I did so, but this was a point of private conscience unrelated to any special obligation as philosopher.

Why, you ask, did I choose philosophy as a career? It was a matter of intellectual curiosity about the basis of mathematics and natural science. I majored in mathematics and I did my graduate study in a philosophy department; but my focus stayed much the same, not shifting to social ills and values. That would have been a good interest too, but the chance association under the word 'philosophy' is immaterial.

You ask how I identify the problems I approach as properly mine. Any critical thinker has enough sense of method and evidence to know roughly where his competence leaves off. I know my competence in parts of logic and my lack of competence in chemistry and sociology. If I am concerned with some problem and it turns out to depend on solving another problem, then I might tackle the latter if competent, and otherwise I might try to develop competence for it or leave it to someone else. Whether the problem is called philosophical is, again, neither here nor there.

Shifting now from the main line of argument for the space of a final remark, I should like on general principles to enter a plea for respect for theoretical creativity. Philosophical and scientific literature is abundant; substantial theoretical contributions are not. Each substantial theoretical contribution is a near miracle. Nobody is under any obligation to bring off anything of the kind. Anyone who somehow contrives to do so simply deserves acclaim, and does not thereby incur some added obligation.

Sincerely yours,
W. V. Quine
Edgar Pierce Professor of Philosophy

SEVENTEEN

THE RELEVANCE
OF REALITY

Herbert Marcuse

Ever since Thales designated the substance, origin, and principle of things as water; ever since Parmenides declared all motion and time as illusion, ever since Plato rejected the objects of sense perception and common sense as mere appearance, ever since Aristotle proposed the "bios theoreticos" as the highest mode of life—the relationship between philosophy and reality was, to say the least, ambivalent. From the analysis of reality, philosophy derived its devaluation: whatever the *given* reality may be, it is not the real thing; whatever knowledge may be attained *in* it, is not knowledge *of* it, is not "science," "the truth." Philosophy, as science, demanded abstraction from the colorful, and painful, world of everyday experience, better still, closing one's eyes on many of its features in order to remain "pure" in thought. Truth and purity became interrelated: life was dirty—thought must be pure: pure science. Socrates' terrible statement that, for the philosopher, death is the beginning of life, was, at least in a figurative sense, to become a signpost in the history of philosophy (though by no means of all philosophy). And Socrates' own death was the voluntary, methodical, philosophically argued surrender to the order of the state whose blatant irrationality

---

NOTE: Slightly extended version of presidential address delivered before the Forty-third Annual Meeting of the Pacific Division of the American Philosophical Association in Portland, Oregon, March 28, 1969. (This paper appeared originally in the *Proceedings of the American Philosophical Association*, 1968–69. It is reprinted here with the permission of the author and the Association.)

he had so effectively demonstrated throughout his life.—Was this great model of the philosopher perhaps also the model of the liberal whose radical criticism terminates in civil obedience when the confrontation with the Establishment finally occurs? We are told (and it makes good sense) that Socrates was searching for the *concept:* which would define what things really *are* in contrast to what they are held to be by the common man, the citizen, and his representatives in the state, the government. No "elitism" was necessarily involved in this philosophy, for the common man himself was thought capable of arriving at the truth—provided only he would start thinking by himself instead of just accepting what was being said and done. But the teacher himself, did he pursue his search for the "concept" to the very end, or did he break it off at the point where the *polis* itself would be subject to question?

For Socrates, the search indeed stops where the concept of "law and order" itself, and not only some positive and posited "case" becomes the object (and terminus) of thought: then, the particular, and not the universal—the given things and conditions, and not their Form, their Idea have the last word. The judges question Socrates whether he did not intend to destroy the city state. Here is his answer (in *Crito*):

> "Yes, I do intend to destroy the laws, because the State wronged me by passing a faulty judgment at my trial."

And "the laws" reply:

> "Was there provision for this in the agreement between you and us, Socrates? Or did you undertake to abide by whatever judgments the State pronounced?"

And the Laws remind Socrates that

> "any Athenian, on attaining manhood and seeing for himself the political organization of the State and us, its laws, is permitted, if he is not satisfied with us, to take his property and go wherever he likes."
>
> (CRITO 50-51)

This argumentation, which Socrates puts in the mouths of his judges, is not less flimsy than today's popular and familiar "if you don't like it here, why don't you go somewhere else?"

A geographical definition of reason and freedom not worthy of a philosopher! By virtue of this definition, the particular triumphs over the universal, established *fact* over the *concept* which is supposed to define and "judge" the fact (the philosophical proposition as judgment, sentence). The search for the universal, as the *arche,* principle, (true) Form of the particular things, is frustrated: it comes to a halt before the power of the *polis.* It is the political power which establishes, and enforces (if necessary, by imposing the death penalty) the meaning of words and the corresponding moral behavior.

Or was Socrates right? Did his surrender, his free decision, testify to the inherent limits of philosophy, its impotence before a reality which offers stubborn resistance to any transcending conceptual analysis, that is to say, an analysis which is directed toward a universality (validity) *higher* than that of the established facts, and of the modifications, extensions, prolongations of them? In the Socratic example, this defining and confining reality was the City State; its political authority turned into philosophical authority forbidding the philosopher to draw certain conclusions from his analysis, to apply the philosophical Logos, Reason to the logic and rationality of the state. For the demand for civil obedience, which Socrates so eloquently defends and so courageously justifies by the sacrifice of his life, goes far beyond the jurisdiction of the court, the tribunal which judges Socrates' crime. Not the judgment of the Court, but Socrates' own unconditional acceptance of it extends the State's authority over the realm of critical thought.

Thus, thinking (in the emphatic sense) becomes a political offense: the crime of civil disobedience begins with the radical questioning, with the destruction of the prevailing *concepts* of piety, courage, justice, etc. *They* are the concepts which guide the citizen's behavior, their common values; therefore, they are the cement that joins them together: the "concrete." And Socrates cannot argue that his *own* (contradicting) concepts are true in theory but inapplicable in practice; he cannot invoke the freedom of thought and the servitude of action. For his concepts are *normative,* the truth is *norma-*

tive and calls for a corresponding mode of behavior in opposition to that required by the city state. To argue for the separation of theory from practice would establish the essential harmlessness of philosophical thought, its essential non-commitment—non-commitment made into a Principle of Non-Intervention, according to which the philosopher is to continue to *think* about the Beautiful, the Good, and the True while refraining from *doing* something about them in reality, outside his academy. Socrates was thus horribly consistent when he said that philosophy is really not of this life, that it comes into its own only with death. Reality becomes irrelevant.

We know that the picture changes with *Plato:* at least since the *Republic,* philosophy and politics are internally linked: the concepts elaborated by philosophy *imply* subversion of the existing political reality. What does it mean: "imply?" Philosophical thought is critical thought: its concepts are *normative;* its definitions are veiled *imperatives.* Already for Heraclitus, the *Logos is Law;* and Plato develops the theory of Ideas as the Forms, not of a given reality but of one *to be attained.* To be attained first in thought: what men and things really are, their "concept" must be determined by a complex interplay of "abstract" analysis and synthesis: abstract in as much as the way of thought leads *away* from the immediately given, to that which is "announced," "in-formed" *in* the given, as the blocked, distorted *potential* of the given, as the *essence.* In this sense, philosophy *is* theory of information, communication: it takes the given, ordinary words, propositions, gestures as signs, symbols of a meaning, a message not exhausted, not adequately expressed by the established vocabulary of words, meanings, "values." To the degree to which philosophy elaborates the universal concepts as against the particular appearance of things, it communicates not only knowledge but also the *imperatif* of *acting* accordingly. The universality of the concept contains the message of concretization: the "ought" is implied in the "is."

Now the normative concept stipulates a twofold universality: the (subjective) universality of Reason, of the rational faculties of man, and the (objective) universality of the human condition. The *Subject* who defines the concept (let's say, the philosopher) must be more and other than a contingent individual; Socrates must be able to show credentials for his claim that the prevailing concepts are false, and that his abstraction from the values of the particular State and its citizens is capable of arriving at an *overriding,* universal validity. And the human condition, without losing its particular concreteness, must be supra-individual, common to such an extent that the validity of the concept can become a practical one— translatable into a reality which is throughout *social* reality. Unless this dual condition prevails, philosophy lacks the denominator, the field of convergence of thought and action, concept and reality: philosophy's relevance to reality would be as slight, as uncommitted as the relevance of reality to philosophy.

The universal validity of the concept, and its twofold, subjective and objective foundation are never given facts, they are projections and evaluations. For the philosophical concepts never govern propositions describing established conditions. The concepts of Reason, Freedom, Knowledge, Good and Evil, etc. circumscribe a range of *possibilities* derived from the analysis of the *actual manifestations* of Reason, Freedom, etc., of given "cases," particular realizations of the universal. And these possibilities terminate in the concept of "that which (the universal) really is"—according to the mind and intelligence of the respective philosopher. And his intelligence is a *historical* condition, and as such a *particular* condition. All philosophy, no matter how abstract and speculative, constructs its conceptual universe with the material provided by a particular *historical* universe, which remains operative even in the purest abstractions and speculations—not as sociological conditioning "from outside," but as the very stuff of which concepts are made. By virtue of this situation, the philosophical concepts remain inextricably *ideological:* their universality remains a particular one, confined by the historical situation. Here are the limits, internal limits of the validity of the "concept." And I believe that this tension between philosophy and history lies behind the contradiction between Socrates' critical enterprise and his abdication to the powers that be.

Philosophical thought confronts the material force of existential conditions which thought can neither master nor change. And the numerous intermediary links which may lead to the translation of thought into action also lead *away* from the established conditions

—into the past and into the future. (For example, in the case of Socrates, to the roots of the "false" reality which remain hidden to the philosopher, namely, the separation of intellectual from manual work, the origin of slavery, the disintegrating imperialist base of the city state.) Philosophy is obstructed by a reality which it can transcend only in thought: reality is left to its own devices, and autonomous philosophical thought terminates in civil obedience.

Let us make the jump from the beginning to the end of philosophy. Precisely at the point where the claim of Hegel's absolute idealism seems to become mere phantasy, philosophy comes to grips with reality. "The Rational is real": man has finally set out to organize his world "in accordance with Reason," "to recognize nothing in a constitution as valid that is not right according to Reason." This is Hegel's judgment of the French Revolution: the existential conditions have attained the level of Reason; Reason comes into its own as historical practice, and history is the development of the Logos. Consciousness, in its inherent "logical" development, becoming ever more fully aware of what its object really *is,* in the historical context in which it has emerged and in which it changes— consciousness turns into Reason: *true* consciousness, capable of constructing a rational and free universe. The *Phenomenology of the Spirit* is the grandiose attempt to read the logic of liberation into the history of servitude. Chronologically, the revolution is at the *origins* of Hegel's philosophy; structurally, at its *end.* The Real is rational: in the *process* of *being made* rational, and for Hegel, this is the realization of freedom. Philosophy comes to a close when man makes himself free to act in conformity with Reason: translation of the concept into reality. The *"Aufhebung"* of philosophy is proclaimed in Hegel's system.

We know that Hegel's announcement of the advent of Reason and Freedom in history was wildly premature (or simply wrong). However, the very notion that philosophy is cancelled by its fulfillment anticipates the decisive trend of the period which begins at the time of his death. The *Phenomenology of the Spirit,* according to Hegel the road to the "absolute idea"—to true philosophy, is in fact the road to its destruction: it spells the demise of idealism. To the degree to which philosophy comprehends history and the philosophical concepts "incorporate" history, philosophy becomes materialistic, and to the degree to which philosophical materialism comes to grips with the basic facts of history, it undermines the abstract sovereignty of philosophy. Hegel's idealistic reconciliation of philosophy with reality was of short duration. In the development of thought from Hegel to Feuerbach and Marx, reconciliation turns into radical activism: the philosophical concepts, "translated" into materialistic ones, are to become the theoretical guide for social and political practice.

We must now ask: what miraculous event has bridged the gap between philosophy and reality? And why does this juncture lead (apparently) to the "negation of philosophy"? There is a familiar answer: reality has "overtaken" philosophy in a very empirical sense: scientific, technical, material progress has preempted the domain of philosophy, or rather of all *"pure"* philosophy which tried to remove from its concepts their historical denominator. Such philosophy seems to be *reduced* to the order of an intellectual exercise; rather removed from the human condition, and only modestly interested *in* the human condition.

What is the point in subtle epistemological investigations when science and technology, not unduly worried about the foundations of their knowledge, increase daily their mastery of nature and man? What is the point of a linguistic analysis which steers clear of the transformation of language (ordinary language!) into an instrument of political control? What is the point in philosophical reflections on the meaning of good and evil when Auschwitz, the Indonesian massacres, and the war in Vietnam provide a definition which suffocates all discussion on ethics? And what is the point in further philosophical occupation with Reason and Freedom when the resources and the features of a rational society, and the need for liberation are all too clear, and the problem is, not their concept but the political practice of their realization?

The weight of reality has become too heavy, its ingression into abstract thought too large for philosophy as a separate discipline—even in terms of the academic division of labor. Today, it seems impossible to think, to analyze, to define anything without thinking, analyzing, defining the language, the behavior, the conditions of the existing society. This is perhaps the hidden rationale of a philosophy which, renouncing all transcendence, faithfully sticks to the analysis of ordinary language; the rationale of Wittgenstein's elegant program for the self-reduction of philosophy, the first phase of which ends in the familiar exhortation to silence *in rebus philosophicis,* since what can be *said,* i.e. the propositions of natural science, is "something that has nothing to do with philosophy." This early radicalism partakes—much more than the later linguistic philosophy—of the total suspicion of all ideology which now seems to extend to all modes of thought which transcend the given reality.

This verdict hits thought itself, thought in the emphatic sense, which is essentially abstract. The abstract universals of philosophy are replaced in reality by the emergence of a *concrete* universal: a common goal—a common fight—solidarity. Marx already sketched it in its two manifestations: establishment of a "world market," and realization of man as *Gattungswesen,* "species-being." The global development of the productive forces tends to dissolve the petrified distinctions and conflicts of class, race, nationality—the entire social division of labor which set man against man, the particular against the universal interest, politically required suppression against possible liberation.

On the material, historical basis provided by the possible conquest of scarcity and blind nature, the translation of Reason and Freedom into existential conditions on a universal scale is within the reaches of man. The abstract, universal *Telos* of the philosophical quest is now translatable into the real Subject of history: it is emerging in the global struggle against the powerful international and national policies of domination and exploitation which tend to converge beyond all boundaries and particularities; and the rebellion against these policies assumes an equally universal character. And behind the particular, immediate grievances and struggles of the peoples in rebellion, lies the one universal demand for human freedom pure and simple—a demand on *all* existing forms of society, capitalist and socialist, democratic and authoritarian, East and West.

The reality which has overtaken and overwhelmed philosophy also affects the relevance of its most concrete and actual discipline:

social and political philosophy. The efforts to elaborate the critical theoretical concepts which could develop political consciousness and guide political practice out of the established society are losing contact with the very reality they want to join. The political philosopher faces, rather embarrassed, the deep-seated suspicion, the contempt for theoretical preoccupation on the part of even some of the most "rational" among the rebellious young intelligentsia— a derogation of thought in favor of immediate and direct action on the part of the militants. They are aware of the fact that this position flatly contradicts Marxian theory, that it is grossly undialectical, "vulgar," etc. They are willing to put up with this accusation; they insist on the absorption of thought in reality; what they are being taught and what they learn must be "relevant to their life here and now" ... Are they right on their own terms, and with respect to their own goals?

The answer to that question depends on that to a larger question: does the contemporary situation which I tried to describe indeed call for the sacrifice (or absorption) of thought, of theory by action? Does it indeed call for the *Aufhebung* of philosophy since reality, by virtue of its own development, its *progress,* has invalidated the historical relevance of philosophy? So that, as Marxian theory predicted, only logic and epistemology remain as its genuine domain?

My answer is negative. Paradoxically, the new relevance of reality, its capability of changing the world, far from making the theoretical philosophical effort superfluous and a luxury, demands a renewed and restructured theoretical effort. Obviously and inevitably, this statement appears as, and is, a declaration *pro domo,* but one's own theoretical house is not necessarily a sanctuary from reality, it may also be a workshop for intellectual weapons offered to reality.

The need for a sustained theoretical effort, for a new abstraction from the immediate experience is suggested by this experience itself, which if raised to the level of critical consciousness, calls for a reexamination of the relation between theory and practice—philosophy and reality. The historical conditions in which Marx confidently proclaimed the "definite negation" of philosophy have changed. He envisaged the convergence of consciousness and existence: the exploited classes would become aware of their inhuman situation and of the necessity and the way to replace it by a free and rational society. He knew that this convergence did not prevail, that it had to be achieved in a long political struggle. Prevailing instead was the *discrepancy* between consciousness and existence.

In 1844, Marx wrote that what matters is not what the proletariat *thinks* it is, but what it *is*. For a long time, in fact in some of the less advanced industrial societies until this very day, this antagonism and contrast between consciousness and existence seemed to be definitely reduced and their unity seemed to be established: the worker *thinks* how and what he *is,* namely, exploited and abused— in spite of, or precisely because of the rising standard of living. However, in the most advanced industrial countries, the political consciousness is suffocated, overpowered by a social reality which, by virtue of its technical and material achievements and capabilities, seems to call for protection, perpetuation, improvement of the status quo rather than for radical change. And yet, critical theory demonstrates the *objective* need for such change, and the practice of the protectors and defenders of the status quo verifies this demonstration ever more emphatically.

Under these circumstances, the analysis and development of a transcending consciousness—the germane task of philosophy—assumes renewed urgency. The more uncompromising, the less "private" the commitment to change, the greater the need for learning the conditions, resources, and prospects for change in the society *as a whole*. And since the laws, the forces which move this society as a whole are still experienced as "blind" forces, operating behind the backs of the individuals, since the appearance still conceals the essence, abstraction from the appearance still is the first step toward gaining concreteness, namely, the new concreteness which is that of liberation. It matters little whether you ascribe this theoretical effort to the philosopher, sociologist, psychologist, or historian: reality has long since superseded even the academic division of labor—they are all in the same boat, or ought to be. More than a hundred years ago, Marx called philosophy "the head of the emancipation of man"— we should be worthy of this compliment!

But if reality itself, the concrete social and political reality now calls for the critical philosophical effort—as a guide for action—this does not mean a mere continuation of the manifold philosophical tradition. To be sure, there is much in this tradition which must be preserved (and restored as against the debunking ideological tendencies which, in the academic establishment, want to discard some of the most advanced concepts of traditional rationalism and empiricism): this tradition must be adequately taught and learned, precisely because these concepts are still antagonistic to the given reality, and project conditions of man and nature which now have become subject to materialization, translation into reality.

However, the preservation of this philosophical tradition, and its defense against the twofold attack by the militant, radical activists on the one side, and the pure and neutral technicians of academic thought on the other, does not mean simple repetition. The brute ingression of reality into conceptual thought demands rethinking, sometimes recantation in cases where philosophy has accepted, with too good a conscience, established conditions and values as the terms and termini of thought. Such rethinking is imposed upon philosophy by a reality *in need of philosophy,* that is to say, in need of modes of thought which can *counteract* the massive ideological indoctrination practiced by the advanced repressive societies of today. This counteracting philosophy would have to sacrifice its puritan neutralism in exchange for a critical analysis which transcends the false consciousness and its universe of discourse and behavior toward its historical "concept." Such a philosophy would be materialistic to the extent to which it preserves in its concepts the full concreteness, the dead and living matter of the social reality; it would be idealistic in as much as it analyzes this reality in the light of its "idea," that is, its real possibilities.

Let me, by way of illustration, suggest some areas in which certain changes in reality become relevant for philosophy and call for philosophical rethinking.

1. *Linguistic analysis.* In reality, language has been made, to a considerable extent, into an instrument of control and manipulation. This transformation affects the syntactical as well as conceptual structure of language, the definition and the vocabulary. The distortion and falsification of the "rationality" of language, and

the way in which it impedes independent thinking (and feeling, even perceiving!) appear as an appropriate field of critical analysis and evaluation: political linguistics as the full concretization—and conceptualization of linguistic analysis.

2. *Aesthetics*. The familiar and periodical "crisis of art" has today assumed a form which jeopardizes the very existence of art as art. The notion of the "end of art" becomes the more realistic the more art, in its most radical and destructive expressions, is smoothly absorbed and incorporated into the very reality it wants to indict and subvert. This situation calls for a renewal of philosophical aesthetics: analysis, not so much of the artist and his creativity, not of the "aesthetic experience," as an analysis of the work of art itself, its ontological and historical place and function in the interaction between art and society.

3. *Epistemology*. The modes and the extent to which society (i.e., objects and "data" as specific historical facts) enters into this process of knowing at all levels (sense perception, memory, reasoning) and blends with physiological and psychological processes requires an investigation which hitherto has been left to the "sociology of knowledge." However, the problem calls for a "transcendental" rather than sociological analysis. Such analysis would differ from Kant in as much as it would treat the "forms of intuition" and the "categories of understanding" not as "pure" but as historical forms and concepts. These would be *a priori* because they would belong to the "conditions of possible experience," but they would be a *historical a priori* in the sense that their universality and necessity are defined (limited) by a specific, experienced historical universe.

4. The *history of philosophy* offers many areas in need of reinterpretation. To mention only one: Plato's demonstration of the best form of government is still easily ridiculed and judged under the dual aspect of its obviously repulsive features and its irreconcilable conflict with liberal and democratic values. But there is another aspect to the *Republic;* namely, the internal relation between the theory of knowledge and the theory of government, political theory. Government is here made conditional upon the attainment of the highest mode of knowledge, and on the actually available possibilities to attain them. If the first part of the premise

242

is accepted, the conclusion seems inevitable: as long as this knowledge is not attainable by all citizens, democracy implies a dangerous reduction (if not abolition) of the qualification for government; authentic democracy presupposes equality in the ways, means, and time necessary for acquiring the highest level of knowledge.

"Relevance to reality" has become one of the slogans by which our militant students oppose the academic establishment. They insist that what is taught and learned should be relevant to their life, here and now. The time-honored hostility against history, but also against abstract thought, theory itself is present again. We should not belittle the justification of this claim: relevant today is the action, the practice that can get us *out of* a society in which well-being, even being is at the price of destruction, waste, and oppression on a global scale. But relevant to this goal is not any private and particular practice; relevant is only a practice in which the universal suffering and the universal protest appear in the particular action—a practice which demonstrates the need and the aim of liberation. And such a practice, if it is to obtain a mass base (that is, to become universal, social rather than particular action), presupposes knowledge of the conditions, limitations, and capabilities of change. They derive from the structure, dynamic, and history of the existing society: to know them as conditions and prospects of action means to understand them in terms of a *theory* of society, of the whole which they form, closed toward the past, open toward the future—open within a given range of alternatives. In this sense, action itself—in order to be able to attain its goal—calls for thought, for theory. The relation between theory and practice is truly a dialectical one: "it is not enough that thought should strive toward its realization; reality itself must also strive toward thought." Today, this is perhaps more necessary than before. False consciousness and truth are inextricably intertwined: the benefits of the affluent society are *real,* technical progress is *real,* the rise in the GNP is *real*—and so are the frustration, waste, oppression, and misery inflicted by the same reality. To be sure, this dialectic of progress is nothing new; new are the deadly efficient (and comforting) controls which bar its awareness; new is the scope of the false consciousness, its all but immediate, direct coincidence, harmony with reality. Change, the changing practice presupposes the break of this harmony, the emancipation of thought—*abstract* thought. For the concepts, images, and goals which are to guide this practice are not yet concrete, cannot be "read off" the existing facts and conditions; they are still transcendent.—Their elaboration involves a reexamination of the past, where the failures as well as the discoveries, the false as well as the true consciousness originated. This means learning, and it requires intellectual discipline and energy—the theoretical discipline and energy which will find concreteness in the discipline and energy of action.

Philosophy was at the origin of the radical historical effort to "change the world" in the image of Freedom and Reason; the effort has not yet attained its end. The famous Feuerbach-thesis never meant that now it is no longer necessary to interpret the world—we can just go about changing it. This undertaking today is even more difficult than before: the world must be interpreted again in order to be changed; and a good part of this interpretation requires critical thought, philosophical thought. *Pro domo* or not— I think we still have a job to be done—an *increasingly serious,* and, I hope, an increasingly RISKY job!

University of California, San Diego

EIGHTEEN

EPISTEMOLOGICAL ENLIGHTENMENT

John Wisdom

A. When I hear or read a philosophical question of the form 'Do X's exist?' e.g. 'Do material things exist?', 'Do any minds other than my own exist?' or of the form 'Do we know anything about X's?' or of the form 'Have we justification for any of the things we say about X's?', I am tempted to say "We all know the answer to that" and then to say "What knowledge, what enlightenment, can an answer to that question bring us?".

B. I have felt the same. Other people have felt the same. Some philosophers have felt the same. Moore, perhaps, would never have bothered with such questions if he hadn't heard other philosophers ask them and then give what he regarded as preposterous answers. Moore gave to these questions their, at least seemingly, obvious answers, backed them with obvious premises and then turned to questions which seemed to him not to have such obvious answers. He liked to present philosophical problems in a concrete form and would ask such questions as 'How do I know that this is a human hand?' and 'What do I mean when I say "Here is a human hand"?'. But one may say that the philosophical questions which interested

---

NOTE: Based on the presidential address delivered before the Forty-fifth Annual Pacific Meeting of the American Philosophical Association in Beverly Hills, March 26, 1971. (This paper appeared originally in the *Proceedings of the American Philosophical Association*, 1970–71. It is reprinted here with the permission of the author and the Association.)

him were of the form 'How do we know what we know about X's?', 'What do we assert when we make assertions about X's?', 'What do we mean when we say the things we do about X's?', and so on. I don't think one can say of questions such as these that each has an answer which is the obvious answer to it.

A. No. But one can say "Nothing can be said in answer to a philosophical question of this sort which isn't already known in practice to anyone who understands the question.". I mean if a person who asks 'What is meant by such a sentence as "The moon was full last night"?' is a philosopher and not a foreigner who doesn't know the meaning of the past tense in English, then he knows in practice the meaning of such sentences as 'The moon was full last night'. And a philosopher who asks 'How do we know the moon was full last night?' knows in practice how we know the moon was full last night.

B. One may say something as to the implications of what is meant by certain sentences to someone who already knows the meaning of those sentences and yet thereby lead him to knowledge which he did not have, even in practice. For instance, a man may know what is meant by the sentence 'The sun is at a great distance from the earth and when it is directly overhead at Aswan it is 7 degrees from the vertical at Alexandria which is 500 miles from Aswan', without knowing what Eratosthenes points out to him by saying "That would imply that the circumference of the earth is about 25,000 miles". One may know the meaning of the sentences which express the premises which imply that there is no greatest prime without knowing that they imply that great truth. A child may know the meaning of sentences such as 'There are here 3 boxes with 12 eggs in each' and of sentences such as 'There are here 36 eggs' without knowing that $3 \times 12 = 36$. The truths conveyed by the multiplication tables are even less thrilling than the truth that there are just four numbers which are the sums of the cubes of their digits, but they are of great value in practice; for the learning of them greatly facilitates thousands of inferences.

A. Ah, mathematics, yes! And the multiplication tables are invaluable. But then as you remarked a child may know the meaning of sentences such as 'There are here 3 boxes with 12 eggs in each' without knowing even in practice that $3 \times 12 = 36$. But can a child know the meaning of sentences in the past tense without knowing in practice all that is true in what philosophers tell him as to the meaning of those sentences, all that is true in what epistemologists tell him as to how the propositions those sentences express can be known to be true or known to be false? In general, can a child know the meaning of any of those sentences about the meaning of which philosophers talk so much without knowing in practice all that's true in what those philosophers say?

B. A person may say to another only what that other already knows in practice and yet thereby bring him some enlightenment. I know in practice that there are times when the end justifies the means and yet it may happen that you find me troubled as to what I ought to do in a certain situation and say to me "There are times when the end justifies the means" and thereby lead me to see in a clearer light that situation, and possibly other situations later.

Dissatisfied with explanations in terms of absolute motion Berkeley remarked, Berkeley insisted, that motion is relative. You may say that this is known, was known to us in practice, but doesn't it appear that it wasn't so well known in practice that it wasn't lost sight of at a critical juncture?

Suppose a philosopher says, "There are occasions when a question of the form 'Is this of kind K?' is at issue and neither the answer 'Yes' nor the answer 'No' can be said to be the correct answer to the question, because the case the question is about is borderline with respect to the question. Further, on many of these occasions, the question is not merely a call for a verbal choice but a call for a better apprehension of the case—a better apprehension of the case which may be gained by hearing arguments on both sides of the case." Does it not sometimes happen that someone loses sight of one or other of these truths?

A. Sometimes. But they are truths well known to us in practice. I wouldn't like to make such remarks to lawyers for fear of looking like a man lecturing to cats on how to catch mice.

B. Still I think that there is a good case for saying that these remarks though not the most typical of philosophical remarks are philosophical and yet can be of value in practice.

A. That much I am happy to admit.

B. What about the remark "There are times when a man who asks a question or makes a statement is giving a somewhat unusually wide or unusually narrow meaning to some word or phrase he is using"? Isn't that a remark which can be useful? Isn't that a remark worth making because it conveys a truth which it is sometimes useful to call to mind, a truth which is sometimes lost sight of. For example, suppose someone like Velchaninov in Dostoefsky's *Eternal Husband* says, "He all along intended to murder me although the idea had never entered his head" and that someone replies "That's impossible" like those who said "That's impossible" when Newton first spoke of action at a distance or when Cantor said that the even integers are equal in number to the integers.

A. I am not saying that no philosophical, epistemological, remark is *ever* of *any* value in practice. But I do submit that what philosophers say about this or that type of knowledge, statement, question, is inevitably of limited value in practice and in fact usually of negligible value in practice. Historians don't bother to read philosophers on our knowledge of the past. Astronomers, actuaries, and those who predict tomorrow's winners don't bother to read philosophers on our knowledge of the future. What a philosopher writes in a book called *The Concept of the Past* or *The Concept of the Future* is of no value in practice to those who have those concepts. Of course such concepts are of great value to us in practice. What our mothers do for us when they introduce to us, when they help us to form, the concept of the past, the concept of the future, the concept of the distant, the concept of mind, is of immense practical value to us. Without those concepts we would not have the knowledge, the apprehension, of the world about us which we have. But mothers for all their valuable work are not awarded the title "philosopher" or "epistemologist". Those titles are reserved for those who represent to us in paradox and platitude what we learned at our mothers' knee. What a philosopher says in response to questions such as 'What is Knowledge of the Future?', 'What is Knowledge of the Past?', 'What is Knowledge?' is of no more value to us in practice than what Aristotle, Keynes, Johnson say in response to the question 'What is a valid syllogism?'.

B. Well but now, haven't we here perhaps the clue we need? For surely what Aristotle said is in *some* way valuable to us, in some way enlightening? One who reads Aristotle, Keynes, Johnson, doesn't learn something he didn't know before like one who learns that the sun is not the center of the Milky Way or that all primes which leave remainder 1 when divided by 4 can be expressed as the sum of two integral squares. The truths set out in his old-fashioned book of logic are not only known to him in practice but so well known to him in practice that his study of them is of little or no value to him in practice, in contrast to his study of the truths set out in the multiplication tables. Nevertheless, his old-fashioned book of logic with its chapter on the syllogism brings him enlightenment in that it gives him an ordered view of the familiar manifold of syllogistic argument which he did not have before.

A. That's true. How does it do it?

B. Well, in the chapter on syllogistic argument he finds a definition of a syllogism and then the general rules of the syllogism which set out the conditions severally necessary and together sufficient for the validity of a syllogistic argument; he also finds the special rules for the four figures of syllogistic argument; and he also finds examples of valid syllogistic arguments in each figure contrasted with examples of invalid arguments. So he is presented with a hierarchy of statements about syllogistic argument, with very general statements at the top, quite specific statements at the bottom, and statements in between which are less general than those at the top and less specific than those at the bottom. Take away the specific statements at the bottom and he won't get so good a grasp of the variety in the manifold of syllogistic argument and in the manifold of valid syllogistic argument. Take away the general statements at the top and he won't get so good a grasp of the unity in the manifold of valid syllogistic argument. It is the whole ordered presentation including both general statements and examples that gives him an ordered and still discriminating view of the familiar manifold of syllogistic argument. All the truths presented to him are known to him in practice and so well known to him in practice that they are of little value to him in practice. But the ordered statement of those truths gives him a view of the manifold they cover which he did not have before.

A. I see that. But is there a book which in a comparable manner gives us an ordered view of the various types of knowledge, discovery, question, statement?

B. No, of course there isn't. But in the first place that doesn't mean there couldn't be. And in the second place I think you underestimate what philosophers have done in that direction. Plato, Descartes, Locke, Berkeley, Hume, Kant, Russell, Moore, Ayer, Carnap, Wittgenstein—I admit that very much of what these men wrote is, if not mistaken, misleading, and if not misleading, bewildering, but I do submit that in conjunction they have done much towards remarking differences and affinities between one type of knowledge and another, one type of statement and another which, though familiar, are not less worth remark than, say, the difference between a syllogism in the first figure and a syllogism in the fourth figure.

A. I don't say that differences and affinities between one type of knowledge and another or one type of statement and another are not worth remark. What I would say is this: If philosophers, if the philosophers you have mentioned, were trying to give us what you call "an ordered view of the familiar types of knowledge", then they made a very poor job of it. I mean half the philosophers you have mentioned don't appear to be even *attempting* to give us what you say their words in fact do give us. They spend half their time on those absurd sceptical questions we mentioned at the beginning of this conversation. I mean questions such as 'Do minds other than my own exist?', 'Do material things exist?', 'Do chairs and tables exist?', 'Is there here a table before me?' and questions such as 'Do we know that material things exist?' and even 'Do I know that I am in pain?'; and such questions as 'Do we have any justification for thinking that the sun will rise tomorrow?', 'Do we have any justification for thinking that all men will die, that all men are mortal?', and even 'Do I have any justification for thinking that there is a human face now before me, let alone a living man?'. It is not only Descartes who asks such questions. Hume does. Russell does.

B. I know, I know. And I am not denying that those who have given sceptical answers to what one may call sceptical philosophical questions have said things misleading, not only to others, but to themselves. I mean, a man who asks 'Do minds other than my own exist?' and seems inclined to answer 'No' or 'I don't know' is bound to give to others, if not to himself, the impression that he is in the condition of one who, faced with the question 'Do ghosts exist?', 'Do evil spirits exist?', or 'Do gods exist?', is inclined to answer 'No' or 'I don't know'. And one who asks the philosophical question 'Do numbers exist?' and is inclined to answer 'No' or 'I don't know' is bound to give to others, if not to himself, the impression that he is like one who faced with the mathematical question 'Do there exist even numbers which are not the sum of two primes?' is inclined to answer 'No' or 'I don't know'. Nevertheless, I submit that when we look at what these sceptical philosophers say in defense of their sceptical answers, we often, indeed nearly always, find that they remark a feature of statements of the type they are representing as false or doubtful or unknowable, which those statements have and *could not but have*. For instance a philosopher who, like Russell, is sceptical about material, sensible, things will point out that one's knowledge that there is bread in one's mouth, that the soup is hot, that one sherry is sweeter than another, is based on one's sense-experience, if it is based on anything, and then point out that while, of course, one statement about a material thing may follow from another no statement about a material thing does follow, can follow, from any statement or statements about sense-experience. And a philosopher, the rare philosopher, who, like Wittgenstein, is inclined to say that a person doesn't know, can't know, he is in pain, will point out that sentences such as 'I am in pain, unless I am mistaken' or 'I think I am in pain but I am doubtful about it' have an absurdity about them which 'I am in Rome unless I'm mistaken' has not. And a philosopher who says that one does not, cannot, know that another is in pain will stress the point (shall we say the platitude?) that one cannot know that another is in pain *as* he knows it.

A. True. But now how about those who have shunned sceptical questions and have asked questions such as 'What is it to know something about a material thing?' or 'What is it to know something about the mind of another?' or 'What do we mean when we say "That's hot"?' or 'What do we mean when we say "Jack is in pain"?' or 'What do we mean when we say "The moon is full"?' They have at least the merit of not talking in a manner which suggests that they are concerned with questions which are still of the same type as interesting questions such as 'Does God exist?', 'Do ghosts exist?', 'Do there exist even numbers which are not the sum of two primes?'. And yet they seem to me a sorry lot whose pronouncements are either preposterous or platitudinous. Take a positivist who says 'A statement about a material thing is reducible to, a disguised form of, a statement about sense-experience' and a positivist who says 'A statement about someone's sense-experience is reducible to, a disguised form of, a statement about a body's response to its environment'. It's obvious that they are both wrong —especially when their so called "theories" are put side by side.

B. Some philosophers, like yourself, have had the merit of pointing out that the things said by positivists are not true.

A. I wouldn't think much of the medical profession if the best of them had only the merit of remedying the mischief made by others. I mean if a philosopher says 'A statement about material things is not reducible to one about sense-experience' or 'A statement about the past is not reducible to one about the present and the future' then what he says is true but is it worth saying?

B. What he says has the merit of combatting what is wrong in what the positivist says. And in so far as he not only says that what the positivist says is untrue but also says just why what the positivist says will not do, then between the two of them they can come as near as you like to saying what will do. After all, when a positivist says that any statement of a certain type, say one about material things, is reducible to a statement of a certain other type, say a statement about sense-experience, there always is a close relation between the way we verify, the way we come to know the truth or falsity of, statements of the one type and the way we verify statements of the other type. What positivists say always has to be abandoned, but they have not only fought the sceptics; they have also done much to remark remarkable affinities between one type of knowledge and another. One may say of positivists what the poet says of King Louis' household cavalry at Fontenoy, "To death they rush, but rude their shock, not unavenged they died".

A. You make a better case for the philosophers than I thought could be made for them. And I will admit that in spite of the fact that often what they say does not even seem to be concerned with types of knowledge and in spite of the fact that when what they say does seem to be concerned with types of knowledge, what they say is often obscure, paradoxical, or platitudinous, nevertheless, their words have contributed, do contribute, to a better view of the types of knowledge. But I think that you will allow that they have not provided us with an account of the various types of knowledge as successful as the account which the old logicians provided of the manifold of valid syllogistic argument or the account which modern logicians have given us of the enormous manifold of deductive argument.

B. Would you say that the account which logicians have provided of inductive argument, or of scientific procedure, is as successful as their account of deductive argument?

A. Not *as* successful, no. There are difficulties in the way of presenting the manifold of good inductive argument or good scientific procedure which don't arise when one attempts an account of deductive argument. With different manifolds different difficulties arise. I would hesitate to offer a "theory" of good pictures, an account of all possible types of good picture, for fear my attempt would do more harm than good.

B. No one has offered an adequate account of the possible, or even the actual, varieties of love and hate. There are difficulties about indicating in words the lights and shadows in that landscape. But I wouldn't say that what novelists, poets, dramatists have written has done nothing for our view of it.

A. No, no, of course not. We may recall Lord Macmillan's words, "The categories of negligence are never closed".

B. One who seeks to present the manifold of knowledge, discovery, question, statement, must meet difficulties which don't arise for one who presents the manifold of syllogistic arguments nor even for one who presents the much larger manifold of deductive arguments.

A. No doubt, no doubt. Have we time to say anything about what these difficulties are?

B. We haven't much time but let's say a few things briefly. First, the question 'In what way or ways can one know to be true any proposition about material things?' is deeper than the question 'In what way or ways can one deduce a proposition about material things from other propositions about material things?'. It is deeper than the difficult and enormous question 'In what way or ways can one deduce a proposition of any given type from propositions of that same type?'.

A. I think I see what you mean. A logician can answer the latter questions without bothering about how we come to know premises about material things from which to deduce conclusions about material things; and he need not bother about how we come to know premises about the past from which to deduce conclusions about the past; or how we come to know premises which could not conceivably have been false in order to deduce conclusions which could not conceivably have been false. But an epistemologist who asks 'How can one know to be true any statement about material things?' must remind us of how we know to be true a statement about material things *without* deducing it from others, and must do so in a way which gives us a better grasp of the differences and affinities between the way one comes to know truths about material things and, for example, the way one comes to know truths about one's own sense-experience or truths about another's sense-experience.

B. That's about it. Second, an epistemologist who is seeking to give us a new view of the relationships between different types, different classes, of knowledge has to combat an already existing, well-tried classification of these classes of knowledge—it is a classification encouraged by metaphors which impregnate our language.

A. What do you refer to?

B. Well, we speak of having knowledge of physical, material things, knowledge of psychological, mental things, knowledge of things in the past, knowledge of things in the future, knowledge of things in the present, and knowledge of things which, like numbers, are neither material nor mental, not in the past or the present or the future, not in time at all.

A. Well, what's wrong with that? It all seems true.

B. It is true. It would not be so epistemologically dangerous if it were not.

A. Why is it dangerous?

B. It does nothing to draw attention to the fact that the differences between the types of knowledge, the species of knowledge, referred to are not differences in subject matter, not differences between the species of thing they are about, in the way in which the difference between knowledge of tigers and knowledge of lions is a difference between knowledge of one species of the felidae and knowledge of another. The difference between knowledge of dogs and knowledge of horses is a difference between knowledge of one "species" or sort of animal and another. As has often been said, your body and your mind are not two species of thing, two species of possession. Real tigers, imaginary tigers, and dream tigers are not three species of tiger, though statements about real tigers, imaginary tigers, and dream tigers are three species of statement. Past roses, present roses, future roses, timeless roses are not four species of rose, though statements about past roses, present roses, future roses, timeless roses, are four species of statement, and knowledge of past roses, of present roses, of future roses, of timeless roses are four species of knowledge. All this has to be pointed out by an epistemologist and it isn't easy to do that. It is not easy to describe the differences between statements about, knowledge about, past roses, present roses, future roses, timeless roses, in words which make it clear that the differences are different from the difference between statements about, knowledge about, dogs and statements about, knowledge about, horses. It is not easy to do this. And yet it must be done if we are to achieve our double, our full purpose. We want (1) to cure the cramp, to dispel the idle but occasionally distressing mystification which is often expressed in a question of the form 'How can we have knowledge of type T?' or 'What is it to have that knowledge of type T with which we are so familiar?'. And we want (2) to transform that mystification as to knowledge of type T into a better grasp of its place in the manifold of knowledge. For instance we want to do these two things when someone asks 'How do, how can, we know things in the past?' and also when someone asks 'How do we know what we know about things as timeless as the number 2 or the idea of a triangle or the property of triangularity?'. We want to do this when someone expresses mystification in some such words as these: "Knowledge of the timeless rose is knowledge of a flower more unfading than those that bloom in time can ever be though they should last till time be done. But how is such knowledge possible?".

A. I see what you mean. Any further difficulty?

B. Yes. An Indian elephant can differ from an African elephant in the way he must if he is to be an Indian elephant, without having any feature adverse to his being an elephant.

A. Certainly.

B. And a valid syllogism in the fourth figure may differ from a valid syllogism in the second figure without having any feature adverse to its being a valid syllogism. In general the differentia of the forms of valid syllogism are not at all adverse to a syllogism's being a valid syllogism.

A. Of course not.

B. But now an occasion when two people are playing handicap chess cannot differ from an occasion when two people are playing non-handicap chess in the way it must differ if it is to be an occasion when people are playing handicap chess, without having a feature adverse to its being an occasion when people are playing chess.

A. This is connected with Wittgenstein's question "Can we play chess without the queen?". But I never properly understood what he meant and I am not quite clear what you mean.

B. Suppose a player A, at the beginning of a game "gives" his queen, as we say, to the other player, B. This feature of the occasion would not, normally, lead us to say 'They are not playing chess'. On the contrary, we would still say 'They are playing chess —handicap chess, chess at odds'. On the other hand this feature of the occasion is not irrelevant to whether A and B are playing chess. It is adversely relevant to the claim that A and B are playing chess in a way which becomes obvious if we think of an occasion when one player gives the other all his pieces except his king. Put it another way: When people are playing handicap chess the occasion must lack a feature which on occasions when people are playing non-handicap chess is part of the basis for saying that they are playing chess.

A. I see what you mean. Chess without the queen is at least close to Hamlet without the Prince of Denmark.

B. And this may lead someone to say, of an occasion when at the beginning of a game a player gives his opponent a queen, 'They are not really playing chess'. A person who says this is not adequately described by saying 'He is marking an unusual feature of the occasion'. If A and B while playing chess are both mounted on elephants the situation has an unusual feature but it's irrelevant to whether they are playing chess.

A. I see all that. But how is it relevant to philosophy, to epistemology?

B. A man or a dog who in his sleep, in a dream, sees a rabbit, hunts rabbits, lacks a feature, lacks several features, relevant to whether he sees a rabbit. Not only is there no rabbit there—that is true when he sees an imaginary rabbit—but also his eyes are closed and, or, he shows little or no awareness of things around him. This would not normally be enough to make us say 'He is not seeing a rabbit in his dream'. But it may lead a philosopher to say 'He isn't really seeing a rabbit at all. He can't be seeing a rabbit'. Again suppose you say 'Last night Bob saw a rabbit in his sleep'. A philosopher may say 'He didn't really. He can't have done so; he was asleep. Of course if you mean only that when he woke he said, "Last night I saw a rabbit" or "Last night in a dream, I saw a rabbit," that's different. No doubt you are right about that'. This philosopher talks in an old-fashioned sceptical and positivist manner but this should not prevent his words' drawing your attention to the fact that when a man sees a rabbit in a dream he lacks features the presence of which on other occasions when a man sees a rabbit provides much of the basis for saying that he sees a rabbit. Take another case. Suppose someone says 'A month from now the moon will be full'. He can't have so complete a ground for this statement about the future as he could now have for the statement 'The moon is full' and as he may have a month from now for the statement he makes if he then says 'The moon is now full'. This would not normally lead us to say 'He doesn't now know that a month from now the moon will be full'. But it may lead a philosopher to say this, and unless he and his hearers recognize that he is taking some license with language in order to point to the fact that when a person knows the future the occasion inevitably lacks a feature F, which often is and always may be part of the basis for a claim of the form *X knows that S* where *S* is a statement about the present, confusion and misplaced conflict may arise. Further even if his hearers recognize this he may still need to make plain to them, and perhaps to himself, what that feature F is. But both these difficulties can be overcome.

A. I see. And of course like difficulties may arise when a philosopher says 'One can't really know the past' or 'One can't really know the mind of another' and so on.

B. And those difficulties also may be overcome. I hope that some day some philosopher or party of philosophers will write a book about the manifold of types of knowledge, in which examples are so well accompanied by comment and general statements that no one is left in a condition in which he can't see the wood for the trees, and general statements are so well supplemented with examples that everyone understands what those statements do and don't mean and apprehends all the variety in what they cover.

Books

Bobik, Joseph (ed.): *The Nature of Philosophical Inquiry*, University of Notre Dame Press, Notre Dame, Ind., 1970.

Broad, C. D.: *Scientific Thought*, Harcourt, Brace and Company, Inc., New York, 1923, Introduction.

Collingwood, R. G.: *An Essay on Metaphysics*, Oxford University Press, London, 1940.

Danto, Arthur C.: *What Philosophy Is: A Guide to the Elements*, Harper & Row, Publishers, Incorporated, New York, 1968.

Hall, Everett W.: *Philosophical Systems: A Categorical Analysis*, The University of Chicago Press, Chicago, 1960.

Heidegger, Martin: *What Is Philosophy?* trans. William Kluback and Jean T. Wilde, Twayne Publishers, Inc., New York, 1958.

Johnstone, Henry W.: *Philosophy and Argument*, The Pennsylvania State University Press, University Park, 1959.

Johnstone, Henry W. (ed.): *What Is Philosophy?* Macmillan & Co., Ltd., London, 1965.

Körner, Stephen: *What Is Philosophy?: One Philosopher's Answer*, The Penguin Press, London, 1969.

Lazerowitz, Morris: *Philosophy and Illusion*, Humanities Press, New York, 1968.

Maritain, Jacques: *On the Use of Philosophy: Three Essays*, Atheneum Publishers, New York, 1969.

Moore, G. E.: *Some Main Problems of Philosophy*, George Allen & Unwin, Ltd., London, 1953, chap. 1.

Newell, R. W.: *The Concept of Philosophy*, Methuen & Co., Ltd., London, 1967.

Ortega y Gasset, José: *What Is Philosophy?* trans. Mildred Adams, W. W. Norton & Company, Inc., New York, 1960.

Randall, John Herman, Jr.: *How Philosophy Uses Its Past*, Columbia University Press, New York, 1963.

Reck, Andrew J.: *Speculative Philosophy: A Study of Its Nature, Types and Uses*, The University of New Mexico Press, Albuquerque, 1972.

Reichenbach, Hans: *The Rise of Scientific Philosophy*, University of California Press, Berkeley, 1951.

Rorty, Richard (ed.): *The Linguistic Turn: Recent Essays in Philosophical Method*, The University of Chicago Press, Chicago, 1967.

Sparshott, F. E.: *Looking for Philosophy*, McGill-Queens University Press, Montreal, 1972.

Articles

(We have not listed any articles which are contained in any of the books included above.)

Broad, C. D.: "Critical and Speculative Philosophy," in J. H. Muirhead (ed.): *Contemporary British Philosophy*, First Series, George Allen & Unwin, Ltd., London, 1924.

Cavell, Stanley: "Must We Mean What We Say?" *Inquiry*, vol. 1 (1958), pp. 172–212.

Chisholm, Roderick M.: "Philosophers and Ordinary Language," *Philosophical Review*, July 1951, pp. 317–328.

Gallie, W. B.: "Essentially Contested Concepts," in Max Black (ed.), *The Importance of Language*, Prentice-Hall, Inc., Englewood Cliffs, N.J., 1962.

Katz, Jerrold, and Jerry A. Fodor: "The Availability of What We Say," *Philosophical Review*, January 1963, pp. 57–71.

Mates, Benson: "On the Verification of Statements about Ordinary Language," *Inquiry*, vol. 1 (1958), pp. 161–171.

Ramsey, Frank D.: "Philosophy," in A. J. Ayer (ed.), *Logical Positivism*, The Free Press of Glencoe, Inc., New York, 1959.

Ryle, Gilbert: "Philosophical Arguments," in A. J. Ayer (ed.), *Logical Positivism*, The Free Press of Glencoe, Inc., New York, 1959.

Schlick, Moritz: "The Turning Point in Philosophy," in A. J. Ayer (ed.), *Logical Positivism*, The Free Press of Glencoe, Inc., New York, 1959.

Stigen, Anfinn: "Philosophy as World View and Philosophy as Discipline," in Raymond E. Olson and Anthony M. Paul (eds.), *Contemporary Philosophy in Scandinavia*, The Johns Hopkins Press, Baltimore, 1972.

Waisman, Friedrick: "How I See Philosophy," in A. J. Ayer (ed.), *Logical Positivism*, The Free Press of Glencoe, Inc., New York, 1959.

INDEX

Catalog

If you are interested in a list of fine Paperback
books, covering a wide range of subjects
and interests, send your name and address,
requesting your free catalog, to:

McGraw-Hill Paperbacks
1221 Avenue of Americas
New York, N.Y. 10020